Machine Musicianship

Machine Musicianship

Robert Rowe

The MIT Press
Cambridge, Massachusetts
London, England

This book was set in Melior by Achorn Graphic Services, Inc., and was printed and bound in the United States of America.

Library of Congress Cataloging-in-Publication Data

Rowe, Robert.
  Machine musicianship / Robert Rowe.
    p. cm.
  Includes bibliographical references and index.
  Contents: Machine musicianship—Symbolic processes—Sub-symbolic processes—Segments and patterns—Compositional techniques—Algorithmic expression and music cognition—Interactive improvisation—Interactive multimedia—Installations—Directions.
  ISBN 0-262-18206-8 (hc. : alk. paper)
  1. Artificial intelligence—Musical applications. 2. Music—Computer programs.
  3. Real-time programming. 4. Computer composition. I. Title.
  ML74.R68 2001
  780'.285—dc21

                                                          00-038699

Contents

Acknowledgments

A text like this is never complete—I encounter new material that relates to it daily. My only comfort is that such a book is not and could never be comprehensive. To my knowledge, easily twice as many projects could have been included. I cannot claim methodological rigor in selecting which things received considerable attention, or little or none. Of course, I wrote most about the things I know best. Another main reason for including something was that I had access to materials—articles, source code, Max patches—that allowed me to document more than my impressions.

All of the work referred to here was supported by material provided by composers and researchers, and I am grateful to all of them for their help. The list of names is too long to recount here; the index probably best reflects its extent. Beyond providing grist, many of these colleagues also read what I had written and helped amend my errors. Mistakes that remain, of course, are all my doing.

I owe a great debt to the Music, Mind, Machine research group at the University of Nijmegen in the Netherlands. Group directors Peter Desain and Henkjan Honing invited me there for my sabbatical from New York University. I spent that time conducting research and writing this book; indeed, I could not have written it without the work I accomplished there. Many stimulating discussions with students and faculty helped hone my ideas and presentation. Particular thanks go to Richard Ashley, Dirk-Jan Povel, Piet Vos, Renee Timmers, Paul Trilsbeek, Yvonne Schouten, Hank Heijink, Huub van Thienen, Rinus Aarts, Chris Jansen, and of course Peter Desain and Henkjan Honing.

The sabbatical year that led to this book was granted to me by New York University, and my experience in the Music Technology

Program of the Department of Music and Performing Arts Professions there provided the preparation necessary to write it. Many people helped me by reading and commenting on various drafts. In particular I would like to thank Kenneth Peacock, George Fisher, Carlos Guedes, Paul Berg, Roger Dannenberg, Lawrence Ferrara, and Ilya Smulevich.

Earlier versions of certain parts of the text were published in *Contemporary Music Review,* Volume 13, Part 2, in an article entitled "Incrementally Improving Interactive Music Systems," *Music Perception,* Volume 17, No. 4, in an article entitled "Key Induction in the Context of Interactive Performance," and in a chapter in *Readings in Music and Artificial Intelligence,* edited by Eduardo Reck Miranda (1999).

I would like to thank my editor at The MIT Press, Douglas Sery, for his support, guidance, and patience through the whole process.

Thanks, too, to my wife Tamara, who managed the move of our family of five across an ocean and back, took care of the kids, took care of me, and gave me time even to think about undertaking this project. *Machine Musicianship* is dedicated with love to my three daughters, Charlotte, Abigail, and Miranda.

Machine Musicianship

1 Machine Musicianship

Machine Musicianship is both an exploration of the theoretical foundations of analyzing, performing, and composing music with computers, and a tutorial in writing software to pursue those goals. The theoretical foundations are derived from the fields of music theory, computer music, music cognition, and artificial intelligence. The intended audience includes practitioners in those fields, as well as composers and interested performers.

The training of musicians begins by teaching basic musical concepts, a collection of knowledge commonly known as musicianship. These concepts underlie the musical skills of listening, performance, and composition. Computer programs designed to implement any of these skills—that is, to make sense of what is heard, perform music expressively, or compose convincing pieces—can similarly benefit from a musician's fundamental level of musicianship.

To be sure, there are many worthy computer music programs that have no basic musical knowledge at all. The usual technique is to implement thoroughly that part of musicianship required for the task at hand. Notation programs must know how many beats belong in a bar; sequencers must be able to transpose enharmonically. In this text we will explore how a more systematic foundation of musical knowledge can further extend such programs' range of use as well as improve their communication with human musicians.

Consider a simple example of this level of functionality: music sequencers can transpose enharmonically, but they cannot execute a command such as "transpose the selected measures to the subdominant." The reason for this limitation is that typical programs have no access to a description of the music in terms of relative harmonic function. Such an extension would be quite straightforward for current sequencers—and there may even be some that do it—though I have not seen any. Even better would be a sequencer that could transpose to the subdominant without the user having to inform the program as to which tonal center is current. That facility is more computationally demanding, but still well within the reach of established algorithms. Examples such as these can be generated at will and doubtless have occurred to anyone who has used music software in any depth. The point is that such programs can become more useful simply by better accommodating the practices of fundamental musicianship.

This book explores the technology of implementing musical concepts in computer programs and how resulting applications can be used to accomplish tasks ranging from the solution of simple musical problems through live performance of interactive music compositions to the design and implementation of musically responsive installations and web sites. These concepts are programmed using both C++ and Max, a graphic programming environment developed by Miller Puckette and David Zicarelli (Dobrian 1997). Some experience with one or both of these is assumed if readers wish to extend the example programs on their own. The accompanying CD-ROM includes working versions of the examples, as well as source code and a hypertext document showing how the code leads to the programs' musical functionality.

Machine Musicianship is not intended as a programming tutorial, however. The processes described in these pages constitute a computational approach to music analysis, composition, and performance that may engage practitioners in those fields whether they are programmers or not. I present the practical examples with programming information in order to help those who wish to write their own, but they can also be used as stand-alone applications by those who do not. It is my hope that interested musicians may even profit from simply reading the text without any use of a computer at all.

1.1 The Motivation for Machine Musicianship

Designing computer programs that will recognize and reason about human musical concepts enables the creation of applications for performance, education, and production that resonate with and reinforce the basic nature of human musicianship. Access to functions such as phrase boundary recognition makes possible operations that simply cannot be accomplished without such capabilities. The realization of norms for the expressive shaping of a phrase by a machine performer, for example, can only be applied once a phrase has been identified as a phrase in the first place. Further, realizing these concepts algorithmically allows us to augment human musicianship with processes and representations that only a computer could implement. A complete record of the program's "listening experience" is immediately available and can be used both to evaluate the algorithm's performance and to direct further analysis.

Beyond the pedagogical and practical value, I believe that there are compelling musical reasons to emulate human musicianship with computers. Readers may determine for themselves on the basis of extensive existing repertoire whether or not computer music programs have contributed to enduring compositions. Those who dismiss machine musicianship tend to argue that algorithmic composition programs (as one example) are more interesting technologically than they are musically. Another prominent source of dissatisfaction with the enterprise derives from a belief that the development of increasingly musical programs forms a real and growing threat to the livelihood of human musicians.

The need for better musicianship in music processing is relatively self-evident when contrasted with the aesthetic and ethical questions surrounding the use of automated composition and performance programs. Computers in music have made possible new kinds of creation at the same time that they have caused upheaval in the social and cultural practice of music making. Music programs are cheap, easy to use, and tireless. These attributes make it attractive to use them for many tasks that previously were performed by human musicians. None of these properties, however, have anything to do with the nature of the music being performed. In other words, a large part of the motivation for making music with computers is that computers are less troublesome to employ than people. This situation has had a dramatic effect on the economic prospects for musicians almost as profound as the proliferation of television and sound recording equipment since the 1940s. One can condemn this trend in a hand-wringing Luddite reflex, but the situation is unlikely to change except in the direction of ever greater reliance on machines.

There are other reasons to use computers in music, however, that have everything to do with the nature of the music performed. My own interest in computer music generally, and interactive music systems in particular, stems from the new compositional domains they open up. Composers have used algorithms in the creation of music for centuries. The speed with which such algorithms can now be executed by digital computers, however, eases their use during the performance itself. Once they are part of a performance, they can change their behavior as a function of the musical context going on around them. For me, this versatility represents the essence of interaction and an intriguing expansion of the craft of composition.

An equally important motivation for me, however, is the fact that interactive systems require the participation of humans making music to work. If interactive music systems are sufficiently engaging as partners, they may encourage people to make music at whatever level they can. I believe that it is critical to the vitality and viability of music in our culture that significant numbers of people continue (or begin) to engage in active music making, rather than simply absorbing reproduced music bombarding them from loudspeakers on every side.

Tod Machover stresses a similar point:

Traditional instruments are hard to play. It takes a long time to [acquire] physical skills which aren't necessarily the essential qualities of making music. It takes years just to get good tone quality on a violin or to play in tune. If we could find a way to allow people to spend the same amount of concentration and effort on listening and thinking and evaluating the difference between things and thinking about how to communicate musical ideas to somebody else, how to make music with somebody else, it would be a great advantage. Not only would the general level of musical creativity go up, but you'd have a much more aware, educated, sensitive, listening, and participatory public. (1999)

We are at an inflection point in the technology of our culture as the trajectories of television and computer usage cross. Already more computers than television sets are sold each year in the United States. Televisions themselves are due to become digital within a matter of years and households are already becoming wired to receive a much higher bandwidth of information than they currently get from a telephone connection. None of this comes as a revelation anymore and has been thoroughly discussed elsewhere. The interesting question for this discussion is whether people using the new computer/televisions will simply look at these devices or be moved to interact with them. I believe that if computers interact with people in a musically meaningful way, that experience will bolster and extend the musicianship already fostered by traditional forms of music education. Ultimately, the goal must be to enrich and expand human musical culture. Certainly, music will continue to be produced in any case, but without the ferment of an actively engaged audience it will lapse into yet another form of consumerism.

Philippe Manoury makes this assessment of the relationship between music and its society:

I am convinced that a certain culture is being lost. Music is increasingly playing the role of a diversion and that scares me. I don't have anything against music as a diversion, but I have the impression that our society, faced with numerous problems and no resolutions in sight, considers diversion as an antidote to those problems. . . . The more society stagnates, the more it distributes this antidote of diversion, in which music plays an important role. There is an overconsumption of the music of diversion and people don't see that music can also be the fruit of a reflection and an internal process, something they recognize more easily in literature. (Derrien 1995, 19–20 [my trans.])

Although it is tempting to believe that one's own approach to music-making will lead to a more engaged society and more fully developed art form, I make no claims of special aesthetic or social virtue inherent to interactive music. However, as computer music is so often accused of leading us to a day when machines will listen only to machines, I feel compelled to observe that many of us are motivated by a much different vision of the computer's potential connection to the community of human musicians.

1.2 Algorithmic Composition

The formalization of processes for generating music has a long and distinguished history in Western art music. From Guido d'Arezzo's chant generation method through the isorhythmic motet to serial techniques and Xenakis' "formalized music," interest in processes that produce music has waxed and waned through several centuries of composition (Loy 1989). Such algorithms move the compositional act to a meta-level where the evolution of the music's character is controlled over time by the manipulation of a limited number of parameters. Computers can now execute these processes so quickly that they can be realized on stage as part of an ongoing performance (Chadabe 1989). Interactive systems change the values of compositional parameters using information from a variety of inputs, including live performance data from multiple members of an ensemble.

Because these systems derive control parameters from a real-time analysis of performance, they can generate material based on improvised input as easily as they can on interpretations of notated music. They become a kind of ligature connecting improvisation to notated composition, just as the same processes used to govern the response to notated music can be employed to generate new improvisations in performance. This possibility expands the domain of composition. By delegating some of the creative responsibility to the performers and some to a computer program, the composer pushes composition up (to a meta-level captured in the processes executed by the computer) and out (to the human performers improvising within the logic of the work).

An interesting effect of this delegation is that the composer must give very detailed instructions to the computer at the same time that she gives up such precise direction of the human improviser. The resulting music requires a new kind of performance skill as much as it enables a new kind of composition. The human player working with an interactive system must learn how to perform with it much as he would learn to play with another human. The very real differences between computer performers and human performers mean, however, that the human also acquires a new degree of freedom in invoking and directing real-time algorithms through different styles of performance. An interactive composition changes and matures as the human and computer performances increasingly intertwine.

Another possibility, of course, is that the composer will take to the stage to perform with the system herself (figure 1.1). One of the notable characteristics of the field is the resurgence of the composer/

Figure 1.1 Mari Kimura improvising

improviser, those musicians who design interactive systems and then improvise with them and/or other players in performance (e.g., Richard Teitelbaum, George Lewis, Chris Chafe, Mari Kimura, David Wessel, Ed Campion, Laetitia Sonami, and many others).

There is very seldom something new under the composition sun. Algorithmic thought is certainly not new, having been in evidence in Western music composition from the beginnings of its notation. Using processes in performance that change their behavior according to an analysis of other players's music, however, was never possible before the advent of computers and interactive music systems. Such systems therefore engender a realm of composition that was unknown only a few decades ago. I believe that this music, however, should not be described as being "in its infancy" or passing through an "experimental" phase. Doing so belittles the very real aesthetic credibility many of these works have achieved and gives composers an excuse to present works that still belong in the studio.

The musical values evinced in interactive compositions are ultimately the same as those underlying a string quartet. By transferring musical knowledge to a computer program and compositional responsibility to performers onstage, on the other hand, the composer of interactive works explores the creative potentials of the new technology at the same time that he establishes an engaging and fruitful context for the collaboration of humans and computers.

1.3 Algorithmic Analysis

There is a certain paradox at the heart of the transfer of musical knowledge to a machine. We must labor mightily to make a computer program perform the analysis required of a freshman music student. Once the work is done, however, the program can make analyses more reliably and certainly much more quickly than the freshman. The computer can deliver complete descriptions of each chord in a dictation within milliseconds of its performance, for example.

The purely quantitative difference of a very great acceleration produces a qualitative difference in the kinds of tasks a machine musician can reasonably be asked to perform. We would not set a novice musician in front of an ensemble with no idea of the piece of music to be played, its key, tempo, character, or form, and expect that apprentice player to follow what was going on very well, let alone contribute to the performance in more than a perfunctory way. Interactive systems whose knowledge of music theory does not go much beyond that of our hypothetical novice are often put into just such situations, however. Because these systems always do what they do correctly and very quickly, a little musical knowledge goes a long way.

The formalization of musical concepts is proceeding apace through research in several fields, including music theory, music cognition, and artificial intelligence. So much work has been done in recent years that it would be inconceivable to document it all in one volume. The work reviewed in this text, then, is delimited by the requirement that the algorithms discussed be able to work in real time as part of a musical performance involving human players. Even with that restriction, this text in no way forms a comprehensive overview of the field.

There is a particularly interesting convergence between the fields of music cognition and interactive composition: as music cognition research becomes increasingly concerned with processes that could account for musical competence in a real musical environment, it gives rise to algorithms that can be adapted and used by composers and improvisers in performance. Whether or not it was a concern of the great variety of developers whose algorithms are described in these pages, all of these programs also pass the minimum threshold of psychological plausibility: they are all capable of execution in real time using only the information that becomes available as it is presented in sequence.

Certainly, some aspects of musicianship do not require such demanding performance in time; analysis is usually carried out over a period of days, not milliseconds, with an open score that allows the analyst to consult the music in any desired sequence. Many excellent systems of algorithmic analysis model this situation, and a suspension of the real-time requirement often allows them to produce better results than their performance-oriented counterparts. To maintain a more manageable scope, however, some such systems will be considered only to the extent that they can be adapted to real-time use.

Figure 1.2 illustrates some of the main processes extant in the literature that can be applied to real-time analysis of musical input. Space from left to right in the figure corresponds roughly to movement from low- to high-level processes in the algorithms. The arrows approximate the flow of information between stages: pitch input is forwarded to root and key identifiers, for example, while segmentation

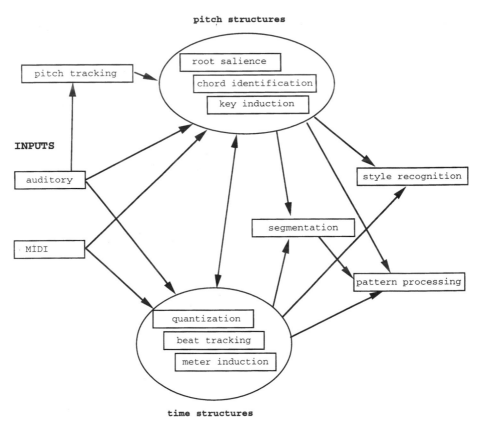

Figure 1.2 Machine musicianship processes

and style recognition rely in turn on the output of those lower-level analyses. This list is not exhaustive, but every element in it is manifested by one or more published algorithms.

My interest in this field is twofold: (1) to implement certain published processes so that they can be executed in performance; and (2) to design control structures within which these components can be combined to produce a more complete account of musical context and to make the cooperating components work better. This figure sketches only those processes related to analysis; there are similar collections that pertain to algorithmic composition and to the generation of expressive performance.

In their article "On the Thresholds of Knowledge," Douglas Lenat and Edward Feigenbaum propose the Empirical Inquiry Hypothesis: "The most profitable way to investigate AI [artificial intelligence] is to embody our hypotheses in programs, and gather data by running the programs. The surprises usually suggest revisions that start the cycle over again. Progress depends on these experiments being able to falsify our hypotheses. Falsification is the most common and yet most crucial of surprises. In particular, these programs must be capable of behavior not expected by the experimenter" (Lenat and Feigenbaum 1992, 187).

The Empirical Inquiry Hypothesis—clearly related to Sir Karl Popper's observations on the nature of science (1992)—suggests that machine musicianship programs should be built to exhibit behaviors that observers can recognize as correct or incorrect. Many, if not most interactive music systems are written to function in an environment of new music performance and improvisation. Their output can certainly be evaluated by their makers and those familiar with the idiom. My previous book, *Interactive Music Systems* (Rowe 1993) and several sections of this one deal with just such examples. A still broader class of musicians can evaluate the performance of algorithms that process standard works, however, and in accordance with the Empirical Inquiry Hypothesis many examples in this text will treat the mainstream classical and jazz repertoires as well.

I should make clear that this is not a psychology text, though the techniques I describe could be used to implement music cognition models or experiments. Psychological theories must address the question of how the processes they propose are realized in humans. My measure of success, however, is not whether these programs match empirical data from research with human subjects, but whether they output structures that make musical sense. I will gauge their performance in those terms by comparing their output with the answers expected from students studying introductory texts in music theory. The software may produce an acceptable answer by using processes similar to those of humans, or by using others that are wildly different. All else being equal, I would prefer that the machine processes resemble the human ones. Whether or not they do is a side effect, however. Ultimately I am concerned with machine musicianship and not a strict emulation of human music cognition.

1.4 Structure of the Text

The programming examples in *Machine Musicianship* are written using two languages: C++ and Max. C++ is an object-oriented programming language that is widely available, well documented, and firmly established as one of the main vehicles for developing computer music applications. As examples are described in the text, I will develop a library of C++ objects that can be used as the basis for the reader's custom programs. This book is not an introduction to C++ programming. As examples are introduced I will summarize a few features of object orientation that are particularly valuable in developing a library for machine musicianship. Beyond that, any computer store will have a shelf full of introductory C++ books to which the reader is referred.

The fact that I will be illustrating concepts with C++ programs does not mean, however, that one must be or become a programmer to follow the text. C++ programs are a compact and complete way of notating algorithms. The algorithms themselves are the topic of interest here and will be explained in the text as they are implemented in code. All of the applications described are included on the accompanying CD-ROM, but only a very small portion of the associated source code is printed in the text. Non-programmers approaching *Machine Musicianship* can then read the theory of the algorithms in question and run the associated applications to test their operation. Programmers can run the applications and modify the source, recorded in its entirety on the CD-ROM, to produce their own variations. C++ fragments in the text are concentrated at the end of each chapter so that non-programmers can skip over the code if they wish.

Max is a graphic programming language developed by Miller Puckette and David Zicarelli. There are a number of compelling reasons to include it as a development language here. First of all, Max has spawned a user community that is the most active and prolific group of interactive music designers working in the world today. There is no good reason to port Max patches to another language when there are probably more readers who know Max than know C++. In fact, I will demonstrate how C++ code is translated into a Max external to suggest how the Max community might make use of the C++ applications introduced here. Another good reason to use Max is the library of objects that has already been written for it and for MSP, a set of digital signal processing extensions. Programmers can quickly write powerful applications by building on the work of others.

Following this introduction, chapter 2 focuses on symbolic representations and algorithms directed toward the processing of pitch material. Issues such as root salience, chord identification, and key induction are addressed there. Chapter 3 continues with subsymbolic processes, notably neural networks, and expands the field of application to include rhythm. Chapter 4 moves to higher-level musical constructs including segments and patterns and discusses systems whose input consists of a digital audio stream. Chapter 5 begins to look at compositional techniques, including score following and algorithmic digital signal processing. In chapter 6 processes for the automatic application of expressive performance techniques are reviewed.

In the remaining chapters I look in detail at some distinctive interactive systems that have been used in performances or installations. The particular techniques of interactive improvisation are the nucleus of chapter 7, leading to a discussion of how such machine performers can collaborate with an ensemble of other players. Chapter 8 looks at extensions of interactive environments to include other media, most prominently graphics, in live performance situations. Chapter 9 presents several interactive installations, where the inherent ability of such systems to deal with unpredictable input contributes to responsive environments exhibiting a variety of behaviors. A presentation of research directions form the conclusion in chapter 10.

1.5 Machine Musicianship Library

The CD-ROM enclosed in this book contains a library of C++ objects that can be used to build interactive programs. The source code of the examples, also listed on the CD-ROM, provides a set of templates for users to follow in writing their own applications. The library includes the files listed in table 1.1.

Many more files are included with their associated projects: the library is a repository of base classes from which specializations are built for almost every program in the book. In object-oriented programming, a *base class* is a generalized encapsulation of data and processes concerned with a particular subset of some application area. Specializations refine those general classes into *derived classes* that address the details of some specific application. All of the analysis processes depicted in figure 1.2, for example, have examples detailed in the text and included on the CD-ROM that are made from a combination of base classes, derived classes, and custom code.

Max programs are referenced as stand-alone applications, but are not included in the *Machine Musicianship* library as the necessary objects already form the heart of Max itself. One fully developed example is ported from the C++ environment into Max as a Max external, and many of the other C++ examples could similarly produce useful

Table 1.1 Machine Musicianship Library

Clock.cp	timing routines
Event.cp	representation of a group of notes
EventBlock.cp	representation of a group of events
File.cp	file handling
Listener.cp	analysis of incoming MIDI events
ListenProps.cp	analysis processes
Mac.cp	macintosh I/O
MMerrors.cp	error reporting
Note.cp	representation of notes
OMSInPort.cp	OMS input routines
OMSOutPort.cp	OMS output routines
OMSSystem.cp	OMS communication
Scheduler.cp	scheduling facilities
Segment.cp	representation of segments
Utilities.cp	miscellaneous

Max objects. Taking programs in the other direction, from Max to C++, should be facilitated by the *Machine Musicianship* base classes.

The danger in producing a set of classes like this, particularly when it includes such entries as Note, Event, and EventBlock, is that it can be taken as a general representation of music. My intention is precisely the opposite—I do not believe that there is a simple and general way to represent all of the aspects of music we might want to process. The representations suggested by the *Machine Musicianship* library emerged from the particular collection of applications described in this book. Other tasks will demand other representations, or at the very least, modifications of these. Rather than a proposal for a generalized solution, the classes described here should be seen as an example of how programmers might design their own. After getting our feet wet with an initial application, in fact, I will discuss the issues of representation design more thoroughly in chapter 2.

2 Symbolic Processes

The general orientation of this text is toward integration. It is a common and useful simplification to consider musical parameters independently—pitch analysis is conducted without consideration of rhythm and vice versa. Such separations are a device to focus musical discussion. The consideration of algorithms may similarly be focused by the separation of symbolic from sub-symbolic processes. Symbolic processes are those based on representations of objects and relationships and manipulations of those representations according to some set of rules. Sub-symbolic processes learn to map a collection of input parameters to a set of output classifications. Once trained, such processes can identify similar patterns in novel input without reference to a system of symbols and rules.

Ultimately I will be concerned with integrating all of these parameters and processes, much as we attend to pitch and rhythm using several strategies simultaneously when we listen. The need to begin somewhere, however, leads to the same simplifications just outlined. In this chapter I introduce several techniques necessary for algorithmic analysis and composition generally, and others required for the treatment of pitch in particular. The general techniques include C++ classes for representing musical events and handling Musical Instrument Digital Interface (MIDI) input and output. Pitch-specific processes include chord classification, the calculation of root salience, and key induction. Moreover, this chapter is restricted to symbolic processes—those that are best characterized as a system of representations and rules. The algorithms introduced in this chapter, then, are symbolic pitch processors.

I believe that it is easiest to grasp the function and significance of programming constructs when they are presented in the context of building an actual application. For that reason we will begin immediately with writing a program and start to explain the classes involved along the way. Readers who prefer to begin by learning all of the base classes involved will find them and an explanation of their function on the CD-ROM.

I conclude the chapter with programming detail about several of the base C++ classes found in the *Machine Musicianship* library. These classes include MIDI input/output routines and low-level representations of music. MIDI I/O classes are purely for bookkeeping and tend to become outdated quickly. Representation of the information encoded in a musical score, on the other hand, is a central issue for the algorithmic processing of music. There is no generally accepted formal representation of music (certainly not MIDI) and I will not propose one here. Rather, I will demonstrate the impact of particular representational choices on the implementation of specific applications and briefly discuss the general issues that emerge as they arise.

2.1 Chord Theory

The study of chords is a basic part of music theory, particularly jazz theory. For the jazz pianist, generating chords from a description of their type is one of the most fundamental skills required. Similarly, students of tonal harmony learn how to identify the types of chords from notation or dictation. At a very elementary level, these skills are taught with reference to pitch information alone, that is, without considering the rhythmic placement of the chord.

Restricting the analysis to pitch significantly simplifies the process. We must always remember what we are doing when we engage in such reduction, however. Though the resulting program may work well within its restricted domain, the context could become so impoverished that the developed algorithm would be incapable of functioning meaningfully with real music. Human music students are quickly confronted with the function of chords in a rhythmic context to ground the abstract discussion of pitch in the reality of the material. Nonetheless, in modeling a highly restricted representation of a problem we may learn much about what is necessary to produce a desired behavior, and what is not. In the course of this chapter I first implement a completely context-independent chord classifier and then gradually introduce elements of context dependence to show how they improve performance.

2.1.1 Triad Classifier

Let us begin our exploration of chord identification by writing a triad (three-note chord) classifier. We make these simplifying restrictions: first, only unique pitch classes of a chord are considered; and second, there are no references made to the rhythm or any other kind of information derived from the surrounding context.

How many three-note chords are there? If all chord members are reduced to pitch classes and no pitch class may be repeated, as we have stipulated, there exist 220 distinct three-note chords. Let us define a normal order for triads as $a < b < c$, where a, b, and c are the three unique pitch classes of the chord. Pitch classes are numbered from 0 to 11 with 0 corresponding to the pitch class C and rising chromatically to 11, corresponding to the pitch class B.

Table 2.1 shows all of the normal order three-note sets that form major, minor, augmented, or diminished triads.

Allen Forte defines a different normal order for pitch-class (pc) sets in his seminal text, *The Structure of Atonal Music* (1973). To establish a normal order in Forte's system, a pc set is evaluated through all of its circular permutations. For example, the pc set [0 1 2] would have two other circular permutations, formed by rotating the item at the beginning of the set to the end: [1 2 0] and [2 0 1]. If the original set is in ascending order, circular permutations can be made to maintain that property by adding 12 to the first element before it is rotated to the end of the list. The permutations of [0 1 2], then, become [1 2 12] and [2 12 13]. Ascending order is necessary for finding the permutation that is in normal order: "the normal order is that permutation with the least difference determined by subtracting the first integer from the last" (Forte 1973, 4). In the prior example, then, [0 1 2] is the normal order because 2-0 is less than 12-1 and 13-2.

Table 2.1 Classifications of Four Basic Triad Types

PITCH CLASSES	NOTE NAMES	ROOT	TYPE	INTERVALS
0 3 8	C E♭ A♭	2	major	3 8
0 4 7	C E G	0	major	4 7
0 5 9	C F A	1	major	5 9
1 4 9	C# E A	2	major	3 8
1 5 8	D♭ F A♭	0	major	4 7
1 6 10	D♭ G♭ B♭	1	major	5 9
2 5 10	D F B♭	2	major	3 8
2 6 9	D F# A	0	major	4 7
2 7 11	D G B	1	major	5 9
3 6 11	D# F# B	2	major	3 8
3 7 10	E♭ G B♭	0	major	4 7
4 8 11	E G# B	0	major	4 7
0 3 7	C E♭ G	0	minor	3 7
0 4 9	C E A	2	minor	4 9
0 5 8	C F A♭	1	minor	5 8
1 4 8	C# E G#	0	minor	3 7
1 5 10	D♭ F B♭	2	minor	4 9
1 6 9	C# F# A	1	minor	5 8
2 5 9	D F A	0	minor	3 7
2 6 11	D F# B	2	minor	4 9
2 7 10	D G B♭	1	minor	5 8
3 6 10	E♭ G♭ B♭	0	minor	3 7
3 8 11	D# G# B	2	minor	5 8
4 7 11	E G B	0	minor	3 7
0 4 8	C E G#	na	augmented	4 8
1 5 9	D♭ F A	na	augmented	4 8
2 6 10	D F# A#	na	augmented	4 8
3 7 11	E♭ G B	na	augmented	4 8
0 3 6	C E♭ G♭	0	diminished	3 6
0 3 9	C E♭ A	2	diminished	3 9
0 6 9	C F# A	1	diminshed	6 9
1 4 7	C# E G	0	diminished	3 6
1 4 10	C# E A#	2	diminished	3 9
1 7 10	D♭ G B♭	1	diminished	6 9
2 5 8	D F A♭	0	diminished	3 6
2 5 11	D F B	2	diminished	3 9
2 8 11	D G# B	1	diminished	6 9
3 6 9	D# F# A	0	diminished	3 6
4 7 10	E G B♭	0	diminished	3 6
5 8 11	F A♭ C♭	0	diminished	3 6

A further rule determines the best normal order for two sets that have the same difference between the first and last integers: "If the least difference of the first and last integers is the same for any two permutations, select the permutation with the least difference between first and second integers. If this is the same, select the permutation with the least difference between the first and third integers, and so on, until the difference between the first and the next to last integers has been checked. If the differences are the same each time, select one ordering arbitrarily as the normal order" (Forte 1973, 4).

Forte's ordering scheme is not entirely algorithmic due to the last instruction of the second rule, but as such cases are very rare, it can certainly be implemented in a functional computer program. The advantage of Forte's classification is that it yields a great reduction in the number of unique pitch-class sets. There are 220 three-note chords delimited only by the requirement that no pc be repeated. This number is reduced to 55 when three-note chords are represented as a set of two intervals rather than three pitch-classes, as I will establish momentarily. Forte's normal ordering yields a list of only 12 three-note pitch-class sets. For a table-lookup algorithm (such as the triad identifier) smaller set lists mean smaller and more manageable tables.

Forte defines pc sets to be equivalent if they are related by transposition or inversion followed by transposition. This equivalence relation means that his set names cannot be easily adapted to the classification of tonal music. For example, the major triad and minor triad are inversions of each other and so are represented by one name. Inversion here means intervallic inversion: if we duplicate the intervals of a C major triad going down from C instead of up we get C-A♭-F, an F minor triad. Since we are interested in tonal distinctions we will continue with a larger classification table. Note, however, that the mechanism introduced here for chord identification could be adapted quite directly to a real-time Forte set recognizer.

Whether using the Forte set list or table 2.1, we can easily write a program that looks for certain pitch class sets and outputs the corresponding label. If we adopt the set list from table 2.1, the same identification can be accomplished even more simply. The last column, showing intervallic relationships of the other members to the lowest pitch class, demonstrates regularity that makes it easier to work with two intervals than with three pcs. For example, to find an augmented chord we need only identify intervals of four and eight semitones above the lowest pitch. Now we are looking for one kind of augmented triad instead of four.

There are no inversions of augmented chords—the intervals are always the same no matter which pitch is lowest. Correspondingly, I have listed the augmented chords as having no root. Another strategy would be to identify the lowest pitch class of an augmented set as the root. Because we have reduced notes to pitch classes and eliminated duplications, however, the lowest pitch class might not correspond to the lowest note in the chord. We have thus encountered the first limiting consequence of our contextual simplifications.

With the other triad types (major, minor, and diminished), notice that inversions do change the intervallic relationships. Major triads represented intervalically have three forms, corresponding to the three possible placements of the root. Root position major triads have the interval set [4 7], first inversion triads [3 8], and second inversion triads [5 9]. Therefore we need to calculate the two intervals above the lowest pitch class.

To make an intervallic representation, we first order the pitches as before, with a < b < c. The interval a-b will then vary between 1 and 10 semitones because the interval between the lowest note and the middle one must always be at least one semitone and not more than a minor seventh, allowing the third member to be higher than the middle. Similarly, the interval a-c will vary between 2 and 11 semitones above the lowest pitch class. Considered from the intervallic perspective, there are only 55 distinct combinations of two intervals above the lowest pitch class—a reduction of 75% from the number of chords considered as pitch class triplets. A table similar to table 2.1 can now be constructed to classify intervalically represented three-note chords and to pinpoint which of the three members is the root. Table 2.2 shows all 55 possibilities.

Table 2.2 Classifications of All Three-Note Chords

| [1 2] | [1 3] | [1 4] | [1 5] | [1 6] | [1 7] | [1 8] | [1 9] | [1 10] | [1 11] |
| maj 7 b9 | major 9th | min/maj 7 | major 7th | dom #11 | dom b9 | major 7th | maj 7 #5 | minor 9th | maj 7 b9 |

| [2 3] | [2 4] | [2 5] | [2 6] | [2 7] | [2 8] | [2 9] | [2 10] | [2 11] |
| minor 9th | dom 9th | minor 7th | dom 7th | dom 9th | half dim 7 | dom 7th | dom 9th | major 9th |

| [3 4] | [3 5] | [3 6] | [3 7] | [3 8] | [3 9] | [3 10] | [3 11] |
| maj 7 #5 | dom 7th | diminished | minor | major | diminished | minor 7th | min/maj 7 |

| [4 5] | [4 6] | [4 7] | [4 8] | [4 9] | [4 10] | [4 11] |
| major 7th | half dim 7th | major | augmented | minor | dom 7th | major 7th |

| [5 6] | [5 7] | [5 8] | [5 9] | [5 10] | [5 11] |
| dom b9 | dom 9th | minor | major | dom 9th | dom #11 |

| [6 7] | [6 8] | [6 9] | [6 10] | [6 11] |
| dom #11 | dom 7th | diminished | half dim 7 | dom b9 |

| [7 8] | [7 9] | [7 10] | [7 11] |
| major 7th | minor 7th | dom 7th | major 7th |

| [8 9] | [8 10] | [8 11] |
| min/maj 7 | dom 9th | maj 7 #5 |

| [9 10] | [9 11] |
| major 9th | minor 9th |

| [10 11] |
| maj 7 b9 |

Of these 55, 10 correspond to the primary triad classifications of Western tonal music: three groups form major triads ([3 8], [4 7], and [5 9]), three groups form minor triads ([3 7], [4 9], and [5 8]), three groups form diminished triads ([3 6], [3 9], and [6 9]) and one group forms augmented triads ([4 8]). Another 21 can be labeled seventh chords (major, dominant, minor, minor-major, half diminished, diminished) in some inversion with one member missing, yielding a total of 31 identifiers. As we continue in this vein, the classifications for the remaining 24 sets become more problematic. For example, I have defined the set [2 A] to be a dominant 9th chord with the lowest pitch class identified as the root. Figure 2.1 shows the notation of such a dominant 9th chord with the missing pitches shown as white noteheads.

Certainly a 9th chord with only three pitches is a very incomplete 9th chord. If one is given only these three pitch classes, on the other hand, there are two choices: one can call it an "unknown" chord, or try to come up with a plausible label. While the dominant 9th interpretation is a plausible label for this set of three pitch classes and will often be the most appropriate, alternate identifications are plausible as well and will sometimes be better. For example, the chord may be a dominant 9th, but with a different root. Consider the chord in figure 2.2.

This interpretation of the three pitch classes C, B♭, and D, again identifies the chord as a dominant 9th, but now shows B♭ as the root.

Figure 2.1 Dominant 9th interpretation of [2 A] set

Figure 2.2 Alternative dominant 9th interpretation of [2 A] set

Figure 2.3 Dominant b13 interpretation of [2 A] set

In other words, the root of the set is ambiguous. Moreover, the type is also ambiguous. Figure 2.3 shows the three pitch classes in a dominant seventh chord plus a flat thirteenth with D as the root. Though less likely than the other two, this interpretation is also correct in some situations.

Because this collection of pitch classes is ambiguous with respect to both type and root, it is clear that these attributes cannot be uniquely determined from pitch class alone. The only way to decide between rival interpretations is to appeal to the surrounding context. A context-dependent identifier might consider the prevailing key, for example, or voice-leading from and to chords immediately surrounding the one to be identified. Even a consideration of the voicing of notes within the chord, though not involving the surrounding context, would require more information than we have allowed ourselves thus far.

Though analysis of the context can be useful for correct chord identification, it also introduces complexity that may affect the speed and consistency of computation. A context-independent identifier will work faster and always produce the same result for the same collection of pitch classes. Moreover, assigning a label based only on pitch classes is not insensitive to compositional norms. Table 2.2, for example, assumes a context of Western tertian harmony that appears regularly in some kinds of jazz and classical music, but does not hold in other styles that do not follow those conventions. Table 2.2, then, is not style-insensitive, but rather encodes a set of assumptions about the contexts in which it will be used. I begin with a table-based approach for its simplicity, and because the technique is commonly used in commercial chord identifiers, which constitute a kind of baseline competence. Before proceeding with methods that do make computational use of the surrounding context, let us see how well this simple table lookup approach can do.

Figure 2.4 shows a small code fragment from a C++ program that performs table-lookup triad identification. (I use triad as a shorthand for three-note chord—most of these pc-sets are not triads in any conventional sense.) At the end of the chapter I describe some of the underlying programming constructs in more detail. For the moment I will use code to illustrate how the program works, both because it shows exactly what happens, and because the code constitutes a high-level notation of the steps of an algorithm. Non-programmers should concentrate on the comments following the double-slash marks (//). These are not part of the program but text explanations of the immediately following code.

An integral part of the process involves a data structure (an array) representing the twelve pitch classes. The first thing the algorithm does is initialize all twelve elements in the array to zero. In the second step, elements in the array corresponding to pitch classes in the triad are set to one. MIDI defines middle C to be note number 60. Other note numbers are generated by adding or subtracting semi-tone distances from middle C: the C♯ above middle C is note number 61, the B below 59, etc. The modulo operator (notated by the symbol "%") divides a number by the argument and returns any remainder. In this case, each MIDI pitch is divided by twelve and the remainder is used as the address into the pitch class array.

Pitch class C in MIDI has the note number 60, as well as integer multiples of 12 above and below 60 (36, 48, 72, 84, etc.). Therefore all notes with a pitch class of C taken modulo 12 will have the address (remainder) zero, all notes with a pitch class of C♯/D♭ will have the address (remainder) one, and so on. Once the pitch class of a triad member is computed, the array element at that location is set to one. Multiple occurrences of the same pitch class in a chord are effectively eliminated—the array position will still be equal to one no matter how many times the pitch class is repeated. Table 2.3 shows the pcs array representing a C major triad: the array members at

```
void Chord::Calculate(Event* event)

{

    register int i;


    // 1. initialize pitch class array to zero

    for (i=0; i<12; i++)

        pcs[i] = 0;


    // 2. put a one in the corresponding pcs slot for each pitch

    for (i=0; i<event->chordSize; i++)

        pcs[event->notes[i]->pitch%12] = 1;


    // 3. count the total number of pitch classes

    int numPcs = 0;

    for (i=0; i<12; i++)

        numPcs += pcs[i];


    CallChordFinder(numPcs);        // 4. find chord type and root

    DrawChordType();                // 5. output onto the screen

}
```

Figure 2.4 Triad identification

Table 2.3 C-Major Triad Pitch-Class Array

ADDRESS	0	1	2	3	4	5	6	7	8	9	10	11
	1	0	0	0	1	0	0	1	0	0	0	0

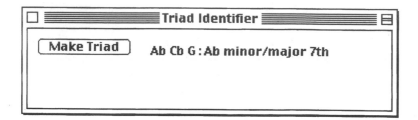

Figure 2.5 Triad identifier application

addresses 0 (corresponding to the pitch class C), 4 (E), and 7 (G) are
set to one while the others are set to zero.

The third step of the triad identification algorithm counts the number of distinct pitch classes in the chord simply by adding all of the
array elements set to one. Another routine, `CallChordFinder()`,
is invoked with the number of distinct pitch classes as an argument.
`CallChordFinder()` computes the two intervals above the first element in the pcs array that is set to one. These two intervals form an
address into a table that contains the type and root for every three-
note chord. The identification table consists of the 55 type/root pairs
shown in table 2.1. Finally the pitch classes found together with the
root and type from the table are printed on the interface (figure 2.5).

The CD-ROM contains the triad application and all of the source
code necessary to compile it. This example program generates random three-note chords when the `Make Triad` button is clicked or
the space bar is depressed. Next we will build a version that recognizes chords played on a MIDI keyboard. Before doing so, let us
consider some of the problems surrounding music representation
generally, and the MIDI standard in particular.

2.1.2 Representations

The issue of music representation is a complex and unsettled one.
Several books (Selfridge-Field 1997a; Marsden and Pople 1992; De
Poli, Piccialli, and Roads 1991; Howell, West, and Cross 1991) and
journal issues (*Computer Music Journal* 17[1–2]) have been devoted
to the question. Carol Krumhansl considers representation from the
standpoint of music cognition:

We come now to the central question about internal representations in music: What kind of information about the musical stimulus is internalized, in what form(s) is it stored, and how is it interpreted and recognized? With regard to visual perception, Kosslyn and Pomerantz (1977) warned against thinking of visual representations as pictures in the head. Similarly, I would warn against thinking of perceived or imagined music as auditory tapes in the head which record sound-pressure variations continuously over time. Visual representations are organized at early levels of processing into objects, properties of objects, and spatial relations between objects; music is organized at early levels of processing into events, properties of events, and temporal relations between events. (Krumhansl 1992, 200–201)

For machines, the difference between untreated audio (closest to Krumhansl's "tapes in the head") and more abstract representations is critical. The most common form of audio input is a lightly structured stream of digital pulse-code-modulation (PCM) samples, such as AES-EBU or SP/DIF signals (Watkinson 1994). The most common abstract representation is MIDI. Devices called pitch-to-MIDI converters attempt to convert an audio stream into a series of MIDI messages. MIDI synthesizers perform the reverse by changing MIDI messages into audio output. Pitch-to-MIDI converters lose a lot of information because they must represent the sound with only two parameters: pitch and velocity (i.e., loudness at the attack). Worse, even this restricted form of representation is often inaccurate: it is difficult to reliably report the fundamental pitch and loudness of a quickly changing audio signal in real time.

In the case of a MIDI stream controlling a synthesizer, information is not so much lost as it is incomplete. MIDI messages say nothing about the timbre of a sound to be produced beyond the selection of a program number. The complete specification of an audio output stream, then, is distributed between the MIDI messages and the program resident in the synthesizer.

Moreover, MIDI represents music as a collection of notes that go on and off with a certain velocity, roughly equivalent to loudness.

As such it is much more a representation of the physical gestures performed on a musical keyboard than it is a representation of the music itself. The activity MIDI represents is really just a step beyond typing—the only difference is that we usually do not record how hard a typewriter key is struck. Beyond limiting what the representation can say about the music, this orientation also effectively restricts input to those parameters that most resemble keyboard playing. Changes in bowing a viola, for example, are simply ignored.

David Huron describes MIDI as a representation of performance activity information (PAI), because it most directly models the physical gestures of a keyboard player (1992). He labels transduction from PAI to sound synthesis information (SSI) *registration* in an analogy to organ registration. Essentially this is the conversion that takes place when a MIDI stream is interpreted by a synthesizer and sound is produced as a result.

I will not continue with a rant about MIDI here. There are fine reviews of the issues involved (Loy 1985; Moore 1988), and I have discussed several aspects of the problem myself (Rowe 1993). Moreover, most of the applications in this book are based on the MIDI standard, warts and all. In general, I will approach representation with the goal of providing a minimal description, and fortunately MIDI is very minimal. Trying to develop a comprehensive representation that can mean all things to all projects often leads to a concoction that serves no one: "Most systems are extensible, but all become cumbersome when they begin to seem like centipedes—with too little core to support a large array of extensions and too few links between extensions to provide an integrated logical foundation for understanding the music as music. Each new addition takes the representation further from the object it attempts to simulate and taxes programming effort as well" (Selfridge-Field 1997b, 5).

Roger Dannenberg makes this observation regarding the possibility of a general music representation: "As an art form, music is distinguished by the presence of many relationships that can be treated mathematically, including rhythm and harmony. There are also many non-mathematical elements such as tension, expectancy, and emotion. Music can contain symbolic or structural relationships existing within and between the dimensions of pitch, time, timbre, harmony, tempo, rhythm, phrasing, and articulation. A further source of complexity is that 'music' can mean printed notation, performance (instrument control) information, or resulting sounds. Finally, music evolves with every new composition. There can be no 'true' representation just as there can be no closed definition of music" (Dannenberg 1993, 20).

I do not believe that a general music representation exists, nor that the particular collection of objects included in the *Machine Musicianship* library approximates one. The representation classes included there emerged from the particular set of applications I describe in this text. Other applications will demand other representations. "The essential point is that in order to represent something, its properties must be interpreted according to some proposed utility. Or more simply expressed, one cannot meaningfully discuss the design of representation schemes without some knowledge of how such a representation is going to be used" (Huron 1992, 10).

David Huron has written extensively on representations (1997) and implemented his analysis ideas in a software environment called the Humdrum Toolkit. Humdrum is a collection of music analysis software that relies on a common representational protocol, called *kern*. Information following the kern protocol can be manipulated and transformed by a variety of tools that perform such tasks as key induction, information measurement, and pattern matching. Of particular interest for the current discussion is the fact that Humdrum adheres to no single representation, but rather describes a format within which many different representational styles can be realized: "Humdrum avoids trying to represent everything within a single scheme. Instead, it encourages the user to break up the representational problem into independent manageable schemes, which are then coordinated. Each specific representation scheme will establish its own limits. While several representation schemes are predefined in Humdrum, users are free to develop their own schemes, tailored to their specific needs" (Huron 1997, 376).

The analysis algorithms of Humdrum are mostly written in awk, and the Toolkit as a whole is closely tied to the structure of the UNIX operating system. In keeping with the UNIX philosophy, for example, analyses with Humdrum are normally accomplished by linking together processes from the Toolkit, rather than by running one stand-alone application with different scores as input. And as is the case with UNIX, a collection of processes designed to work together can be used to realize a great variety of analyses, including many never specifically foreseen by the author of the tools.

Although Humdrum facilitates exploratory investigations, Humdrum is best used when the user has a clear problem or question in mind. For example, Humdrum allows users to pose and answer questions such as the following:

- *In Bartók, are dissonances more common in strong metric positions than in weak metric positions?*
- *What passages of the original* Salve Regina *antiphon are preserved in the settings by Tomas Luis de Victoria?*
- *In Urdu folk songs, how common is the so-called "melodic arch"—where phrases tend to ascend and then descend in pitch?*
- *Which of the Brandenburg Concertos contains the B-A-C-H motif?*
- *What are the most common fret-board patterns in guitar riffs by Jimi Hendrix?*

(Huron 1994, 7)

Interestingly, Miller Puckette conceives of Max in terms of a collection of connectable processes in the spirit of UNIX as well: "Max occupies a niche in the ecology of music-making tools which is similar to that which a shell ('sh', etc.) occupies in UNIX. It's probably possible to write a Bourne Shell program to find the nth prime. I wouldn't do it that way—I'd use C. I wouldn't use Max to do it either—I'd write a C extern. (To tell the truth, if I knew that $1 < n < 25$, I'd just use a table.) Either Max or the shell might be a very suitable environment for invoking this program, though. Max or 'sh' are good ways for fitting things together" (Puckette 1993, 6).

There are several compelling proposals for a successor to MIDI, directed either toward synthesizer control (Wright and Freed 1997) or sound description more generally (Wright et al. 1998). Some such systems have an explicit mechanism for converting from MIDI into the new representation, and vice versa. Therefore, we may hope that minimal representations may easily be ported to a more powerful and modern format when available. Moreover, there is a strong branch of current research that begins not with a quasi-structured representation like MIDI at all, but rather with a raw audio input stream. We will review some of this work in section 4.3. In many cases, such systems are able to derive information from the audio that at least duplicates the level of MIDI and often surpasses it. This is not always the case, however, as I have already mentioned the difficulties of converting pitch-to-MIDI in real time. But to the extent that analyses of audio inputs can be made to replicate the information MIDI conveys, we again might continue to use algorithms developed for MIDI even when a more powerful input source replaces it.

In this section I introduce the software interface necessary to input MIDI messages. We then will use that interface to build a MIDI chord recognizer based on the triad classifier described in section 2.1.1.

2.1.3 MIDI Chord Recognizer

To receive and transmit MIDI events using the serial port of a computer, a device driver and a set of system calls are needed. When a device driver is involved, there is almost always a hardware dependency built in to the software, and this unfortunately is the case with MIDI drivers. On the Macintosh the situation is even worse because there are competing standards for the same function. Apple long ago abandoned its leadership in this area when development of the Apple MIDI Manager was discontinued. The MIDI I/O package I will describe here, then, is the Open MIDI System (OMS) distributed by Opcode, Inc. OMS is widely used, readily available, and well documented. It has been implemented under both Windows and the MacOS, which means that software written using it can be ported between the two operating systems relatively easily.

```
typedef struct {

    long time;

    unsigned char status;

    unsigned char data1;

    unsigned char data2;

} MIDIEvent;
```

Figure 2.6   MIDIEvent struct

There are three OMS classes defined in the Machine Musicianship library. The first is OMSSystem, which provides the initial layer of communication with OMS. Any application using MIDI will need to include the OMSSystem class. This is accomplished simply by adding the OMSSystem.cp file to the project and allocating an instance of the class (see the CD-ROM for an example). To receive MIDI input or transmit MIDI output we need to allocate an input or output port, respectively, using the classes OMSInPort and OMSOutPort. The OMSInPort class provides buffering for MIDIEvents, a structure whose definition is shown in figure 2.6.

A MIDIEvent packages a MIDI channel voice message into a group of bytes. Channel voice messages always have a status byte and one or two data bytes. These are recorded in the corresponding fields of the MIDIEvent. In addition, a MIDIEvent records a timestamp that is set to the time in milliseconds at which the MIDIEvent arrived at the device driver. The buffer of the input port, then, is an array of these structures.

OMSInPort fills the buffer in the interrupt routine called by OMS and empties it in the main event loop of an application. The *Machine Musicianship* library assumes that the buffer will be read by an object of another class called Listener (described at the end of this chapter). The interaction between OMSSystem, OMSInPort, and Listener can be examined in the MIDI I/O application on the CD-ROM. In this simple example, incoming MIDI note messages serve

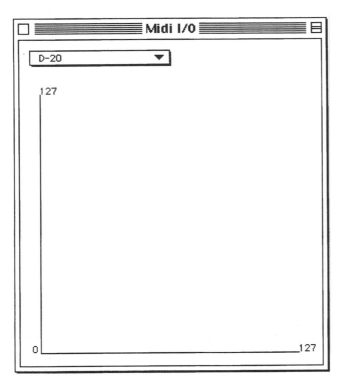

Figure 2.7 MIDI input application

only to draw or erase a line on the screen. The result is a little bar graph of incoming MIDI activity (figure 2.7). Simple though it is, such an application can be very useful in making sure that MIDI is being transmitted properly through the serial port and operating system to the application level.

With the addition of MIDI input, we can now modify the triad identifier of section 2.1.1 to analyze chords arriving from a MIDI device, such as a keyboard or sequencer, as well as those generated randomly by the program itself. The triad program discussed in section 2.1.1 is aimed at a very specific kind of harmony: the triadic chord construction usually found in beginning jazz piano texts. Even in that narrow context, the triad identifier treats a very limited range of possibilities. Bill Dobbins's *Jazz Piano Harmony*, for example, concentrates initially not on three-note but on four-note chords: "I chose to begin with four-note chords for two very practical reasons. First, four notes are a sufficient number to express a wide variety of harmonies, especially when the possible four-note chords are later combined with different bass notes. Second, four notes are a small enough number that any well motivated pianist can soon become fairly facile at working creatively with chords of this density, even in an improvising situation" (Dobbins 1994, 9).

To program the knowledge of chords possessed by a novice jazz pianist, then, we need to be able to identify and generate at least four-note chords, and preferably more. How many chords are there? Using the same restrictions governing the triads (no repeated notes, all notes considered as pitch classes) we find the totals to be those listed in table 2.4.

With three pitch classes (pcs), there are 55 distinct chords when considered intervalically, as we know from the discussion in section

Table 2.4 Chord Counts

PCs	NUMBER OF CHORDS	INTERVAL REPRESENTATION
1	12	1
2	66	11
3	220	55
4	495	165
5	792	330
6	924	462
7	792	462
8	495	330
9	220	165
10	66	55
11	12	11
12	1	1

2.1. Similarly, there exist 165 four-note chords. Note that the greatest variety is for six- and seven-note chords, which have 462 intervallic possibilities. Above seven notes the possibilities decrease again, since the increasing number of pitch classes reduces the number of possible intervals between them. Just as there is only one chord with one pitch class (the unison), there is only one twelve-note chord (the chord of all pitch classes). The symmetry continues from both ends towards the middle, peaking at 462 varieties for sextads and septads.

The MIDI chord application generates an identification of the root and type of any collection of pitches, not only three-note chords. The basic algorithm remains the same, however. Chords, reduced to pitch classes and then to intervals above the first pc in the array, are used as an address to look up stored roots and types in a table. The application and all of its associated source code is found on the CD-ROM.

The first test of the program is to examine its analysis of the four-note chords listed in Dobbins's *Jazz Piano Harmony* (Dobbins 1994, 13). All the five basic seventh chords are correctly identified in all inversions. These include major sevenths, dominant sevenths, minor sevenths, half-diminished sevenths, and diminished sevenths. The basic seventh chords exhaust 17 of the possible 165 chords (not 4*5 or 20 because the diminished seventh has the same set of intervals regardless of inversion).

Later examples in the Dobbins text show seven common altered seventh chords: the major seventh ♯5, the major seventh ♭5, the dominant seventh ♯5, the dominant seventh ♭5, the dominant seventh suspended fourth, the minor/major seventh, and the diminished/major seventh (1994, 54). Of these, the identifier again consistently labels every chord in every inversion. There are two deviations from the text identifications: the chord Dobbins labels a dominant seventh with a suspended fourth I call a dominant eleventh, and the chord he labels a diminished major seventh I call a dominant with a flat ninth. Only the surrounding context or the voicing of the chord itself could lend weight to one interpretation over the other, and these are both sources of information that the application currently ignores.

Adapting it to conform completely to the text would simply require changing a few entries in the table.

These altered seventh chords represent another 26 of the possible 165 chords (not 4*7 or 28 because the dominant seventh with a flat fifth has only two inversions). We have tested, then, 43 of the 165 in all or about a quarter of the possibilities. Certainly we could continue with a test of all 165 but I think the point is clear: such a chord identifier can quickly and consistently label all possible four-note constructions. However, by restricting the chord representation to pitch classes, and performing the analysis without reference to the surrounding context, some chords must be arbitrarily identified, and those identifications will as a consequence be incorrect in some situations.

To implement a complete chord identifier, then, one could simply build tables for all 2048 possible chords. Even if one were willing to invest the effort, however, it is not clear what many of the multi-note identifications should be. If we continue to reckon chord names following the conventions of triadic harmony, we start to encounter some very exotic identifications after six or seven pitch classes. A chord with seven pitch classes could include some form of the root, third, fifth, seventh, ninth, eleventh, and thirteenth. *Jazz Piano Harmony* contains no chords with members above the thirteenth, for example. The reason is obvious enough: after the thirteenth the next third up takes us to the root again, two octaves above its first appearance, and the succession of thirds begins again. A chord with eight distinct pitch classes, then, becomes difficult to analyze in this system without declaring chords to have a minor and major third, perfect and sharp fifth, or other such concoctions.

The MIDI chord application on the CD-ROM therefore does not use tables for all possible chords. Rather, it encodes the most common and important identifications in the tables and uses another process to reduce more complex chords that the tables do not contain. The reduction is carried out by repeatedly finding the most dissonant member and removing it until the chord is reduced to one found in the tables.

Figure 2.8 Overloaded chord

The algorithm for finding the most dissonant tone (KickOut-Member) supposes that the chord member with the smallest interval classes relative to the other members of the chord will be the most dissonant. In other words, a chord member with predominantly minor and major second relationships to the other chord members will be heard as more dissonant than another chord member having primarily major and minor third relationships. Distance is calculated between interval classes rather than intervals, meaning that any interval larger than a tritone is considered in its inverted form. Therefore a major seventh will also be counted as a minor second, reinforcing the idea that smaller interval classes are the more dissonant.

Consider figure 2.8. The lowest note of the chord, C, has the following intervallic relationships: augmented second (3 half-steps), major third (4), perfect fourth (5), and minor second (1). Because interval classes are measured rather than intervals, the interval C–G is considered a perfect fourth (inverted perfect fifth) and the interval C–B is considered a minor second. If we add together all of these intervals, the total interval distance of the C relative to the chord is 13. Repeating the procedure for every note in the chord, we arrive at these totals: C(13), D♯(12), E(13), G(16), and B(14). The note with the smallest total is D♯. Eliminating this note from the chord, we arrive at a C major seventh.

With the addition of MIDI input, the chord identifier interface appears as shown in figure 2.9. The pulldown menu comes courtesy of OMS and allows the user to select one of the possible MIDI input devices as that which is read by the program. Now a chord may be input to the application either by clicking on the Make Chord button, as before, or by playing a chord on a MIDI keyboard. The program spells the members of the chord followed by a colon, the name of

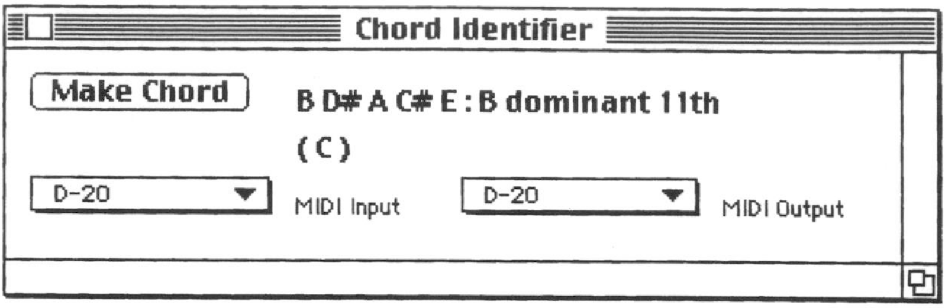

Figure 2.9 MIDI chord identifier

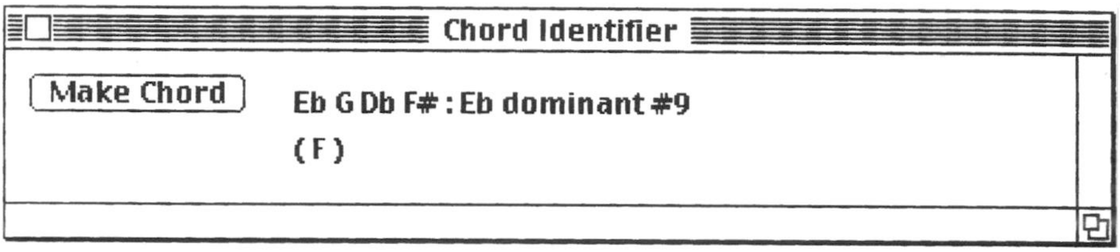

Figure 2.10 Problematic reduction

the root, and the chord type. Chord members that were eliminated by KickOutMember() are listed below in parentheses. The chord shown in figure 2.9 is a B-dominant eleventh chord with a missing fifth. The pitch class thrown out by KickOutMember() was a C natural, in this case a good choice for elimination.

The KickOutMember() algorithm is not an ideal solution, however, and often throws out members that are best retained. In figure 2.10, for example, the process kicks out the F located a major ninth above the root (with a score of 9), instead of the F♯, which is the sharp ninth (with a score of 10). One way to deal with particularly egregious errors caused by KickOutMember() is to simply add a new table entry for any chord that is being incorrectly reduced. The algorithm works well enough to fashion a reliable chord identifier in any case and is not even invoked until the chord has reached a fairly exotic state.

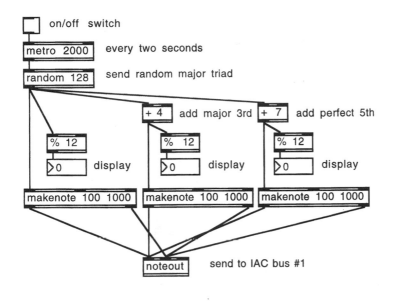

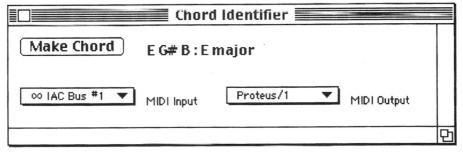

Figure 2.11 Chord reading from IAC bus

We may use the OMS input port to route chords from a keyboard to the chord identifier. One may also generate chords in some other application and send them to the program through one of the OMS inter-application communication (IAC) busses. Shown in figure 2.11 is a Max patch that randomly generates major triads. Every two seconds (the interval specified in the metro object) the patch generates a random number that becomes the root of a triad. The plus objects add a major third (+4) and a perfect fifth (+7) above that root. (The modulo [%] objects and number boxes are only there for us to see which pitch classes result from the operation). All three pitch numbers are then routed to makenote objects and sent to noteout. When noteout is set to transmit to IAC Bus #1, and the chord identifier is directed to read from that same bus, the chord application receives MIDI messages from and identifies every triad banged out by the Max patch.

Of course an even better way to integrate the chord identification process with Max would be to encode the identifier as a Max external. Then it could be used as simply another Max object within the environment as a whole. Section 4.4 demonstrates how such C++ applications can be recast as Max externals.

2.1.4 Chord Spelling

In figures 2.9 and 2.10, notice that the members of the chord are spelled correctly by the application: e.g., the major third above B in figure 2.9 is spelled D♯ and not E♭. This makes the output of the program much easier to read and verify, and also mimics the training of human musicians learning the same skill. The distinction is not available from the MIDI representation: as far as MIDI is concerned, there is one pitch number 63. The standard is unable to distinguish between 63 as a D♯ and 63 as an E♭.

The member function of the Chord class that correctly spells chords is SpellChord(). The routine first prints the name of the chord's root. I have adopted the convention that every root with an accidental will be spelled in its flat form (D♭, E♭, G♭, A♭, and B♭). Maintaining this regularity makes the rest of the job easier, but we will consider other ways to approach root naming momentarily. A NameClasses array of character strings is maintained by the Chord class and used to produce the correct letter names for members of the analyzed chord. When the root name is produced, its index in NameClasses is stored. If we then need to generate the name of the third, for example, we take the NameClass two places above the name of the root.

SpellChord() looks for and names successive thirds stacked above the root. To spell the third, for example, the algorithm assumes that a given chord will have a minor third or a major third, but not both. It first looks for a major third by checking the pcs array for a positive entry four semitones above the root. If one is found, that place in the pcs array is set to zero. This ensures that the same pitch will later not be spelled as something else. It is difficult to imagine for what other interval a major third might be mistaken, but a minor third could be taken for a sharp ninth, for example, were it not erased from the array.

It turns out that the spelling of stacked thirds can be largely, but not wholly, determined by simple rules keyed to whether the root and/or upper member are on "black keys," i.e., must be spelled with an accidental (D♭, E♭, G♭, A♭, and B♭). For a minor third, all members landing on a black key should have a flat appended to the name. This covers B♭–D♭, C–E♭, E♭–G♭, F–A♭, and G–B♭. If the third does not fall on a black key but the root does, the minor third name should also have a flat appended to it (as in D♭–F♭). Finally, if the root is G♭, the minor third needs two flats after the letter name (B♭♭). Such root-specific rules are clumsy but necessary, and these three rules produce correctly spelled minor thirds in every case.

Remember that this only works if we assume that roots falling on an accidental will always be spelled in their flatted form. Considered in isolation, it is better to spell the triad G♭–B♭♭–D♭ as F♯–A–C♯, since A is easier to read than B♭♭. Moreover, the choice between a G♭ and F♯ minor chord should be made based on the surrounding chords and, ultimately, the key in which the sonority is embedded. David Temperley proposes a more principled way of dealing with the spelling of both chord members and their roots (Temperley 1997) as implemented in the Serioso Music Analyzer (Temperley and Sleator 1999).

Before passing to a consideration of Serioso, let us consider another attribute of the spelling process that is perhaps more valuable than the spelling itself: SpellChord() comes up with the same identification of a chord's type as does the table entry, but by an independent process. Though the chord identifier as it stands looks in precompiled tables to determine the type, it could also build the type definition algorithmically as it spells the chord. Sequentially extracting thirds stacked above a defined root is a clear and quite reliable way of computing a chord's type from the standard tertian tradition. This is interesting to notice because it means that the only real contribution of the chord tables is the identification of the root. If the root is known, the chord type can be determined automatically. Therefore the identification capability of SpellChord() can be appended to processes that only locate a root (such as Temperley's) to add a classification of type.

The Serioso system makes a distinction between a "neutral pitch class" (NPC) and a "tonal pitch class" (TPC). NPCs are undifferentiated pitch classes (such as the numbering system used in MIDI) in which no difference between enharmonic spellings such C♯ and D♭ is recognized. TPCs, on the other hand, do preserve these enharmonic differences (Temperley 1997, 43). Serioso takes pitch numbers and their metric placement as input and outputs a series of named "chord spans" in which both harmonic roots and all of the input pitches are spelled as tonal pitch classes.

Both the conversion to TPCs and identification of chord roots depends on a concept called the "line of fifths." Pitches, or chord roots, are organized along a line on which neighboring pitches are a perfect fifth apart. The line of fifths is similar to the circle of fifths except that it extends infinitely in either direction (figure 2.12).

Serioso changes the problem of correctly spelling NPCs to one of finding the smallest distance along the line of fifths. For example, the interval 60–63 (in MIDI pitch numbers) could be spelled C–D♯ or C–E♭. The tonal pitch classes C and D♯ are nine places apart along the line of fifths while the TPCs C and E♭ are removed by only three places. Serioso, then, would clearly prefer to spell the interval C–E♭, following the smaller distance.

Let us implement chord spelling using the line of fifths idea. The algorithm here is my own version and is greatly simplified from the

---

··· Db   Ab   Eb   Bb   F   C   G   D   A   E   B   F#   C#   ···

Figure 2.12   Line of fifths

much more complete program found on Temperley and Sleator's website (http://bobo.link.cs.cmu.edu/music-analysis/). It is based on the observation that enharmonically equivalent TPCs are always 12 spaces apart on the line of fifths. Therefore the nearest TPC for any pitch class will always be less than 12 steps away from any other. For the moment we will only spell chords relative to themselves, as the SpellChord() process does. The routine NpcToTpc() takes an anchor TPC and returns the TPC corresponding to the input PC argument that is closest to the anchor (figure 2.13).

We can define the root from the identification table to be the anchor TPC of a chord. Since we are only spelling the chord rela-

```
int Chord::NpcToTpc(int anchor, int inputPC)

{

        /* find TPC closest to root on the line of fifths */

        int tpcCandidate = FindMinimumDistance(anchor, PcToTpc(inputPC));

        if (abs(anchor-tpcCandidate) < 12)    // if distance is less than 12

                return tpcCandidate;           // use this TPC


        if (anchor-tpcCandidate > 0)           // otherwise go up or down 12

                while ((anchor-tpcCandidate) > 12)

                        tpcCandidate += 12;    // until distance is < 12

        else

                while (abs(anchor-tpcCandidate) > 12)

                        tpcCandidate -= 12;


        return tpcCandidate;                   // return nearest TPC

}
```

Figure 2.13 NpcToTpc() function

tive to itself, the convention of spelling black key roots in their flat form can be maintained. Then it is simply a matter of calling `NpcToTpc()` for every member of the chord above the root to find the TPC spelling. The `LineOfFifths` application on the CD-ROM does exactly that.

There are two problems with `LineOfFifths`, one related to my implementation of the idea and one arising from the method itself: for jazz chords, the correct spelling of chord members is determined not only by proximity on the line of fifths, but by the alterations made to extensions in a stack of thirds. A C chord with a sharp ninth, for example, should be spelled with a D♯, not an E♭, to indicate an altered ninth. Because E♭ is closer to C than is D♯ on the line of fifths, however, the `NpcToTpc()` function will always return the TPC for E♭. At least for jazz chords, it seems that the TPC idea shows more promise for the spelling of roots in a chord progression than it does for spelling individual chord members.

The problem arising from my simple implementation has to do with the fact that TPCs should not be calculated without reference to the context. A tritone, for example, will be equidistant along the line of fifths whether it is spelled C–F♯ or C–G♭. Temperley writes "it seems that the current event should be labeled to maximize its closeness to *all* previous events, with more-recent events being weighted more than less-recent ones. In the current model, a 'center of gravity' is taken, reflecting the average position of all prior events on the line of fifths (weighted for recency); the new event is then spelled so as to maximize its closeness to that center of gravity" (1997, 44). With this step, we leave the realm of context independence. Now, the spelling of pitch classes depends not only on relationships within the current event, but on the context established by all the material leading up to it.

2.2 Context Sensitivity

Serioso not only labels pitch classes but identifies and spells the roots of harmonic areas as well. As indicated earlier, this too depends on the line of fifths: "Before beginning the process of harmonic analysis, the algorithm chooses a TPC label for each pitch event; in so doing, it maps each event onto a point on the line of fifths. This is the TPC level of the algorithm. The algorithm then proceeds to the harmonic level, where it divides the piece into segments labeled with roots. At this stage, too, it maps roots onto the line of fifths, attempting to choose roots so that the roots of nearby segments are close together on the line" (Temperley 1997, 45).

The full Serioso model is stated in a group of five preference rules. Preference rules, as established in the *Generative Theory of Tonal Music* (Lerdahl and Jackendoff 1983), indicate which of a number of legal structures will correspond most closely to the experience of human observers. There are two that concern line of fifths distance, called the pitch variance and harmonic variance rules. The full set is listed in figure 2.14 (this is the version published by Temperley and Sleator in 1999, which is somewhat different from the one published by Temperley in 1997).

2.2.1 Virtual Pitch

The Compatibility Rule is similar to a tradition of proposals for finding the most salient pitch in a collection. Salience refers to the perceptual prominence of one member among a group of elements: for example, the root of a major triad has a unique and prominent role relative to the other pitches of the chord. As we know from acoustics, any pitched sound is composed of a number of frequencies that are related as integer multiples of the fundamental. The auditory system is so strongly tuned to this phenomenon that the brain will supply the fundamental to a set of integrally related frequencies that are missing the lowest member: we "hear" the missing fundamental as the pitch of the set even if it is not physically present. Figure 2.15 shows the harmonic series above the fundamental C_2.

Because the perceptual system supplies a missing fundamental, virtual pitch theory looks for certain intervals within a collection of pitches and uses them as evidence for a heard fundamental that may or may not be part of the collection. In figure 2.15 we see intervals of a perfect fourth, major third, and minor third between the third, fourth, and fifth harmonics. Virtual pitch theory takes these intervals

Compatibility Rule—prefer roots that result in certain pitch-root relationships. The following relationships are preferred, in this order: 1, 5, 3, b3, b7, b5, b9, ornamental.

Ornamental Dissonance Rule—in labeling events as ornamental, prefer events that are (1) closely followed by another event a half-step or whole-step away, and (2) metrically weak.

Harmonic Variance Rule—prefer roots such that roots of nearby chord spans are close together on the line of fifths.

Pitch Variance Rule—prefer spellings for pitch events such that nearby events are close together on the line of fifths.

Strong-Beat Rule—prefer to start chord spans on strong beats.

Figure 2.14 Serioso preference rules

Figure 2.15 Harmonic series

(at the pitch locations of the figure) as evidence that the fundamental is C, since this is the pitch that the ear would supply. (For an influential version of this theory, see Terhardt et al. [1982]).

Richard Parncutt has continued the tradition with a series of publications (1988; 1989), and he extended the model to account for the contextual effects of voicing and tonality (1997). The virtual pitch component of the model uses a concept of *root-support intervals*. These intervals are derived from the first members of the harmonic series when repeated pitch classes are eliminated and appear in decreasing order of importance: the perfect unison, perfect fifth, major third, minor seventh, and major second. Note in figure 2.15 that the first pitches of the series are C, G, E, B♭, and D when repetitions are omitted.

The vector of weights attached to root-support intervals is: $w = [\ 10, 0, 1, 0, 3, 0, 0, 5, 0, 0, 2, 0\ ]$. To calculate a chord root, the vector w is multiplied by a vector representing the notes of a chord where a 1 indicates the presence of a pitch class and a 0 indicates its absence (like the pcs array in the Chord application). A pitch class vector representing a C major triad, for example, would be $[\ 1, 0, 0, 0, 1, 0, 0, 1, 0, 0, 0, 0\ ]$. Multiplying a C major triad by the vector w yields 18: $1 \times 10 + 0 \times 0 + 0 \times 1 + 0 \times 0 + 1 \times 3 + 0 \times 0 + 0 \times 0 + 1 \times 5 + 0 \times 0 + 0 \times 0 + 0 \times 2 + 0 \times 0$.

Note that this result is obtained by lining up the root-support weight vector so that the unison weight (10) is multiplied by the pitch class C. Because we want to compute the effect of all possible alignments, the next step is to rotate the weight vector such that the unison weight is aligned with C♯, then D, and so on. The calculated salience of the chord multiplied by the rotated weight vector is then stored with the pitch class of each potential root in turn. For example, a root position C major triad contains the pitch classes C, E, and G. After multiplying the chord by the root-support weights for all rotations of the set, the root saliencies calculated are:

C	C♯	D	D♯	E	F	F♯	G	A♭	A	B♭	B
18	0	3	3	10	6	2	10	3	7	1	0

We have already gone through the calculation that assigns a salience of 18 to the root C. The others are found when the weight vector is rotated to align with the corresponding candidate root's pitch class. The root E gets a salience of 10, for example, because the vector w has been rotated to the position { 0, 0, 2, 0, 10, 0, 1, 0, 3, 0, 0, 5 } (aligning the unison root-support interval against the pitch class E), yielding $1 \times 0 + 0 \times 0 + 0 \times 2 + 0 \times 0 + 1 \times 10 + 0 \times 0 + 0 \times 1 + 1 \times 0 + 0 \times 3 + 0 \times 0 + 0 \times 0 + 0 \times 5 = 10$.

The saliencies are then normalized to make the average salience for all twelve roots equal to ten. Normalizing the above collection yields:

C	C♯	D	D♯	E	F	F♯	G	A♭	A	B♭	B
34	0	6	6	19	11	4	19	6	13	2	0

Virtual pitch theory is interesting in that it assigns root energy, as it were, to pitch classes that are not present in the sounding chord. In the case of a C major triad, C♯ and B, the pitch classes one half-step away from the actual root, are the only ones to receive no weight at all. Even the pitch class a tritone away from the root (F♯) receives some activation—more, in fact, than the minor seventh (B♭).

The calculation thus far takes no account of voicing or tonal context and therefore roughly corresponds to the algorithm published by Parncutt in (1988). The version we are concerned with here, however, also regards voicing: in particular, it looks for the lowest note of the chord and gives it additional weight. Parncutt justifies the amendment in part by appealing to jazz chord theory: "In jazz, it is standard practice to notate D–F–A–C as Dm7 (not F/D) and F–A–C–D as F6 (not Dm7/F), implying that the root depends upon which note is voiced in the bass" (1997, 181). The model therefore adds a value of 20 to the lowest note of the chord. Adding the voicing adjustment to our ongoing C major triad (root position) analysis, we arrive at:

C	C♯	D	D♯	E	F	F♯	G	A♭	A	B♭	B
54	0	6	6	19	11	4	19	6	13	2	0

The final step in Parncutt's algorithm is to add weights representing the influence of a tonal context on the perception of the chord. These weights are derived from the pc-stability profiles published by Krumhansl and Kessler (1982). These profiles were determined through experimentation with human subjects using the "probe-tone technique," which has become established as one of the central experimental paradigms of music cognition.

The technique arose from the observation that certain pitches sound as though they finish an incomplete scale while others are less stable. The series of tones C-D-E-F-G-A-B will sound complete when followed by C, for example, but less so when followed by non-tonic pitches of the C major scale, and still less complete when followed by pitches that are not in the C major scale at all. "This, then, suggested that a way to quantify the hierarchy of stability in tonal contexts would be to sound incomplete scale contexts with all possible tones of the chromatic scale (which we call 'probe tones'), and ask listeners to give a numerical rating of the degree to which each of the tones completed the scale" (Krumhansl 1990, 21).

The Krumhansl and Kessler stability profiles, then, came from the numerical ratings assigned by human subjects to certain pitches with respect to a given scale. Parncutt normalizes the profiles for this algorithm in two steps: (1) a constant is subtracted such that the minimum value of a profile becomes zero; and (2) the pc-weights are then multiplied by a constant to make the average of all profiles equal to 10. The resulting normalized values are shown in table 2.5.

Parncutt applies the stability profiles as follows: "To account for the effect of prevailing tonality on the root, the pc-salience profile of

Table 2.5 Normalized PC-Stability Profiles

	0	1	2	3	4	5	6	7	8	9	10	11
major	33	0	10	1	17	15	2	24	1	11	0	5
minor	28	3	9	21	3	9	2	17	12	3	8	6

a chord is rotated around the pc-cycle until its first element corresponds to the prevailing tonic, and then added to the stability profile of the prevailing tonality. The resultant profile is the predicted goodness-of-fit tone profile of the chord in context. The peak of the resultant profile is the predicted root of the chord in context'' (1997, 189). To complete the example of our root-position C major triad, the final set of saliencies after addition of the stability profile for C major (assuming, therefore, that the chord is the tonic of the key) is:

C	C♯	D	D♯	E	F	F♯	G	A♭	A	B♭	B
87	0	16	7	36	26	6	43	7	24	2	5

Figure 2.16 lists the C++ code of a Parncutt-style root calculator. After some initialization, the algorithm converts the notes of the chord to pitch classes and stores them in a pcs array, just as the triad and chord identifiers did. At the same time, the variable lowVoice keeps track of which pitch class was at the bottom of the chord. The double loop (after the comment "for all pcs and all rotations of the weight set") adds the product of all possible rotations of the root-support weights multiplied by the pcs array to a set of sums for each pitch class. The variable bigSum is simultaneously updated to record the total salience distributed across all twelve pcs. A normalization factor is computed by dividing 120 (10 * the number of pitch classes) by bigSum. The sums are multiplied by the normalization factor and the resulting saliencies are saved. Voicing and key context adjustments to the saliencies are then made if the user has chosen to activate those effects.

Figure 2.17 shows the interface to the Virtual Pitch application found on the CD-ROM. The input is a C major triad in root position. Both the voicing and tonal context buttons are on, so the saliencies calculated for the chord are equal to those shown in the final calculation of our previously developed example. Chords can be generated randomly using the Make Chord button (or the space bar) or they can be played in from a MIDI keyboard. Turning the voicing and context buttons on or off will recalculate the most recent chord with

```
void Parncutt::Calculate(Event *event)
{
        register int i;
        int sum[12];
        int lowVoice = 128;      // set lowest note equal to high pitch


        for (i=0; i<12; i++) {
            pcs[i] = 0;          // initialize pitch class array to zero
            sum[i] = 0;          // initialize weight sums to zero
        }


        // put a one in the corresponding pcs[] slot for each pitch
        // and store lowest absolute pitch in lowVoice
        for. (i=0; i<event->ChordSize(); i++) {
            int pitch      = event->Notes(i)->Pitch();
            pcs[pitch%12] = 1;
            lowVoice       = min(lowVoice, pitch);
        }
        lowVoice %= 12;          // convert lowVoice to pitch class


        int bigsum = 0;          // the sum of all weights


        // for all pcs and all rotation of the weight set
        for (i=0; i<12; i++)
                for (int j=0; j<12; j++) {
                    int product = pcs[j] * intervalWeights[((12-i)+j)%12];
                    sum[i] += product;       // save salience sum for pc
```

Figure 2.16 Virtual pitch Calculate routine

```
        bigsum += product;        // add in to total sum
    }


// compute normalization so that the average is 10
float normalize = 120.0 / (float)bigsum;


// normalize all pitch class saliencies
for (i=0; i<12; i++)
        saliencies[i] = round((float)sum[i] * normalize);


// add voicing weight if voicing is on
if (voicingOn) saliencies[lowVoice] += 20;


// add in Krumhansl profile if key context is on
if (contextOn)
        for (i=0; i<12; i++)
                if (profileMode == ParncuttMac::kMajor)
                    saliencies[(i+currentKey)%12] += majorProfile[i];
                else
                    saliencies[(i+currentKey)%12] += minorProfile[i];


Display();
}
```

Figure 2.16 Continued

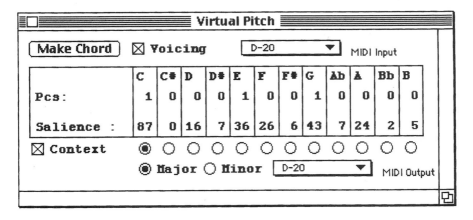

Figure 2.17 Virtual pitch application interface

or without the voicing or context effects so that the user can see the impact of these rules on the calculation.

Figure 2.18 shows the roots output by the Parncutt algorithm for chords in the first eight bars of the Largo con Gran Espressione of Beethoven's *E♭ Major Piano Sonata, op. 7* (the slow movement is in C major, not E♭). There are four possible context combinations: (1) no context, (2) voicing active, (3) tonality active, and (4) voicing and tonality active. For each chord, the root shown in figure 2.18 is the one calculated with both the voicing and tonal contexts active. Most of the analyses are relatively stable no matter which rules are on: of the 15 chords shown, 12 (80%) give the same root in either all of the combinations or in three out of four combinations. In the cases where one of the four does not agree, it is usually because the voicing effect without considering tonal context has elevated the lowest pitch class to the highest score.

The remaining three chords are interesting as an illustration of the various rules' contribution to the analysis. The first, marked "X" in figure 2.18, consists only of the two pitch classes D and F♯. The most salient pitch is found to be either D (when voicing is off) or F♯ (when it is on). Let the strength of the salience rating be the percentage of the highest rating relative to the sum of the two highest ratings. When

Figure 2.18 Beethoven virtual pitch analysis

there is no voicing and no context, for example, chord X indicates D as the most salient pitch with a strength of 56%. Activating voicing alone shifts the root to F♯, with a strength of 56.9%. F♯ is also the root when both voicing and context are active, but with a strength of only 52%. In any case, we can see from the strength analysis that the most salient pitch is ambiguous since it has only a small amount of weight above that of its closest rival. The root position C major triad that opens the movement, by way of contrast, indicates a root with a strength of 67% (when both the voicing and tonal contexts are active).

The chord marked "Y" in figure 2.18 would normally be classified as a dominant seventh chord in third inversion with a suspension in the upper voice. The Parncutt algorithm describes it as a G chord when voicing and tonal context are not considered, an F chord when voicing is on (either with or without context), and a C chord when seen in tonal context but without voicing. The complete model, then, calls chord Y an F chord, but with a strength of only 50.8%. Though it is recognized as ambiguous, the ambiguity is between interpretations of F and C, not the dominant G. The difficulty for the algorithm comes from the suspension, particularly since it is the tonic pitch that is suspended. Whenever the tonic pitch of the key is present, it will tend to have a large activation due to the contribution of the Krumhansl and Kessler stability profile. Note that Parncutt announces the intention to add a consideration of voice-leading to the context-sensitivity of the model, which presumably would treat the suspension of the C, but this extension was not implemented in the version described (1997).

The last ambiguous chord, marked "Z" in figure 2.18, illustrates the same difficulty. Traditional music theory would regard it as a double suspension above a D minor chord in first inversion. The Parncutt algorithm analyzes it as an A, F, or C chord according to the rules that are active. The full model (with voicing and context) calls it an F chord with a strength of 55%. None of the cases finds chord Z to have a root of D.

The Parncutt root salience algorithm is an important contribution to machine recognition of harmony. For our purposes, it is also particularly interesting because it functions well in real time. How may we incorporate it in an analysis system for use in live performance? There are two areas of extension I wish to address here: (1) determination of chord type, and (2) interaction with key induction. Use of the Parncutt algorithm in performance has a third limitation as well—it assumes that all members of a chord will be presented simultaneously (which accounts for the mislabeling of chord X in figure 2.18). Any kind of arpeggiation must be reconciled elsewhere before a chord can be presented to the algorithm for analysis. Other harmonic analysis systems (Winograd 1968; Maxwell 1992) have the same requirement: "The most important limitation is that they are unable to handle cases where the notes of a chord are not stated fully and simultaneously, such as arpeggiations, incomplete chords, and unaccompanied melodies" (Temperley 1999, 10). Because that kind of reconciliation falls under the general heading of segmentation, this third extension will be discussed in chapter 4.

2.2.2 Determination of Chord Type

Though the models presented by Temperley and Parncutt represent sophisticated techniques for identifying the root of a chord, they say nothing about the type of the chord lying above the root. In other words, though we may learn that a chord is based on the pitch-class C, we will not know whether it is in a major or minor mode. I suggested in section 2.2 that the chord spelling algorithm described there could be used to determine the type of a chord from a given root. Accordingly, we will now add type identification to the Parncutt root analysis.

Jazz theory, following Rameau's scale-step theory, tends to regard the root of a chord as the lowest note in a series of stacked thirds.

Musicians commonly identify each chord with a capital letter describing the pitch that serves as its root . . . beside each letter of each chord or its roman numeral are arabic numbers describing additional elements or tensions that supplement the basic triad. Artists name them in terms of their numerical positions in a stack of thirds built up from the chord's root, either diatonically (in the initial key) or with chromatic alterations. Reflecting the conventions of the past several decades, chords typically include selective mixtures of the pitches of a major or minor triad (the first, third, and fifth degrees of its related scale), the triad's diatonic upper extensions or tensions (its seventh, ninth, eleventh and thirteenth degrees), and the triad's altered extensions (its flatted-ninth, raised-ninth, raised-eleventh, and flatted-thirteenth degrees). (Berliner 1994, 74)

The table-lookup chord identification method described in section 2.2 includes a rather extensive mechanism for spelling the contents of a pitch-class array as a series of stacked thirds above a root. The Chord application works by table lookup unless there are too many pitch classes in the chord, in which case it throws out pitch classes until it has reduced the input to a size that fits the tables. The spelling processes then identify the intervals above the root according to a stacked-thirds model. In fact, since the spelling algorithm arrives at the same classification of the chord intervals as do the tables, the only contribution that comes from the tables alone is the determination of the root. Accordingly we may substitute the Parncutt algorithm to choose the root of a chord and apply the spelling processes to name the intervals above it.

The process is very simple: we first calculate the address of the pitch class that is a major third above the computed root. Then we look in the pcs array to see if that pitch class is present. If it is, the mode of the chord is declared to be major. If it is not, we look for the minor third. If the minor third is present (and we know that the major third is not), we declare the chord to be minor. If neither one is there, we arbitrarily call it major.

The next step looks for variants of the fifth above the root, again in order of importance to the type definition. In other words, if both a perfect and sharp fifth were present in the pcs array, we would rather use the perfect fifth to calculate the chord type. Whenever an interval is classified, the corresponding pitch class is removed from the pcs array to prevent identifying the same interval as something else later on. With each interval identification, the classification of the type is further refined.

For example, these are the possibilities if the step analyzing the fifth finds a flatted fifth: if the current designation is major, it is refined to major+flat5; if the current designation is minor, it is refined to diminished. The code also addresses the case in which no designation is current by calling the chord flat5. This situation will not arise in the version on the CD-ROM as FindThird() subroutine always calls a chord major unless only a minor third is found. The designation of flat5 demonstrates how other strategies could be implemented: one might prefer to think of a chord as minor when a flat fifth is found and there was no third, for example.

For the moment, however, we are only interested in the distinction between major and minor modes. To add a simple classification of mode to the Parncutt algorithm, then, we look for intervals of a third above the root and generate a classification accordingly. The output of the process is set to (root*2 + chordMode). This yields 24 output values, ranging from 0 to 23. Even values represent major chords and odd values are minor. Now let us look at how roots combined with mode can assist in a determination of tonality.

2.3   Key Induction

Knowing the root and type of a chord is useful information for jazz analysis and improvisation, but becomes much more powerful when processed in the context of functional harmony. To move from raw identification to harmonic analysis, we must be able to relate a chord's root and type to a prevailing tonic. Identifying the tonic of a set of chords is the task of key induction.

2.3.1   Interaction with Key Induction

One limitation of the Parncutt algorithm with respect to real-time applications is that it requires the input of a key and mode in order to apply the Krumhansl and Kessler stability profiles. We would prefer, in an interactive situation, that the program determine the prevailing tonality for itself. To achieve this functionality, we must perform a process analogous to calculating root salience on a higher structural level. Root salience finds the pitch that is most central to the harmonic function of a collection of notes. Key induction finds the pitch that is most central to the harmonic function of a collection of roots.

For the purposes of the current discussion, we will use a simple key induction process that I developed to supply part of the harmonic analysis performed by my program, Cypher (Rowe 1993). There exist other and certainly better methods but my focus here is not so much on that process as it is on the interaction between root finding and key induction, regardless of the specific algorithm used. The Cypher key finder applies weights associated with 24 major and minor chord roots to a set of 24 major and minor key theories. A C major chord, for example, will reinforce theories for which that chord is functionally important (C major, F major, etc.) and penalize theories to which the chord is alien (C minor, B major, etc.). At any given point the key theory with the highest score is taken to be the tonality of the musical context at that moment.

It appears straightforward to send the output of a key induction process to the Parncutt root finder and thereby activate the tonal context rule. However, the circularity of this method becomes clear when one considers that the output of the root finder will itself be the input to the key induction process. In *Music and Schema Theory*, Marc Leman outlines the problem from a more general perspective:

The context-sensitive semantics in music has particular properties implying an interaction between three elements: (i) the object, (ii) the context in which the object appears, and (iii) the schema or structure that controls its perception. In this perspective one may wonder how both

- *the meaning of a tone (or chord) can be determined by its context, while*
- *the context itself is determined by the constituent tones (chord).*

In other words, what is determined by the context is itself part of that context, and as such, also contributes to the emergence of that context. (Leman 1995, 4)

With this observation, Leman points to a phenomenon that becomes a very concrete problem in designing the flow of control between chord and key analysis processes: How does one calculate chord roots with respect to a tonal center while simultaneously computing a tonal center from the incoming chord roots?

Let us first try the most obvious strategy: incoming chords are sent to the root finder and interpreted without tonal context. When a chord root and mode have been calculated, these are sent as inputs to the key finder. The output from the key finder is then sent back to the root algorithm, setting the key and mode of the tonal context and turning on the context sensitivity. Subsequent chords continue to be analyzed with that key and mode until the key finder switches

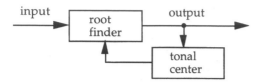

Figure 2.19 Key induction feedback

Table 2.6 Output of Key Induction Process

	C	c	C#	c#	D	d	Eb	eb	E	e	F	f	F#	f#	G	g	Ab	ab	A	a	Bb	bb	B	b
C	**4**										2	2			1									
G	**6**	2		1							2	1			5									
G	**8**	4		2							2				**9**									
C	**12**	1									4	2			10									
C	**16**										6	4			11									
D	**16**			4											13	2			1					
F#	**9**		1												8								2	2
F	**10**										4				2				2	2				
C	**14**										6	2			3				2	1				
G	**16**	2		1							6	1			7									
C	**20**										8	3			8									
F	**21**										12				2				2	2				
C	**25**										14	2			3				2	1				
G	**27**	2		1							14	1			7									
d	**28**	3		4							14				6				1					
C	**32**										16	2			7				1					
C	**36**										18	4			8				1					

interpretations. Whenever the key finder computes new values, these are used to reset the context variables of the Parncutt algorithm and the process continues (figure 2.19).

Table 2.6 lists the output of an application combining key induction with the Parncutt chord identification analysis described earlier. The input was a live performance of the first eight bars of the Largo from Beethoven's *Piano Sonata in Eb*, op. 7 (see figure 2.18). Time advances as we descend through the figure from top to bottom. The leftmost column shows the root and mode of each incoming chord as it was determined by the Parncutt algorithm plus mode classification. The letter represents the root and the case represents the mode, where upper case letters are major chords and lower case letters are minor (e.g., C is C major and c is C minor). The remaining columns show the amount of key salience attributed to each potential tonal center. These are labeled across the top with the same case convention as that used for the chords, yielding 24 columns (two for each of the twelve pitch classes, one for major and one for minor). With some hesitation at the outset, the key is correctly identified as C major and that identification remains stable through the entire fragment (the key theory with the most points in any row is shaded).

With this particular example the process works quite well. Although the passage is somewhat ambiguous (the D and F♯-major chords in measures 3–4 do not belong in C major), the winning key theory is correct in all cases but one: the second G-major chord in measure 2 propels the key of G major to the leading position for exactly one chord.

The C++ code for the key finder algorithm is listed in figure 2.20. We find the current chord classification by querying the input event. Chords are identified by an integer ranging from 0 to 23, where the root pc is found by dividing the value by two, and the mode (major or minor) by taking the value modulo two. The modulo operation is performed to select the correct weight set: minorWeights are used if the input chord is minor, and majorWeights if it is major. Once a weight set is chosen, the weights for that chord relative to each of the 24 key theories are added to the running key scores. The resulting key scores are sorted and the key with the most weight is selected as the current tonic. Finally, the key and mode are fed back to the Parncutt algorithm and its key context sensitivity is switched on.

The Cypher key-finding weight set was developed by hand through a process of trial and error in which tonal music was played to the system and the calculated key theories saved in a trace file. The traces were examined to find chord progressions that led to incorrect key

```
void Key::Calculate(class Event* event)
{
    register int i;
    // get root classification from NoTable
    int chord = event->FeatureValue(PSpellListener::kRoot);
    if (chord < 0) return;


    // use weights corresponding to input chord mode (major or minor)
    int* weights = (chord%2)?minorWeights:majorWeights;


    // start adding weights at the location set by the chord
    for (i=0; i<24; i++) {
        int rotate   = (chord+i)%24; // rotate through all 24 weights
        keys[rotate] += weights[i];    // add weights
        if (keys[rotate] < 0)  keys[rotate] = 0; else
        if (keys[rotate] > 60) keys[rotate] = 60;
        orderedKeys[i].key       = rotate; // save values for sort
        orderedKeys[i].weight = keys[rotate];
    }


    // sort routine
    bool swaps = true;
    while (swaps) {
        swaps = false;
        for (i=0; i<24-1; i++)
                if (orderedKeys[i].weight < orderedKeys[i+1].weight) {
                    SortRecord tmp   = orderedKeys[i];
```

Figure 2.20 Key finder listing

```
                orderedKeys[i]    = orderedKeys[i+1];

                orderedKeys[i+1] = tmp;

                swaps = true;

            }

    }


// weight of the first sorted record in max

int maxWeight = orderedKeys[0].weight;

int newKey    = 0;

// look to see if more than one entry has maximum weight

for (i=0; orderedKeys[i].weight == maxWeight; i++)

    if (orderedKeys[i].key == value) {// if yes

            newKey = value;         // and last key was one of them

            break;                  // keep it

    } else

            // otherwise arbitrarily choose last

            newKey = orderedKeys[i].key;


value   = newKey;

Root* r = (Root*)listener->Feature(PSpellListener::kRoot);

r->SetKey(value/2);                 // set tonic in root finder

r->SetMode(value%2);                // set mode in root finder

r->ContextOnOff(true);              // turn on key sensitivity

if (file) WriteKeys(chord);         // write weights to output file

}
```

Figure 2.20 Continued

identifications and the weights were then adjusted accordingly. Iterating this process led to the realization that negative weights were often more important than the positive ones; that is, it is critical for chords that lie outside a particular tonality to quickly reduce the weight given to their corresponding theories. Only with such strong negative influences was it possible to make the process recognize modulations quickly enough.

The process traced here works well enough on the Beethoven example but does not account for many other structural aspects of tonality in Western music. For example, it does not follow the contribution of scales to the establishment of a tonal center. Let us turn now to a more recent proposal that does address these effects.

2.3.2 Parallel Processing Model

The Krumhansl and Schmuckler key induction algorithm uses the Krumhansl and Kessler pitch-class stability profiles (1982) to estimate the key of a collection of pitch classes. Briefly, the process compares histograms from the target passage and the stability profiles, and predicts that the key associated with the best-matching profile will be heard as the tonal center of the passage. As Krumhansl has documented (1990), the technique does a good job of predicting tonal centers from excerpts as short as four notes.

The algorithm correlates pc distributions without regard to the order of their presentation. David Butler points out that order can be decisive for key perceptions, however, in that the same collection of pitches can indicate two different tonal centers depending on their sequence of presentation (1989). Similarly, "it is easy to create passages with the same root progressions that imply different keys (C-Dm-G7 implies C major, C-D7-G implies G major)" (Temperley 1997, 63). Neither pitch distributions nor chord progressions alone, then, would seem to comprise all of the information used in key recognition.

In their 1996 article, "A Parallel-Processing Key-Finding Model," Piet Vos and Erwin Van Geenen propose a symbolic algorithm in which "scale-specific information and chord-specific information are processed simultaneously and . . . key cues from both streams of information additively contribute to key inference" (1996, 187). The input to the model (abbreviated PPM for parallel-processing model) consists of notes reduced to pitch classes with attached durations. The duration of a pitch class is used to calculate its contribution to particular scalar or chordal interpretations.

Vos and Van Geenen consider key finding an instance of inductive reasoning "in the sense that a structural regularity in a sequence of events (a key in the present case) has to be inferred from a few events (tones)" (1996, 187). Because key finding is inductive, the accuracy of the model depends on its fidelity to the psychological states of human listeners. That is, the key found by the model should match the key experienced by a human listener when hearing the same input. For this reason, Vos and Van Geenen are interested in developing "a computational model of key finding that is able to process tonal music in order to infer its key in a psychologically and music-theoretically plausible way" (1996, 186–187).

Two primary mechanisms from which psychological plausibility arises are the primacy factor and memory constraints. In many kinds of human induction, the first few items of a series of elements have a privileged position with respect to establishing the inference (Brown, Butler, and Riess Jones 1994; Marslen-Wilson and Tyler 1984). This emphasis on early members of the series is referred to as the primacy factor. Memory constraints comprise the other characteristic consistent with human psychology, as the effects of short-term memory on induction tasks like key-finding have been widely discussed (Craik and Lockhart 1972; Butler and Ward 1988).

Let us review the functioning of the algorithm. When a pitch event is submitted, the scale processing component adds the duration of the input to the scale score of each of the 24 keys to which the pc belongs. Durations are expressed in 64ths of a whole note. Thus, one eighth note is given a value of 8. Table 2.7 shows the addition to the scale totals of all 24 keys when a pitch class of 0 (C) with a duration of an eighth note is input to the model. Notice that the pitch class 0 refers not only to all occurrences of C, but also to enharmonic

Table 2.7 Point Contributions of C Pitch Class to 24 Scales

SCALES	POINTS
C Major	8
C minor	8
C♯ Major	8
C♯ minor	8
D Major	0
D minor	8
E♭ Major	8
E♭ minor	8
E Major	0
E minor	8
F Major	8
F minor	8
F♯ Major	0
F♯ minor	0
G Major	8
G minor	8
A♭ Major	8
A♭ minor	0
A Major	0
A minor	8
B♭ Major	8
B♭ minor	8
B Major	0
B minor	0

equivalents such as B♯. That explains why pc 0 contributes to the scale theory of C♯ major, for example, since the scale of C♯ major includes B♯.

All three minor scale forms (natural, harmonic, and melodic) are used to calculate the association of a pitch class with a minor key. Because this conjunction is in effect, there are only three intervals that are not included in the minor scale for any particular tonic: the minor second, major third and tritone. Accordingly, in table 2.7, the only minor scales that do not get points for a pitch class of C are B minor (relative to which, C is the minor second), A♭ minor (relative to which, C is the major third), and F♯ minor (relative to which, C is the tritone). Every pc, then, contributes to 16 different scale theories: seven major scales and nine minor.

Each of the 24 keys has a melodic (scalar) score associated with it that is updated by the process just described, and there are additional calculations due to primacy effects that we will review momentarily. Each key also maintains a harmonic score derived from an analysis of the membership of incoming pcs in certain functional chords within the key. The functions tracked by the algorithm are the tonic, subdominant, and dominant seventh chords of each key. As in the case of the scale analysis, a weight equal to the duration of the note is added to the score of each of the functional chords to which a pitch class belongs. When a pc belongs to two chord functions, the activation is divided between the two scores. Table 2.8 shows the contribution made by the pitch class 0 (C) to three possible key interpretations. Keep in mind that these are not the only key theories affected.

The total contribution of the incoming pitch class is the same in each case: 8 points, or the duration of an eighth note, equal to 8 64ths. Notice the difference in distribution, however, among the three cases. Because pitch class C is a member of both the tonic and subdominant triads in C major, the activation is split between those two scores. In F major, the pitch class C is a member of the tonic triad

Table 2.8 Point Contributions of C Pitch Class to 3 Key Theories

	C MAJOR	F MAJOR	A♭ MAJOR
Tonic	4	4	8
Subdominant	4	0	0
Dominant7	0	4	0
Total	8	8	8

and dominant seventh, so those two scores are each augmented by half of the activation. In A♭ major, C is a member of only the tonic triad, and all of the weight goes to that score.

The Vos and Van Geenen model is parallel in that both the scalar and chordal analyses are conducted for all incoming pitch classes. When the maximum scale and chord weights of all 24 possible keys are associated with the same key theory, that key is held to be the prevailing tonality. If the chord and scale analyses produce different leaders, the key is ambiguous.

Primacy effects complicate the algorithm considerably, but I will not describe them in full here as they are outlined by Vos and Van Geenen (1996) and can be seen at work in the source code for the PPM application on the CD-ROM. I will, however, describe a few primacy effects to clarify their function. The first effect changes the contribution of an initial pc to the scale and chord theories: "The first input is initially assumed to be the key's root by assigning a weight equaling the duration of the first input to the scalar- and chord-scores of the keys whose root matches the input's pc" [Vos and Van Geenen 1996, 191). Since the normal procedure is to add the pc's duration to the scale or chord score, the effect of this primacy rule is to double the contribution of the first pitch class.

The doubling effect entails a special treatment of the very first input to the system. The other effects cover a primacy span of several of the first inputs. Vos and Van Geenen set the primacy span equal to the first five events. One of these effects will remove any accumulated scale weight from a key if a pc arrives that is not a member of the key's scale. For example, if the scale weight for C minor is 8 and an E-natural pitch class arrives (one of the three pcs that does not belong to any version of the C-minor scale), the scale weight does not simply stay at 8 (as it would outside the primacy span) but is reset to zero.

Figure 2.21 lists the code for the scale processing component of the PPM application. Most of it is implemented with the conditional `if (ScaleHas(PC)) UpdateScale(duration);` which simply adds the duration of the input to the scale score if the pc is in the

```
int TKey::ScaleProcess(int PC, long duration)

{

    if (ScaleHas(PC)) {

        if (vos->NumInputs() == 0) // if this is first input

            if (PC == tonicPC)    // and the pc is the tonic of the key

                duration *= 2; // double the duration weight

        UpdateScale(duration);        // add the duration to the scale weight

    } else                        // else pc is not in this key's scale

    if (vos->NumInputs() < vos->PrimacySpan()) {

        melodicScore = 0;         // if in primacy span, zero scale score

        if (hasInitialWeight) {    // if this key got initial chord weight

            tonicChord -= vos->InitialWeight(); // remove it

            hasInitialWeight = false;

        }

    }

    return melodicScore;          // return score for this scale

}
```

Figure 2.21 Listing of TKey::ScaleProcess()

scale of the key. Everything else in ScaleProcess() is there to deal with primacy effects. If we are handling the first input to the model, for example, we check to see whether the pc is the same as the tonic pitch class of the key under consideration. If it is, we double the duration weight used to update the scale. If the pitch class coming in is not in the key's scale while the primacy span is still active, we zero out any accumulated melodic score and remove the additional weight from the tonicChord score as well.

Figure 2.22 shows the score of the opening of Schubert's song *Gretchen am Spinnrade*, D. 118. The excerpt is interesting for its

Figure 2.22 *Gretchen am Spinnrade*

Step	Scalar Profile	Chordal Profile	Key Inference
1	F,f (16)		
2	F,f (24)		
3	F(56)	F(48)	F(104)
5	F(72)	F(56)	F(128)
6	F(104)	d(116)	
10	F(184)	d(196)	
11	F(192)	d(204)	
12	F(216)	F(220)	F(436)
13	F(232)	F(236)	F(468)
14	F(240)	F(244)	F(484)
15	c,d(264)	c(260)	c(524)
16	c,d(272)	c(268)	c(540)
23	c,d(400)	c(396)	c(796)

Figure 2.23 PPM analysis of *Gretchen am Spinnrade*

tonal complexity, as Claude Palisca notes: "The piano part suggests not only the whirr of the spinning wheel by a constant sixteenth-note figure in the right hand and the motion of the treadle by the repeated rhythmic pattern in the left hand, but also the agitation of Gretchen's thoughts, her peace gone, as she thinks of her beloved in Goethe's epic poem *Faust*. The restlessness is also reflected in the harmony, in the tension between D minor and C major and suggestions of C minor in the opening stanza" (1996, 399).

Figure 2.23 lists the output of the PPM for the soprano line alone. An analysis of the soprano without the accompaniment is an unfair test, since the piano establishes so much of the harmonic context of the work. It is interesting to see what the PPM makes of it, however, as a guide to devising strategies for combining it with concurrent analyses.

The model begins with a scale theory of F (major or minor) because of the initial weight accorded to the first pitch class heard. The chordal profile agrees once the second member of an F major triad arrives with the A in m. 3 (simultaneously eliminating F minor as a scalar candidate). F major is the best answer for the soprano alone— it is the additional context in the piano accompaniment that tells us we are in D minor. What is interesting is that the PPM, following the soprano alone, becomes confused between F major and D minor as soon as the primacy span has passed with step 6 (the downbeat of m. 4).

The reason for this confusion is that beyond the primacy span, the tonic, subdominant, and dominant seventh scores for each key are added together to determine the chordal profile, while within the primacy span only contributions from the tonic triad are considered. The repeated A pcs in the first three bars of the soprano line contribute to the chordal profile of F major as part of the tonic triad, but to the profile of D minor as part of both the tonic and dominant. Once the dominant score is considered, and particularly when the large weight stemming from the long A at the beginning of bar 4 is added in, the D minor chordal profile runs ahead. The PPM continues to find the key ambiguous until step 12, the arrival of the soprano C on the downbeat of m. 7. Since C contributes to both the tonic and dominant chord scores of F major, but not to the harmonic weight of D minor, F major is established as the unambiguous tonal center once again.

The B natural on the downbeat of m. 8 (step 15) throws us quite suddenly into a confirmed C minor. As Palisca notes, the score demonstrates a D minor/C major ambiguity throughout this first section. We only know that it is C major from the accompaniment, so the PPM's estimate of C minor is quite well taken. The only reason the PPM does not consider C major, in fact, is the B♭ of the soprano in

m. 3. As the B♭ falls within the primacy span and outside the C major scale, all of the scalar points C major had garnered to that point are erased. Through these bars we can see the value of the parallel tracks in the PPM: D minor has a melodic weight equal to that of C minor, but is not output as the most salient tonality because it is not confirmed by the harmonic analysis.

The Parallel Processing Model is very well suited to real-time applications because it is efficient and causal. A recent extension to the algorithm (not implemented in my version) uses dominant-tonic leaps at the outset of a melody to further focus the identification of key (Vos 1999). The scope of the PPM's application, however, is limited by two characteristics: first, it relies on quantized durations to calculate the salience scores; and second, it only works with monophonic music.

The PPM adds weights to the scalar and harmonic scores that are calculated as integer multiples of 64th note durations. For example, as we have seen, an eighth note will generate a score of 8, since the duration of one eighth note is equal to the duration of eight 64th notes. This is troublesome for real-time processing because, first, we must wait until the release of a note to calculate its effect. That means that any interaction based on key input cannot take place at the attack, but only after a delay equal to the duration of the input. Since key is a relatively high-level percept, processing based on it can often generate a response quickly enough to be musically convincing even after such a delay. We are forced to accept it in any case if we wish to use the algorithm.

We then must face the other complication, which requires that we also run a real-time quantizer, without which we will have no quantized durations available. The function of the algorithm, however, does not depend on quantization as such because it is quite sensitive to the relative values of the durations, no matter what the notated values might be. In other words, if we were to multiply or divide all durations in a melody by two, the algorithm would produce precisely the same results. We can use this observation to develop a method for calculating weights based on the relative durations of the input. Suppose the first actual duration of a performed event is 500 milliseconds. We can compute a constant divisor that will set the millisecond value to eight: `float div = 500/8`. Eight is chosen because it is a common duration value in PPM, but any other value could be substituted. Now this and all subsequent inputs can be divided by the constant and truncated to an integer to derive a normalized PPM weight. Though no longer expressed in milliseconds, the relative duration lengths are preserved.

The PPM does a good job on the Schubert excerpt even when considering the soprano alone. It seems clear, however, that an even better analysis could be performed if the piano part were treated as well. We cannot realize this aspiration with the PPM as it stands, however, because it is designed to handle only monophonic input. The monophonic restriction is not a particular problem for real-time processing, then, but rather a limitation on the range of inputs to which this algorithm can be applied.

How might we couple it with other processes to widen its scope? One strategy would be to invoke the PPM whenever the input is determined to be monophonic, and use some other technique for chords. In fact we could use this possibility to our advantage in combination with the Parncutt algorithm of the previous section. We noted there that the virtual pitch process assumes that chords will be presented simultaneously. Arpeggiation causes each chord member to be considered independently, which means essentially that each individual pitch will be found to be its own root, thus skewing the key finding process. We could instead use the virtual pitch method to compute chord roots that are fed to the harmonic analysis track of the PPM, and use the scalar component as it is. I have not constructed such a program, but I hope the examples already developed give an idea of how it could be realized by reusing the components already at hand. For the remainder of this chapter I will address the C++ programming that underlies these components in greater detail. Those readers who wish to concentrate on the musical issues may prefer to move ahead to chapter 3.

2.4 C++ and Object Orientation

C++ is an object-oriented computer language. Texts discussing object orientation generally are widely available, and Stephen Pope's collection, *The Well-Tempered Object* is a good introduction to its musical use in particular (1991). A key concept of object orientation is the *base class*—a general encapsulation of data and methods that can be specialized for particular applications. The *Machine Musicianship* library is primarily a collection of base classes that can be used directly, or specialized as the building blocks of interactive music applications.

2.4.1 The Note Class

One of the most fundamental base classes is the Note class. The Note class is basically an encoding of the MIDI representation of a note with some additional timing information. That is, a Note is held to consist of a pitch number and an onset velocity, or loudness (following the MIDI standard in which velocities are represented in seven bits and range between 0 and 127). Both pitch and velocity are encoded as integers, however, which means that the Note class does not require that their values stay within seven bits. Some programs may require more precision, and that additional storage is already allocated in the class (figure 2.24).

The Note class makes two additions to the MIDI standard: first, each Note has associated with it a duration in milliseconds. MIDI separates the attack and release of a note into two separate messages: Note On and Note Off. It does not record either the onset or release time of a note. The Note class maintains the duration of each note, allowing a release time to be calculated at the time of attack. The other addition to the MIDI specification is a pointer to a surrounding Event—another class that is made up of a collection of Notes. An Event maintains the onset time of the enclosed Notes, as we see next. All Notes in an Event attack at the same time. Because durations are encoded in the Notes and not the Event, however, each note in a chord can be released individually.

```
class Note {

protected:

        class Event* event;             // surrounding event

        int         pitch;              // MIDI pitch number

        int         velocity;           // MIDI velocity

        long        duration;           // duration in msec


public:

        Note(class Event *event);       // constructor

        Note(const Note& rhs);          // copy constructor

        Note& operator=(const Note& rhs);


        // access to data members

        class Event* Event  (void) const { return event;    }

        int         Pitch   (void) const { return pitch;    }

        int         Velocity(void) const { return velocity; }

        long        Duration(void) const { return duration; }


        // modification of data members

        void        SetPitch   (int newPitch) { pitch    = newPitch; }

        void        SetVelocity(int newVel)   { velocity = newVel;   }

        void        SetDuration(int newDur)    { duration = newDur;   }

};
```

Figure 2.24 Note class

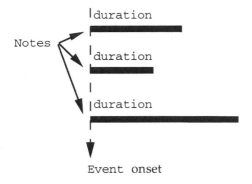

Figure 2.25 Event / Note attack and releases

Figure 2.25 provides a graphic illustration of the organization of attacks and releases in an Event/Note combination. The onset of the Event gives a common attack time to all member Notes. The release of each Note is independent and calculated by adding the duration field of the Note object to the onset time of the Event. This is of course only one of several ways to organize temporal relations between Notes and Events. The right configuration for any particular application will depend on how these constructs are used. If one wanted block-style chords that always attacked and released together, the duration field could be migrated up to the Event level to provide a single release time for all member Notes.

One advantage of proposing these representations in C++ is that they can easily be modified by the reader. All data members of the Note class are declared as protected variables, for example, which means that user classes derived from Note will have access to them. If they were declared to be private, derived classes would not have direct access to the data members. To make an Event/Note configuration in which duration was encoded at the Event level, for example, one could simply delete the duration member and its associated functions from the Note class and add them to Events. (In that case the new classes would not be derived but simply user-modified versions of the originals).

2.4.2 The Event Class

The Event class consists of a collection of Notes and a number of facilities for manipulation of the collection as a whole. An Event could be thought of as the representation of a chord, since it encapsulates a number of Notes. Recall, however, that even single Notes are wrapped in an Event in this scheme. In the middle of the Event definition is a pointer to an array of Notes, the size of which is determined during the construction of the Event. The variable chordSize indicates how many notes are actually present.

An Event has two ways of representing its onset time: the time field records the number of milliseconds elapsed since the application's clock started ticking. The offset field contains the number of milliseconds elapsed since the previous Event—it is the inter-onset-interval (IOI) between the current Event and the one before it. The Event class is listed in its entirety in figure 2.26.

The Event class allows us to deal with chords as a single entity. One Event can contain from one to maxNotes of Notes. Such capability takes us further away from the MIDI standard, which has no facilities for indicating the time at which notes are to occur, or have occurred. Consequently, there is no way in MIDI itself to indicate that a group of notes are meant to sound together as a chord. Such timing information is added by MIDI sequencers, and this addition is in fact one of their main functions. On the CD-ROM is a program that will read standard MIDI files and capture their timing and note information using the Event and Note classes.

Carol Krumhansl suggests a representation for music that is quite close to the Event class: "For purposes of discussion, let us adopt the following formalism for musical events: Event$_{time}$ (pitch, duration, loudness, timbre). The subscript notation is used to indicate that musical events are indexed in time. This mathematical convention is adopted as a way of specifying a value (time) for each event with respect to which it is ordered relative to other events" (1992, 201). The time index is analogous to what we record in the time field of an Event. Pitch, duration, and loudness are also available from a MIDI stream and are recorded within an Event's constituent Notes.

```
class Event {
protected:
   Event*     prev;
   Event*     next;

   enum       { kMaxFeatures = 32 };

   const int maxNotes;        // max number of notes in this Event
   long      time;            // the absolute time of the event
   long      offset;          // IOI between this and prev
   int       numChans;        // how many output channels
   int       whichChans[16];  // which channels they are
   int       bendStart;       // pitchbend at the attack
   long      eventDuration;   // averaged duration of event
   int       chordSize;       // how many notes actually present
   class Note** notes;        // array of Note pointers
   int       featureVals[kMaxFeatures];

   class EventBlock* eventBlock;
   class Segment*    segment;

public:
   Event(void);
   Event(class EventBlock* block);
   Event(const Event& rhs);
   Event& operator=(const Event& rhs);
   ~Event(void);
```

Figure 2.26 Event class

```
void        CalculateEventDuration(void);


// access to data members

Event*      Next(void)              const { return next;              }

Event*      Prev(void)              const { return prev;              }

int         MaxNotes(void)          const { return maxNotes;          }

long        Time(void)              const { return time;              }

long        IOI(void)              const { return offset;            }

int         NumChans(void)          const { return numChans;          }

int         WhichChans(int w)     const {

    if ((w>=16) || (w<0)) return 0; else return whichChans[w];}

int         BendStart(void)         const { return bendStart;         }

long        EventDuration(void)   const { return eventDuration;   }

int         ChordSize(void)         const { return chordSize;        }

class Note* Notes(int n)          const {

                if ((n>=0) && (n<maxNotes)) return notes[n];  }

int         FeatureValue(int id) const { return featureVals[id];}

class Segment* Segment(void)      const { return segment;           }


// modification of data members

void        SetNext(Event* newNext) { next   = newNext; }

void        SetPrev(Event* newPrev) { prev   = newPrev; }

void        SetTime(long newTime)    { time   = newTime; }

void        SetIOI(long newIOI)      { offset = newIOI;  }

void        CopyChans(int numChans, int* whichChans);

void        SetChans(int nc, ...);
```

Figure 2.26   Continued

```
void        SetBendStart(int newBendStart)

                              { bendStart = newBendStart; }
void        SetChordSize(int newChordSize)

                              { chordSize = newChordSize; }
void        SetFeatureValue(int id, int value)

                              { featureVals[id] = value;   }
void        SetSegment(class Segment* s)

                              { segment = s; }


bool        IsBefore(Event^ other);

bool        IsAfter(Event* other);

bool        IsConcurrent(Event* other);

bool        Overlaps(Event* other);

int         NumEventsTo(Event* other);

};
```

Figure 2.26 Continued

There is no field for timbre, however, because the MIDI messages
from which Events are constructed bear no timbral information.

Krumhansl continues her proposal by noting the special status of
time within the framework: "the unidirectional aspect of time (prog-
ressing forward) is reflected in the fact that, although possible, it is
difficult to recognize a melody played backwards, whereas other
transformations such as transposition in pitch range, change of
tempo, change of dynamics, and change of instrument, leave the melody recognizable" (1992, 202). The importance of time ordering
is reflected in the Event class by the two fields used to represent
its passage (time and offset) as well as by the Boolean functions
used to locate one Event relative to another (IsBefore, IsAfter,
IsConcurrent, and Overlaps).

```
class EventBlock {

protected:

        Event**              all;

        Event*               head;

        Event*               tail;

        const int            numEvents;


public:

        EventBlock(int size=128);

        ~EventBlock(void);

        inline Event*    Member(int m)    const { return all[m];       }

        inline Event*    Head(void)       const { return head;         }

        inline Event*    Tail(void)       const { return tail;         }

        inline int       NumEvents(void)  const { return numEvents;    }

};
```

Figure 2.27 EventBlock class

Figure 2.27 lists the definition of the EventBlock class. An EventBlock contains numEvents Events (the default value of numEvents is set arbitrarily to 128). The array all is initialized to hold the Events. Then all of the Events in the block are connected into a doubly linked circular list. Now the Prev() and Next() member functions of the Event class can be used with the Events in the block to access their neighbors. When the end of the block is reached, a Next() call will wrap around back to the beginning. Figure 2.28 illustrates the relationships between an EventBlock, its constituent Events, and the Note objects the Events contain.

Note, Event, and EventBlock form a group of hierarchically related classes that represent music as transmitted through MIDI mes-

EventBlock

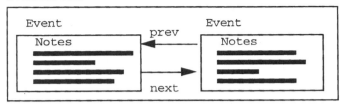

Figure 2.28 Note / Event / EventBlock

sages with the addition of several forms of timing information. Another base class, the Listener, organizes incoming MIDI messages into Notes and Events and supervises their analysis.

2.4.3 The Listener Class

The Listener class pulls the elements we have discussed thus far together in working applications. Whenever new MIDI messages arrive, the OMSInPort class calls Listener to process the input. The Listener function Hear() packages raw MIDI messages as Events. Recall that Events extend the MIDI standard by grouping notes into chords and saving their durations. Figure 2.29 lists the code for Hear().

Hear() is primarily a straightforward filling-in of the values of an Event. The most involved aspect of it concerns determining which MIDI events belong together in a single Event object (that is, which MIDI events form part of a chord) and what their duration is. A related problem involves deciding when the rest of the program should be made aware that a new Event has been formed. The conditional

```
if (((localTime-lastAttack)>100L) || (chordSize>=e->MaxNotes()))
```

determines when a new Event should begin. The first part of the conditional says that when 100 milliseconds have elapsed since the onset of the last Event, any new input should form the onset of a new Event. The second part of the conditional ensures that when an Event has been filled with the maximum number of notes, any additional inputs cause the allocation of a new Event.

```
void Listener::Hear(MIDIEvent *m)
{
    long localTime = m->time; // get time event arrived
    Note*  n;
    Event* e;
    int    address;

    if (((m->status&kCommandMask)==kNoteOn) && Velocity(m)) {
        e = Incoming; // note on
        int chordSize = e->ChordSize();


        // if IOI is over 100 ms or prev is full, start new event
        if (((localTime-lastAttack)>100L) || (chordSize>=e->MaxNotes())) {
            Incoming = Incoming->Next();
            e        = Incoming;
            scheduler->ScheduleTask(Now+50L,0,2,0, NotifyInput, this);
            e->SetTime(localTime);          // record onset time
            if (lastAttack > 0)             // record IOI
                e->SetIOI(localTime - lastAttack);
            else
                e->SetIOI(0);
            e->SetChans (1, Channel(m)); // record input channel
            n = e->Notes(0);                // initialize note pointer
            e->SetChordSize(1);             // first note
            lastAttack = localTime;
        } else {
            n = e->Notes(chordSize);        // chord member
```

Figure 2.29 Code listing for Hear ( )

```
            e->SetChordSize(chordSize+1); // increment chordSize count
    }
    address = Pitch(m)%kNumPitches;
    notesOn[address] = 1;                  // record that note is on
    n->SetPitch(address);                  // record pitch
    n->SetVelocity(Velocity(m));           // record velocity
    n->SetDuration(-1);                    // provisional duration
    durations[address] = n;
} else {                                   // note off
    address = Pitch(m)%kNumPitches;
    notesOn[address] = 0;                  // record that note went off
    if (durations[address])
        n = durations[address];            // get back note pointer
    else
        return;
    // calculate real duration
    long realDur = localTime - n->Event()->Time();
    if (realDur < 20L) realDur = 20L;
    n->SetDuration(realDur);
    n->Event()->CalculateEventDuration();
    durations[address] = NULL;
}
}
```

Figure 2.29 Continued

Even when a new Event has been created, however, the line

scheduler->ScheduleTask(Now+50L, 0, 2, 0, NotifyInput);

will delay notification of its formation to the rest of the program for 50 milliseconds. The reason for the delay is to allow additional chord members to arrive. These two durations—100 milliseconds to form a new Event, 50 milliseconds to notify the rest of the system—are critical to the performance of a real-time analysis system. It might seem that the lapse between onset and notification should be the same as the duration within which new chord members may arrive. This makes the analysis unacceptably sluggish for performance situations, however, since there would always be a 100-millisecond delay between what the player does and when the program responds. That is why these durations are different: the time lapse before notification determines the responsiveness of the system, and the duration within which chord members can arrive affects how accurately the program will group together pitches that were meant to be played as a chord.

A similar pragmatism affects how note durations are calculated. At onset time, all notes in a chord are given a duration of -1, to serve as an indicator to the rest of the system that the note has no real duration yet assigned. When the notes of the chord are released, the real duration of each note is determined and used to overwrite the -1 marker. The Event function CalculateEventDuration() computes the duration of the Event as a whole by taking the average of all its constituent Note durations. Because duration is not known at the time of attack, any listening processes that are sensitive to duration and that are executed at the attack time must use some surrogate—the duration of the most recent complete Event, for example, or the moving average of the durations over a recent collection of Events.

2.4.4 The `ListenProp` Class

When the `Listener` signals that new input has arrived, the constructed `Event` is sent to a collection of `ListenProps` determined by the application. `ListenProps` analyze musical features of `Events`. They are so called because they construct a property list of feature classifications.

The `ListenProp` (figure 2.30) is a base class that maintains the three basic items of information needed for an analysis process in this system: an identification number, a value, and a resolution.

```
class ListenProp {

protected:

        int    id;          // identifier of analysis type

        int    value;       // calculated feature classification

        int    resolution;  // number of possible values


public:

        ListenProp(int id, int value, int resolution) :

                id(id), value(value), resolution(resolution) {}


        virtual void Calculate(class Event* event) = 0;


        // data member access functions

        inline  int PropID(void)      const { return id;         }

        inline  int Value(void)       const { return value;      }

        inline  int Resolution(void)  const { return resolution; }
};
```

Figure 2.30 `ListenProp` class

The ID number identifies which of the possible analysis types a ListenProp object represents. The value is the quantitative classification of a musical feature resulting from a class's analysis. The resolution records how many possible classification values may be output from a given ListenProp. An Event object contains a featureVals array that lists the classifications calculated for that Event by some number of ListenProp objects. In other words, the featureVals of an Event are copies of the values calculated by all active ListenProps.

Notice the declaration of the virtual void function Calculate(). A virtual function is one that can be replaced by another definition in derived classes. Calculate() is a pure virtual function because there is no default code for it in the base class. Since ListenProp contains a pure virtual function, it is an abstract class that cannot be used to instantiate objects. Derived classes that use ListenProp as a base and do define the functionality of Calculate(), on the other hand, can be used to instantiate objects. The Chord class used in the triad identifier, for example, is a derived ListenProp. The Calculate() function of the class was listed in figure 2.4. The MIDI chord identifier and PPM calculator were also derived from the ListenProp class.

The advantage of replacing a virtual function with specific definitions in a derived class is that the derived classes can all be handled according to the characteristics of the base class. We will write a great variety of analysis processes during the course of this study, but as long as they are written as descendants of the ListenProp class, higher-level routines can access them all through a common interface and continue to function unchanged no matter which collection of analyzers is currently active. The higher-level class that primarily takes advantage of the uniform interface to ListenProps is the Listener. The Listener function Level1_Analysis() (shown in the listing on the CD-ROM) illustrates how ListenProps are called.

In this chapter we have established a number of base classes for the representation and processing of music. The object-orientation of the analysis routines and their control processes allows us to combine various algorithms and put them into communication with one another. Techniques of chord identification, root salience computation, and key induction were all implemented within the same basic framework. In the remaining chapters the utility of such compound analysis techniques is further explored. We have in many published algorithms proven techniques for limited domains—the PPM is one example of a process that works well, but only for monophonic inputs. With an integrated and consistent control structure, we can easily augment it with other processes that address the limitation. The problem then becomes one of coordinating concurrent processes and managing the parallel and sometimes conflicting streams of information they produce.

3 Sub-symbolic Processes

The techniques developed in chapter 2 all used some kind of symbolic processing. That is, symbols representing features of the musical context were manipulated by algorithms that made inferences about their relationships based on knowledge of the objects they represent in real music. The Vos and Van Geenen Parallel Processing Model, for example, uses knowledge about scales and chord functions to update saliency ratings for 24 possible major and minor tonalities. Rules of the sort found in ScaleProcess() (see figure 2.21) determine how the knowledge is applied.

Sub-symbolic processes are those that use regularities learned from prior inputs as a way to characterize and predict subsequent inputs. Two main properties distinguish sub-symbolic processes from symbolic ones, as these terms are generally used: first, sub-symbolic processes learn their behavior from exposure to material; and second, this learning engenders models that do not rely on a fixed set of rules. Probably the best-known sub-symbolic processes used for music are neural networks.

3.1 Neural Networks

Neural networks are a class of algorithms that learn relations between inputs and outputs. Their structure is derived from a schematic model of the neurons of the brain. Brain neurons consist of dendrites, a soma or cell body, and an axon. Dendrites carry activation to the soma which then transmits activation through the axon to other cell bodies as a function of its inputs. Neural network simulations similarly employ some number of input and output nodes. In the most common configuration, each input node is connected to every output

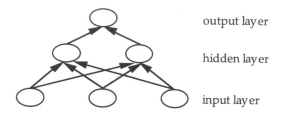

output layer

hidden layer

input layer

Figure 3.1 Schematic of typical neural network

node, or, alternatively, to every node in a middle layer called the hidden layer. If the hidden layer is present, each of these nodes is then connected to every output node. The proliferation of connections arising from such a topology gives rise to the term *connectionism,* another common appellation for neural network research. Figure 3.1 illustrates the structure of a typical neural network.

The network as I have drawn it here is *feedforward*—that is, nodes are connected only to the nodes in the next layer up. Such networks are the most straightforward to analyze and implement, but are not the only possibility. Other architectures use various forms of feedback or resonance between layers, and in fact we will explore one such model in more detail when we take up sequential neural networks. For the moment, consider this sketch as descriptive of feedforward models.

Placed on each connection in a neural network is a weight. Activation traveling from one node to another across a connection is multiplied by the weight before reaching its destination. All activations reaching a node (after multiplication by the weights) are summed together. The activation sum is input to a nonlinear *transfer function* that determines the output of a node relative to its total activation. The simplest transfer function is a threshold: if the total activation exceeds the threshold, the node becomes active (e.g., is set to 1.0). If not, the node remains inactive (is set to 0.0). "Note that the nonlinearity of the function f is crucial in endowing the network with real computational (i.e., decision-making) power. The nonlinearity allows quantitative changes in the inputs to produce qualitative changes in the output (i.e., the output can switch from off to on instead of simply changing in direct proportion to the input)'' (Dolson 1991, 4).

Initially the connection weights are set to random values. One of the great attractions of neural networks is that they are able to learn weight sets that will reliably associate input patterns with output patterns. To accomplish this, a training set of input examples with correct answers (configurations of output activations) attached is presented to the network. Over the course of a training session, the connection weights are gradually adjusted by the neural network itself until they converge on a set that correctly relates outputs with the corresponding inputs of the training set. If the training set captures the regularities of a wider class of inputs, the trained network will then be able to correctly classify inputs not found in the training set as well. Such a process is an example of supervised learning, in which a teacher (the training set) is used to guide the network in acquiring the necessary knowledge (connection weights).

The adjustment of the weights is accomplished through a learning rule. An example is the delta rule: first, an error is computed by subtracting the output of a node from the desired output encoded in the training set. The delta rule uses the error to calculate a new link weight as shown in figure 3.2.

One of the simplest neural network types is the ADALINE, developed in 1963 by Bernard Widrow (1963). An ADALINE has some number of input nodes and one output node. The output can be either +1 or −1, which means that an ADALINE is a simple classifier that can sort input sets into one of two classes. Since the possible outputs are +1 and −1, and the desired outputs in the training set will be restricted to these two values as well, the error can be

```
error     = desiredOutput - output;

newWeight = weight + (learningRate*error*inputValue);
```

Figure 3.2 Delta rule

either −2 (when the desiredOutput is −1 but the calculated output is +1), zero (when the desiredOutput and calculated output agree), or +2 (when the desiredOutput is +1 but the calculated output is −1).

The learning rate is a constant that specifies the percentage of change that can be made to a weight on each pass. Suppose that the learning rate is initialized to .25, meaning that each training pass can effect a 25% change to the weight. The learningRate * error, then, will be either −0.5, 0, or +0.5. The input determines the magnitude and sign of this term: as the absolute value of the input approaches one, the learning change will be greater. Finally the change is added to the existing weight and the weight on the link is updated. Subsequent learning passes will continually invoke the delta rule on the weights until all the training examples are correctly classified.

In addition to the learning rule, the behavior of a node in a neural network is determined by its transfer function. In the ADALINE the transfer function is a simple thresholding process: if the sum of the inputs is less than one, the node outputs a value of −1, otherwise it outputs a value of +1 (figure 3.3).

Backpropagation is a term describing a form of supervised learning in which errors are propagated back through the network (from the outputs to the inputs), changing the connection weights as they go. A common transfer function for backpropagation neural networks, the type that we will implement first, is the sigmoid function (figure 3.4). The sigmoid is an S-shaped curve that yields values between 0.0 and 1.0 no matter how high or low the sum of the inputs may be.

$$f(x) = \begin{cases} -1.0 \; \textit{if } x < 0 \\ 1.0 \; \textit{otherwise} \end{cases}$$

Figure 3.3 ADALINE transfer function

$$f(x) = \frac{1.0}{1.0 + e^{-x}}$$

Figure 3.4 Sigmoid transfer function

It fulfills the requirements of backpropagation learning: the transfer function must be nonlinear, defined for all input values, and differentiable (Rogers 1997).

The preceding description is clearly a minimal account of neural networks, but is all that the scope of this book accommodates. Many excellent texts provide a comprehensive introduction to their design and use (Rumelhart and McClelland 1986; Rogers 1997), and others detail the application of neural networks to several areas of musical modeling (Dolson 1991; Todd and Loy 1991; Leman 1992; Griffith and Todd 1999; and Bharucha 1999). Beyond these texts, the internet is an excellent resource for information, code, and neural network simulators. Our first neural network, in fact, will be developed from a program called QuickProp that I first found from an internet search. We will program a complete backpropagation neural network based on a C++ port of the QuickProp code to establish exactly how such an algorithm works and how it can be trained to work with musical materials.

Another common approach is to work with an established Artificial Neural Network (ANN) simulator. With a simulator, the user specifies the topology of the network, some learning characteristics, and a training set. The output of a simulator depends on the application; the most useful ones for our purposes are those that output a computer program (C code or other) to perform the calculations of the trained net. An internet search for neural networks will turn up several ANN simulator resources.

A final observation concerns the suitability of ANNs for real-time applications. Neural networks are justly famous for their computational demands, and the training process of an ANN can be quite lengthy, depending on the topology of the network and the size of the training set. Once a network is trained, however, its classification work is quite fast, certainly fast enough to be used as part of a real-time analysis environment. Indeed, many examples of this method can be found: a group at Waseda University in Japan reports training a neural network to recognize grasping gestures applied to a custom input device. Once trained, the net can find new occurrences of the gestures in real time and use its recognition to control the algorithmic generation of MIDI output (Sawada, Onoe, and Hashimoto 1997). Our strategy here, then, will be to develop performance networks that have already undergone a training phase before being used onstage.

3.1.1 Neural Network Key Induction

The CD-ROM lists a number of neural network–based analysis applications. These are all built on the Network class, a base class included with the *Machine Musicianship* library. The Network class has methods for constructing, training, and running a neural network, and supports two types of units, one with a symmetrical sigmoid output varying between −1.0 and +1.0 and the other an asymmetrical output that varies between 0.0 and +1.0. We will use the asymmetrical units in these examples. The Network constructor is called with a specification of the desired number of input, hidden, and output nodes.

Let us construct a neural network with twelve input nodes. These nodes will be used to represent the root of an event, or if the event has only one note, its pitch class. Similarly, the output layer of the network will contain twelve nodes for the pitch classes of the twelve possible tonics. Now, there are two remaining issues: the design of a training set and the ultimate topology of the network. In this training set, we will define a set of chords that together indicate a particular major key. I, IV, and V (tonic, subdominant, and dominant) chords are commonly used to establish a sense of key. An ear-training instructor, for example, will play a chord sequence such as I-IV-I-V-I to establish a sense of key for his students. Let us write a training set that associates the tonic, subdominant, and dominant chords with the key of the tonic input. An input of C, F, and G chords, then, will be associated in the training set with an output of C major.

The ability of the network to learn the training set helps determine its topology. Hidden nodes, for example, can increase the range of patterns that networks are able to learn. Let us allocate a network with an equal number of input, hidden, and output nodes, fully connected (the source code of the MajorNet application on the CD-ROM

```
;C  C#  D   D#  E   F   F#  G   G#  A   A#  B

1.0 0.0 0.0 0.0 0.0 1.0 0.0 1.0 0.0 0.0 0.0 0.0 ; input values

1.0 0.0 0.0 0.0 0.0 0.0 0.0 0.0 0.0 0.0 0.0 0.0 ; output values
```

Figure 3.5 C-major training set

demonstrates how such an allocation is made). Next we need to input the training set and train the network.

The training set is maintained in a text file with the following format: a line of twelve floating point values that are fed to the input nodes is followed by a line of twelve more values that represent the outputs the network should learn to associate with the given inputs. Since we are looking for a simple association of I, IV, and V with the tonic, we can use twelve patterns such as the one shown in figure 3.5 for C major. (Note that anything after a semicolon in the training file is considered a comment).

The interface presents the user with two buttons, one that is used to train the network and another to test it. The training button launches the function call: `network -> Train(100);` which causes the trainer to go through the backpropagation process on the network one hundred times (each pass is called an *epoch*). The effects of each pass are cumulative, which means that each push of the training button will further improve the performance of the network on the training set. Statistics on the progress of the learning are displayed on the interface every ten epochs, as shown in figure 3.6. In the figure we see that the trainer had run for 1095 epochs, after which the network correctly classifies the input {C, F, G} as indicative of C major.

A second text file is used to record test patterns. For tests, we need only supply values for the input nodes—the network will compute output values based on the weights learned. If learning has gone well, we can at least read the input values from the training set and expect to see the answers that were originally associated with them output (as is verified in the test shown in figure 3.6). The real test comes when the training set captures enough regularity to cause the network to correctly identify patterns that were not in the set. For example, let

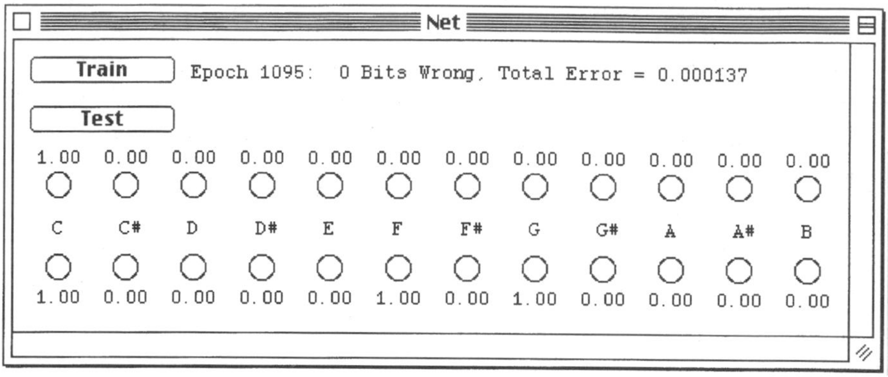

Figure 3.6 Neural network interface

```
;C   C#   D   D#   E   F   F#   G   G#   A   A#   B

1.0 0.0 1.0 0.0 1.0 1.0 0.0 1.0 0.0 1.0 0.0 1.0 ; input values
```

Figure 3.7 Network test

us present our newly trained network with the input pattern shown in figure 3.7.

In this example, we present the network with the seven pitches of the C-major scale, rather than just the tonic, subdominant, and dominant. What key does the network think this represents? In fact the network outputs C as the most likely tonic of this input set (as shown in figure 3.8), although with a much lower score than is produced by running it with the original C major training example (0.37 instead of 1.0). It is interesting, however, that no other candidate achieves a significant score; even though the C major output score is low, the network has still clearly identified C as the tonic of the input set.

Using an input that differs from the training set, we have obtained an identification that is nonetheless consistent with it. Other studies with neural networks have explored their ability to complete partial patterns after training. If a network is trained to recognize a C-major scale, for example, presentation of an input with some members missing will still cause the network to recognize C major.

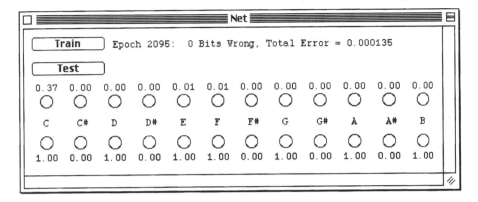

Figure 3.8 C-major scale test

The MajorNet application on the CD-ROM implements the network discussed so far; the reader can experiment with other training and test sets by editing the files trainset.dat and testset.dat.

3.1.2 Sequential Neural Networks

The neural network application just developed can readily be used as a classification module within a real-time analysis system. Training a neural network can be quite time-consuming, though this one learns relatively quickly. Once the network is trained, however, the treatment of input is very fast, certainly fast enough to be used in performance.

As it stands, the model is designed to receive all the input at once: if given the tonic, subdominant, and dominant roots, or all pitches of the scale simultaneously, it outputs a matching key estimation. We have stipulated, however, that the processes eligible for machine musicianship must be able to work with information as it is presented in sequence. Fortunately there exists a substantial literature on the adaptation of neural networks to work just so. One version is described by Jamshed Bharucha:

As a piece of music unfolds, patterns can be composited over time by the accumulation of activation, creating a temporal composite memory. Suppose, for example, that the features of interest are pitch *classes. When a musical sequence begins, the pattern of pitch classes that are sounded at time t_0 constitute a vector, $\mathbf{p}_0$, in 12-dimensional pitch-class space. If at a later time, t_1, another pattern of pitch classes is sounded, represented by vector $\mathbf{p}_1$, a composite, $\mathbf{c}_1$, covering a period of time ending at t_1, can be formed as follows: $\mathbf{c}_1 = s_1\mathbf{p}_0 + \mathbf{p}_1$, where s_1 ($0 \leq s_1 \leq 1$) is the persistence of $\mathbf{p}_0$ at t_1. (Bharucha 1999, 420)*

The temporal composite memory demonstrates one of two common modifications made to neural networks that equips them to handle sequential patterns. The addition of $\mathbf{p}_0$ with $\mathbf{p}_1$, after multiplication by a persistence factor s, introduces a resonance to the input units by which prior inputs continue to exert an influence that decays over time. Figure 3.9 displays this resonance on the input units at the bottom of the figure as a feedback path from each input unit to itself.

The other modification is similar and is shown in figure 3.9 as feedback from the output nodes at the top of the figure to the input nodes at the bottom. (Only the leftmost nodes of figure 3.9 are fully connected to simplify the graphic—the reader should consider that all nodes are similarly connected to every other one at the next level up). As the temporal composite memory multiplies prior inputs by a persistence factor, a similar decay mechanism is applied to activation coming back around from the output to the input. The complete

output feedback

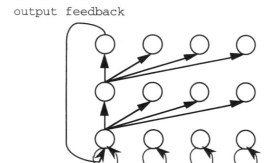

input feedback

Figure 3.9 Sequential neural network

activation applied to an input node in such a model, then, is $i_n +$ $i_{n-1} * decay_i + o_{n-1} * decay_o$ where i_n is the input at time n, $decay_i$ is the input decay factor, o_n is the output at time n, and $decay_o$ is the output decay factor.

I will refer to networks with some version of this architecture as *sequential neural networks*. Because such networks are no longer strictly feedforward, "the backpropagation learning algorithm is no longer valid in this situation, but many investigators have obtained successful results by employing it anyway" (Dolson 1991, 10). Jordan has published one of the most influential models using backpropagation on sequential networks (1986), and such architectures are sometimes called Jordan networks as a result.

Many musical applications of sequential neural networks are extant, including several that are designed specifically for harmonic recognition. Bharucha's MUSACT developed expectancies of chord progressions in a tonal context using a network with decaying input activations (1987). "After repeated exposure to [chord] sequences, the net learns to expect (i.e., produce as output) the schematic distribution of chords for each successive event in a sequence. This net will not learn individual sequences, but will learn to match the conditional probability distributions of the sequence set to which it is exposed. In other words, each output vector approaches a probability vector representing the schematically expected distribution of chords following the sequence context up to that point" (Bharucha and Todd 1989). Here the authors refer to Bharucha's distinction between *schematic* and *veridical* expectancies: schematic expectancies are those arising from the sequential regularities of a corpus or style while veridical expectancies emerge from familiarity with a particular work.

The net described by Scarborough, Miller, and Jones (1991) models simple connections between pitches and certain chords, and between chords and certain keys. In other words, the network is not fully connected: the pitch class C is only linked to the major chord root nodes C, F, and A♭, for example. They use feedback on the input nodes as well as a derivation of activation strength from duration: "The amount of activation provided by an input note is proportional to the note's duration: i.e., a half-note has more influence than a quarter-note. Second, once a note stops, the activation of the corresponding pitch node does not stop immediately but rather decays with time" (Scarborough et al. 1991, 55). The assignment of activation strength to an input as a function of duration is similar to the technique used in Vos and Van Geenen's Parallel Processing Model (section 2.3.2).

Peter Todd describes a sequential neural network used in an algorithmic composition application (1991). His architecture includes both input feedback and feedback of the prior output to the context nodes before the following step. Because he was training the net to reproduce specific melodic sequences, he also used a group of "plan nodes" that were clamped to fixed values during the learning of each training melody. The plan nodes eliminate Todd's architecture for improvisational purposes because they provide a priori indication of what the network should expect. However, many other aspects of Todd's model do work well for us, and I will review here those features of his approach that are most profitable.

We begin with the technique of pitch representation in the input and output nodes. The nodes of a network could represent pitch in either a localist or distributed way. In a localist representation, each node is assigned to a particular pitch class individually. For example, a network designed to deal with four distinct pitch classes would have four input nodes and four output nodes, one for each pitch class. (This is the technique we used in the MajorNet application described in the previous section.)

In a distributed representation we could encode the same number of pitch classes with only two nodes: in this case, we regard each node as one bit in a binary representation of the four possible inputs. In the localist representation the set of possible inputs would be {0001, 0010, 0100, 1000} while in the distributed representation the set would be {00, 01, 10, 11}.

The distributed representation has the advantage of using fewer nodes. The disadvantage is that it introduces similarities among the members of the set that do not correspond to relationships between the pitch classes being represented. As far as the network is concerned, the combinations 01 and 11 are more similar than 00 and 11, for example, because 01 and 11 differ in only one position while 00 and 11 differ in two. I will substitute these values in a similar example provided by Todd that explains the problem:

This difference would have an effect while training the network. For example, using the values just given, if [01] is produced as output instead of [11], this would be a lesser mistake (since they are more similar) than producing [00] for [11]. As it learned, the network's knowledge of musical structure would begin to reflect this (probably) erroneous difference. Thus this distributed coding imposes a similarity-measure on the network's outputs that we probably do not want—there is no a priori reason to designate [01] and [11] as more similar than [00] and [11]. The localist pitch representation, which does not impose this differential similarity on the outputs, works better. (1991, 179)

Let us allocate a neural network with 12 input, hidden, and output nodes, as before. The nodes encode the twelve pitch classes in a localist representation. The network is now sequential because decayed inputs and outputs of the previous step are added to the input before each pass through the network, as illustrated in figure 3.9.

The sequential neural network object is virtually identical to the one described in section 3.1. The main difference is in the operation of the `ForwardPass()` method (figure 3.10), which makes use of the two data members `inputDecay` and `outputDecay`. Because the decay constants are variables, we may easily experiment with different settings to watch their effect on learning. We may even change the architecture of the network by setting one or both of them to zero: if both are zero, this network is identical to the one in section 3.1, since no activation is fed back. Similarly, either the input or output feedback paths may be individually eliminated by setting the corresponding decay parameter to zero.

Once the network has been established, the next step is to develop a training set of examples from which the network can learn. For the

```
void Network::ForwardPass(float* input)

{

  register int i;


  for (i=0; i<nInputs; i++) {

      // input + decayed prior input

      Nodes[i+1]  = input[i] + (Nodes[i+1] * inputDecay);

      // add in decayed prior output

      Nodes[i+1] += (Nodes[firstOutput+i]  * outputDecay);

      if (Nodes[i+1] > inputLimit)

            Nodes[i+1] = inputLimit; // limit to maximum activation

  }


  // For each unit, collect incoming activation and pass through sigmoid

  for (int unit=firstHidden; unit<nUnits; unit++) {

      float sum = 0.0;

      for (i=0; i<nConnections[unit]; i++)

            sum += (Nodes[Connections[unit][i]] * Weights[unit][i]);

      Nodes[unit] = Activation(sum);

  }

  DrawNodes();

}
```

Figure 3.10 ForwardPass function

purposes of the current discussion we will train a network to recognize some elementary progressions of Western tonal harmony with the idea that recognizing these progressions may allow the network to induce the tonality of musical material as it arrives. Because now we are interested in the succession of chord roots as much as we are in the roots themselves, a training set must be devised that will induce the network to learn the sequences relevant to the establishment of a key.

Figure 3.11 lists the set used to train the network to recognize a I-IV-V-I progression in C. There are four input/output pairs that make up the set for this tonal center. The full training set includes I-IV-V-I progressions for all twelve possible tonic pitch classes, yielding a collection of 48 examples. In each pair, the upper line is the set of values given to the twelve input nodes, and the line below it the desired values at the twelve output nodes, as before.

```
;C  C#  D   D#  E   F   F#  G   G#  A   A#  B

1.0 0.0 0.0 0.0 0.0 0.0 0.0 0.0 0.0 0.0 0.0 0.0 ; C activates itself

0.5 0.0 0.0 0.0 0.0 0.0 0.0 0.0 0.0 0.0 0.0 0.0


0.0 0.0 0.0 0.0 0.0 1.0 0.0 0.0 0.0 0.0 0.0 0.0 ; F after C activates F

0.5 0.0 0.0 0.0 0.0 1.0 0.0 0.0 0.0 0.0 0.0 0.0 ; strongly, C somewhat


0.0 0.0 0.0 0.0 0.0 0.0 0.0 1.0 0.0 0.0 0.0 0.0 ; G after F-C reinforces

0.5 0.0 0.0 0.0 0.0 0.5 0.0 0.0 0.0 0.0 0.0 0.0 ; only them (not G)


1.0 0.0 0.0 0.0 0.0 0.0 0.0 0.0 0.0 0.0 0.0 0.0 ; C after C-F-G

1.0 0.0 0.0 0.0 0.0 0.0 0.0 0.0 0.0 0.0 0.0 0.0 ; strongly indicates C
```

Figure 3.11 Simple dominant to tonic training set

The design of the training set captures some low-level characteristics of tonic/dominant relationships in tonal music. When the first chord of a progression arrives (i.e., no other context is established), it is taken as relatively weak evidence that the root of the chord is the tonic of the key. We can see the assertion expressed in the first two lines of the training set, in which the inputs show only the pitch class C set to one and every other node set to zero. The associated output should produce an activation of 0.5 for C and zero for the rest. The second pair represents a progression from a C chord to an F chord. Because this could be a I-IV progression in C, the C tonality interpretation is maintained with an activation of 0.5. The progression could also represent V-I in F, however, and in this set of examples we want to demonstrate to the network that dominant-to-tonic progressions are particularly important. Therefore we set the desired output to weight the key of F heavily and the key of C somewhat. The third line establishes that a G after an F–C progression should continue to activate those two theories, but not G itself. Finally, when the I-IV-V-I progression is completed with a return to C, the key of C should be firmly established as the tonality.

Table 3.1 shows the output of the sequential neural network when fed chord roots from the Parncutt algorithm during a performance of the Beethoven Largo shown in figure 2.18. Though the training set does not include an explicit example of I-V-I, the network correctly identifies C major as the key through the initial I-V-V-I progression and maintains that classification through the entire passage. Moreover, the key of C is held through the repeated G chords in measures 1–2, avoiding the error committed by my handmade weights in table 2.6.

As in table 2.6, the chord roots progress down the leftmost column and the activation present in each of the twelve tonal centers is shown across the grid from left to right. Note that in this example there is no consideration of mode, either in the chord interpretations or in the key possibilities. It is interesting to observe the rival keys entertained by the network during the analysis, such as G in bars 2–3 and F in bars 5–6. Apparently it has learned to consider the F-C progression in measure 6 as a possible modulation to F, though this

Table 3.1   Sequential Net Beethoven Analysis

	C	C#	D	Eb	E	F	F#	G	Ab	A	Bb	B
C	0.50											
G	1.00							0.17				
G	0.95							0.31				
C	1.00							0.15				
C	1.00							0.15				
D	1.00							0.67				
F#	0.99								0.02			
F	1.00											
C	1.00								0.01			
G	1.00								0.02			
C	1.00								0.02			
F	1.00					0.37						
C	1.00					0.66						0.02
G	1.00					0.11						
D	1.00					0.02						
C	1.00											
C	1.00											

interpretation wanes when the potential dominant is followed by a G chord in measure 7.

This simple example shows that a sequential neural network can successfully be trained and used in a real-time analysis structure with other concurrent components, but little more. Much remains to be done with more complete training sets (including modulations) and a greater diversity of chord and tonality types. That such a restricted training regime can already yield a network able to follow relatively straightforward types of tonal harmony encourages the pursuit.

That the function, and therefore the recognition of a tonal center in Western music is style-dependent presents an acute problem for key induction. There are several versions of the very definition of tonality that change with the type of music being studied and the theoretical outlook of the analyst (Vos 1999). Wallace Berry offers an interesting version in his book, *Structural Functions in Music:*

Tonality may be thus broadly conceived as a formal system in which pitch content is perceived as functionally related to a specific pitch-class or pitch-class-complex of resolution, often preestablished and preconditioned, as a basis for structure at some understood level of perception. The foregoing definition of tonality is applicable not just to the "tonal period" in which the most familiar conventions of tonal function are practiced (roughly the eighteenth and the nineteenth centuries), but through earlier modality and more recent freer tonal applications as well. (1976, 27).

The comprehensive nature of Berry's proposal is appealing, but difficult to envision algorithmically. Sub-symbolic systems are particularly attractive for their ability to learn rules of correspondence on their own. In this case, if the analyst is able to prepare training examples that indicate a "pitch-class of resolution" for a given succession of pitch events, a network can learn to make such associations without the formulation of a wild proliferation of style- and period-dependent rule sets.

3.2 Time Structures

To this point we have built symbolic and sub-symbolic processes for the real-time analysis of pitch structures. While music often can be dismantled into harmonic and rhythmic components, we clearly do not experience music as an assemblage of independent parts. Even the analyst who makes such divisions recognizes them as a procedural simplification: "It is important to realize that when [Leonard] Meyer analyzes rhythm he is not simply considering one aspect of music and ignoring the others. Instead he is using rhythmic accentuation as a means of clarifying and notating his response to the music as a whole" (Cook 1987, 77).

Though their outputs ultimately must be combined, the decomposition of analysis into parallel independent systems echoes the organization found in the brain itself: "There is convincing physiological evidence that the subsystems underlying the attribution of various characteristics of sound become separate very early in the processing system. . . . Such evidence would lead us to hypothesize that auditory grouping is not carried out by a single mechanism but rather by a number of mechanisms, which at some stage act independently of each other" (Deutsch 1999a, 301).

The initial independence of subsystems requires that at some later point their contributions be synthesized. The gradual coordination of information seems to correspond to the emergence of higher-level percepts: "Investigations into mechanisms of visual shape perception have led to a distinction between early processes, in which many low-level abstractions are carried out in parallel, and later processes, in which questions are asked of these low-level abstractions based on hypotheses concerning the scene to be analyzed. . . . The distinction between abstractions that are formed passively from "bottom up" and those that occur from "top down" is important in music also" (Deutsch 1999b, 349).

We will maintain the analytical separation of pitch and time for the moment because such decomposition makes it easier to design and discuss processes appropriate to the corresponding dimension. It is worth noting at this point, however, that the ultimate goal is to integrate them into larger structures that consider both simultaneously. The work with key induction is a good example: clearly an important cue to our understanding of harmony is the relationship of pitch materials to an ongoing metric hierarchy. If we can similarly coordinate the pitch analysis processes with others that follow rhythmic development, we may reasonably expect the system's performance to correspond more closely to our own.

With this larger perspective in mind, let us proceed to the implementation of temporal analyses. When considering pitch, we moved progressively up a hierarchy extending from individual chord roots and types to large-scale keys and modes. Now consider a hierarchy of temporal structures ranging from a simple pulse up to a meter in which some pulses are periodically recognized as being more important than others. Conceptually, this hierarchy extends in both directions, down to subdivisions of the pulse and up to phrase groupings in which collections of strong beats form yet larger periodic units.

For the moment we will consider the middle levels of the rhythmic hierarchy: the formation of a regular pulse, and the differentiation of those pulses into the strong and weak beats of a meter.

3.2.1 Quantization

Standard notation of Western music assumes a temporal grid of bars, beats, and subdivisions of beats. This notation reflects an essentially automatic cognitive process in human listeners whereby a pulse is extracted from a regular sequence of musical events. The phenomenon of pulse is manifested in the tapping of a foot in time to the music, for example, or in the beat of a conductor's baton. Rhythm perception builds on the foundation of pulse to form hierarchies in which some pulses (beats) are more important than others. Meter is the notational device used to indicate such hierarchies: a meter of 4/4, for example, represents the occurrence of a strong pulse once every four beats.

Western rhythmic notation, then, is a hierarchical system that multiplies and divides simple pulse durations by small integer values. Multiplication of beats produces measures; division of beats produces subdivisions. Within a measure some beats are stronger than others, and within a beat some subdivisions are stronger than others. This economy of notation is directly related to the cognition of musical time—we experience music with even minimal temporal regularities as conforming to a metrical grid.

The correspondence of notation and perception does not extend to the duration of events as they occur in performance, however:

In performed music there are large deviations from the time intervals as they appear in the score (Clarke 1987). Quantization is the process by which the time intervals in the score are recovered from the durations in a performed temporal sequence; to put it in another way, it is the process by which performed time intervals are factorized into abstract integer durations representing the notes in the score and local tempo factors. These tempo factors are aggregates of intended timing deviations like rubato and unintended timing deviations like noise of the motor system. (Desain 1993, 240)

The "noise of the motor system" refers to the fact that humans are physically incapable of producing movements that are exactly equally spaced in time. This deficiency is of no great consequence while we listen to music because the variations are small, and our perceptual system effectively filters out the discrepancies, anyway. It does mean, however, that a computer looking at a series of human finger motions (e.g., from a performance on a piano keyboard) will not see a sequence of numbers that can be directly measured as a series of simple integer multiples of an underlying pulse.

The inaccuracies caused by muscle jitter are a small but significant obstacle to quantizing performance information. They become much more formidable, however, when added to the purposeful deviations introduced by musicians in the expressive performance of a work of music. As we shall see in chapter 6, players use a number of temporal manipulations to impart cues about the structure and content of a composition in performance. We as listeners are able to distinguish the structural and expressive factors activating the resulting percept from the underlying meter. The problem of quantization is to perform the algorithmic analog in a machine musician: separate structural rhythms from expressive variations. Ideally we would like to pre-serve and use both, but for the moment we will concern ourselves with deriving a series of integrally related time points from undiffer-entiated performance data.

Commercial sequencers perform quantization by rounding tempo-ral measurements to the nearest quantized grid point. The grid used is computed from a global tempo setting and a specification of the smallest permissible duration. Both of these values are entered by the user. In many systems, the user must also indicate whether "tuplet" (i.e., triplet, quintuplet, etc.) divisions of the beat may be mixed with simple power-of-two divisions. Anyone who has used a sequencer knows that this method yields results that require a lot of editing for any but the most simple of rhythmic styles. In any event, such a technique is useless in a real-time situation because there is no pre-existing grid. The only way to get one would be to require the musicians to play along with a metronome, something that would defeat the entire purpose of playing with an interactive system. Clearly we need to use a different technique.

The Connectionist Quantizer developed by Peter Desain and Henkjan Honing gradually modifies time points in a list of events to bring them into simpler temporal relationships. It is connectionist in that it consists of "a large number of simple elements, each of which has its own activation level. These cells are interconnected in a complex network, with the connections serving to excite or inhibit other elements" (Desain and Honing 1989, 151). The model differs from the backpropagation networks we implemented earlier, however, in that it does not learn. The convergence between cells that it performs is already coded into the system. We can consider the quantizer as a constraint propagation network in which neighboring durations constrain each other to values that increasingly approach integer multiples. For example, two neighboring durations of 1.1 and 0.9 will be gradually pulled by the model into the equal values 1.0 and 1.0.

Let us implement a C++ port of the Connectionist Quantizer, starting from the algorithm as it has been published in Lisp. We refer to the point in time at which an `Event` occurs as its onset. The duration between the onsets of two `Events` is called the inter-onset-interval, or IOI. Desain and Honing model inter-onset-intervals as cells in a network. These are called *basic cells*. An *interaction cell* is connected bi-directionally to two basic cells. "Each interaction cell steers the two basic cells to which it is connected toward integer multiples of one another, but only if they are already near this state" (Desain and Honing 1989, 152). The `Interaction()` function returns a change of ratio for two intervals that will move them toward an integer relationship if they are close to having one already.

Beside the interactions between basic cells, the model operates on *sum cells* as well. "These cells sum the activation levels of the basic cells to which they are connected. The interaction of a sum cell with its basic cells is bidirectional; if the sum cell changes its value, the basic cells connected to it will all change proportionally" (Desain and Honing 1989, 154). Figure 3.12 lists all of the functions used in the C++ connectionist quantizer.

```
/* return change of two time intervals */

double Quantizer::Delta(double a, double b, double minimum,

                        double peak, double decay)

{

    bool inverted = (a <= b);

    double ratio = inverted?(b/a):(a/b);

    double delta_ratio = Interaction(ratio, peak, decay);

    double proportion = delta_ratio / (ratio + delta_ratio + 1);

    if (inverted) proportion *= -1;

    return (minimum * proportion);

}


/* return change of time interval ratio */

double Quantizer::Interaction(double ratio, double peak, double decay)

{

  double goal = round(ratio);

  double position = 2 * (ratio - trunc(ratio) - 0.5);

  double result =

      (goal - ratio) * pow(abs(position), peak) * pow(goal, decay);

  return result;

}


/* quantize data of inter-onset intervals */

void Quantizer::Quantize(int length, ...)

{

    va_list  args;

    va_start(args, length);
```

Figure 3.12 Connectionist Quantizer

```
        double* intervals = new double[length];

        double* changes  = new double[length];

        register int i;

        for (i=0; i<length; i++)

                intervals[i] = va_arg(args, double);

        va_end(args);


        int     iterations = 20;

        double  peak        =  5.0;

        double  decay       = -1.0;

        double  minimum     = 100.0;


        for (i=0; i<length; i++) {

                changes[i] = 0.0;

                if (intervals[i] < minimum) minimum = intervals[i];

        }

        for (i=0; i<iterations; i++)

                Update(intervals, minimum, changes, peak, decay, length);


        delete [] changes;

        delete [] intervals;

}


/* update all intervals synchronously */

void Quantizer::Update(double* intervals, double minimum,

                        double* changes, double peak, double decay,

                        int length)
```

Figure 3.12 Continued

```
{
    for (int a_begin=0; a_begin<length-1; a_begin++) {
        double a_sum = 0.0;
        for (int a_end=a_begin; a_end<length-1; a_end++) {
            a_sum += intervals[a_end];
            double b_sum = 0.0;
            int b_begin = a_end + 1;
            for (int b_end=b_begin; b_end<length; b_end++) {
                b_sum += intervals[b_end];
                double delta = Delta(a_sum, b_sum, minimum,
                                            peak, decay);
                Propagate(changes, a_begin, a_end,   delta/a_sum);
                Propagate(changes, b_begin, b_end, -(delta/a_sum));
            }
        }
    }
    Enforce(changes, intervals, length);
}


/* derive changes of basic intervals from sum-interval change */
void Quantizer::Propagate(double* changes, int begin,
                                    int end, double change)
{
    for (int i=begin; i<end; i++)
        changes[i] += change;
}
```

Figure 3.12 Continued

```
/* effectuate changes to intervals */

void Quantizer::Enforce(double* changes, double* intervals, int length)

{

        for (int i=0; i<length; i++) {

                intervals[i] *= (changes[i] + 1);

                changes[i] = 0.0;

        }

}
```

Figure 3.12 Continued

```
(a)     1.1 2.0  (b)
(a)     1.1 4.9  (b+c)
(a+b)   3.1 2.9  (c)
(b)     2.0 2.9  (c)
```

Figure 3.13 Inputs to `Delta()`

Let us trace through the quantization of a list of three inter-onset intervals: 1.1, 2.0, and 2.9 (note that these values correspond to those used as an example by Desain and Honing [1989]. The Quantizer application on the CD-ROM implements the process with this example. The quantizer is constructed using the number of offsets, followed by the offsets themselves. We use the C/C++ variable argument list conventions described further in section 5.1. Following through the `Quantize()` process, note that the critical calculations are made in `Delta()` and `Interaction()`. `Update()` takes care of exhaustively presenting all of the base and sum node combinations to `Delta()`, which computes the required value changes. The complete list of values presented to `Delta()` is shown in figure 3.13.

These four possibilities exhaust the set of basic and sum cell combinations present in a network of three onset values. As running the

Quantizer example application demonstrates, at the end of twenty iterations the base nodes a, b, and c have indeed converged toward the integer values of 1.0, 2.0, and 3.0.

The process just traced corresponds to the Connectionist Quantizer as it was published in 1993. Although it is fast enough, this version is unsuited to real time because it requires a complete sequence of onsets: "A model that takes a whole temporal sequence into consideration at once is not feasible when the aim is to develop a cognitive model. Luckily, it proved quite simple to design a version of the quantizer which operates upon a window of events" (Desain 1993, 242). To function as a machine musician component, we want the quantizer to treat events as they arrive. We can adopt the technique recommended by Peter Desain: incoming events are added to a window of events that are continually processed as new ones arrive. The window has a fixed length—when it is full of events, the oldest one is removed from the window whenever a new one is added (first in/first out).

Beyond adopting a windowing technique, we must also cast the quantization process as a `ListenProp` so that it may be called with other analysis routines from the `Listener`. Figure 3.14 shows the `Calculate()` routine that prepares input from the `Listener` for treatment by the quantizer.

We must first wait until enough onsets have arrived to make the quantization meaningful. Once we have at least three events, we continually enlarge the size of the quantization window until it includes a maximum of ten inter-onset intervals. The very first IOI becomes a point of reference for the quantizer, since the intervals input to the process need to be expressed as multiples of some base value. We calculate these ratios by dividing each successive IOI by the base IOI. When the intervals and changes arrays have been initialized, the connectionist quantizer is run on them. Finally the base IOI is updated to provide a baseline closer to an integer multiple of the window values.

The Quantizer application on the CD-ROM uses the `ListenProp` implementation just described. The interface to it is shown in figure 3.15. A user can play music on a MIDI device or hit the space bar to

```
void Quantizer::Calculate(Event *event)

{

    if (event->IOI() == 0) return;          // only one event, go back

    if (event->Prev()->IOI() == 0) return;// only two events, go back


    register int i;

    static int countIOI = 0;

    if (countIOI == 0)

        baseIOI = (double)event->IOI();// take first IOI as base

    if (++countIOI > kMaxWindow)

        countIOI = kMaxWindow;   // maximum window of 10 events


    numCells = countIOI;

    for (i=0; i<numCells-1; i++)  // go back to beginning of window

        event = event->Prev();


    for (i=0; i<numCells; i++) {

        intervals[i] = (double)event->IOI()/baseIOI;

        changes [i] = 0.0;

        event = event->Next();

    }

    Quantize();                         // run connectionist quantizer


    baseIOI *= intervals[0];       // adjust base IOI

}
```

Figure 3.14 Quantizer::Calculate()

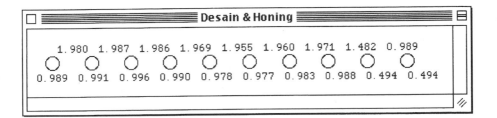

Figure 3.15 Quantizer interface

generate incoming events. As the quantization window size increases, ovals representing the events within it are added across the
display. Below each oval is shown the quantized ratio of its corresponding IOI. Above and between two ovals is the sum of their ratios,
representing the interaction cell based on the two lower IOIs.

As we see in figure 3.15, the quantizer pulls IOIs in the window
into increasingly integral relationships with one another. The input
to the program that produced the output shown was a series of performed quarter notes, effectively, with two eighth notes at the end.
We can read this from the bottom line of values in which the first
eight are all nearly one while the last two are both nearly one-half.

Using the quantizer in real time means that the process will probably not be able to converge to a stable state before the contents of the
window have changed. If the quantizer continued to iterate on the
values shown in figure 3.15, it would tend to converge on a state in
which the first eight ratios would be equal to 1.0 and the last two
equal to 0.5. Because the next input will shift out the first value and
shift in a new one that has not undergone any iterations yet, it is
likely that the remaining intervals will not arrive at their optimal
values before they too are shifted out.

From the example shown, however, it is clear that some averaging
and thresholding can tell us nearly enough the value to which a ratio
is moving. All of the ratios in the window are within 3% of their
ideal value. Whether or not 97% accuracy is good enough ultimately
depends on the process within which the quantized values are to be
used.

3.3 Beat Tracking

Quantization brings performed time-points into alignment with an underlying grid of pulses. Beat tracking (or beat induction) finds the underlying pulse of a sequence of time points. These are two aspects of the same problem: if we can quantize a sequence of intervals, one of the integer multiples from the sequence can be considered the beat. If we have a beat pulse, we can perform quantization by moving all time points in the sequence into alignment with it. In fact, many rhythm analyzers do not decompose the problem into quantization and beat tracking phases. Even where such a decomposition is algorithmically possible, it is not clear which phase should come first: quantization could make beat trackers work better, but having a beat as a starting point makes quantization much easier.

It has even been proposed that beat tracking might be easier if performed without any quantization stage at all:

The small number of models that operate directly on performance data—and allow for changes in tempo and expressive timing . . . —often consider timing as jitter or timing noise; they process this information by some kind of quantization method. . . . In our model the performed pattern (i.e., with expressive timing) is used directly as input. . . . Moreover, in performances often meter and beat are communicated, among other means, by the timing. . . . Thus beat induction models that take performance data as input may actually perform better if they make use of the information present in the expressive timing, instead of attempting to get rid of it. (Desain and Honing 1994b, 93–94)

Separating quantization, beat tracking, and meter induction, then, makes it possible not only to experiment with different orderings of the processes but to leave out some in order to gauge the effect on other stages as well.

As key induction is to chord identification, metrical analysis is to beat tracking. That is, once we have a pulse of evenly separated beats, we would like to identify which of them has greater structural importance—in other words, which ones are the downbeats.

In the past, computational analysis of rhythm has generally been divided into two problems. One is quantization: the rounding off of durations and time points in a piece to multiples of a common beat. . . . The other is metrical analysis: imposing higher levels of beats on an existing lower level. Models that assume a quantized input (such as Lerdahl and Jackendoff's) are really only addressing the second problem. However, an important recent realization of music artificial intelligence has been that quantization and meter finding are really part of the same process. In imposing a low level of beats on a piece of music, marking the onsets of events, one is in effect identifying their position and duration in terms of integer values of those beats. (Temperley and Sleator 1999, 14)

In this chapter we address what I see as three aspects of the analysis of a rhythmic hierarchy: quantization, beat tracking, and meter induction. I make a tripartite division because these tasks have been treated relatively independently in the literature. That is, quantizers (such as Desain and Honing's) operate without beat tracking and beat trackers are written to operate without quantization. Both tasks rarely make reference to a metric level. Metric analysis does rely on the other two, to varying degrees because it operates on a higher hierarchical level and depends on a lower level for material to organize. Consequently we first will review some beat tracking systems and then pass to methods for organizing their pulses metrically.

As often happens with the transfer of human knowledge to computer programs, there are striking differences between what is easy for a human to do and what is easy for the machine. When considering rhythm, for example, musicianship texts assume that a student, no matter how untrained, can tap her foot to music. The perception of a pulse in music is one of the most basic and universal of human musical skills. It is, however, notoriously difficult to accomplish the same "sense" with a computer program.

In their article, "Computational Models of Beat Induction: The Rule-Based Approach," Peter Desain and Henkjan Honing describe some of the attributes that make computational beat induction hard: "Only after a few notes (5–10) a strong sense of beat can be induced (a 'bottom-up' process). Once a beat is induced by the incoming material it sets up a persistent mental framework that guides the perception of new incoming material (a 'top-down' process). This process, for example, facilitates the percept of syncopation, i.e., to 'hear' a beat that is not carried by an event" (1999, 29).

Because of the fundamental nature of the task, many researchers have addressed the problem. A famous session at the 1994 International Computer Music Conference tested the success of software from several contributors in tapping a mechanical shoe to a common input stream (Desain and Honing 1994). As in the case of pitch algorithms, both symbolic and sub-symbolic proposals for beat tracking are extant and both types were presented at the 1994 session.

Todd Winkler introduces a number of techniques for following the temporal presentation of musical events in his book *Composing Interactive Music* (1998). One of the most basic of these is a patch for finding the inter-onset interval between note attacks (figure 3.16). The notein object receives both note on and note off messages from a MIDI input stream. Stripnote eliminates the note off messages and sends a velocity through to bangbang only when it is greater than zero (that is, a note on). Because of Max's right-to-left execution order, the right bang from bangbang will first stop the run of the timer and output the time in milliseconds that was mea-

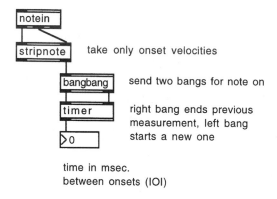

Figure 3.16 Inter-onset interval detection on Max

sured. Then the `bang` sent to the left inlet of the timer starts another measurement that will be terminated by a subsequent `note on`.

Winkler's inter-onset interval patch performs in Max the same calculation that is part of the `Listener::Hear()` procedure listed in figure 2.16. Once IOIs are calculated, they can be used as input to a number of temporal analyses including beat tracking and density estimation. See chapter 6 of *Composing Interactive Music* (Winkler 1998) for a beat tracker written entirely in Max.

3.3.1 Multiple Attractors

I have published a beat tracking technique (1993) that I now shall port to the `ListenProp` design. I previously presented the algorithm as resting on a connectionist foundation. It is connectionist in that a number of inputs are multiplied by a set of weights and summed at the output nodes to find a leading beat candidate. It deviates significantly from the networks we have used thus far, however, in that it does not learn. I call this version of the beat tracker "multiple attractors" in reference to its technique of maintaining a collection of pulse theories that are awarded points according to how accurately they predict the timing of incoming events.

The process fundamentally assumes that beat periods will occur within a certain range: between 300 and 1500 milliseconds long, corresponding to 200 and 40 beats per minute, respectively. These tempi mark the upper and lower limits of a common metronome. Metronome boundaries are not arbitrary; they emerged from many years of performance practice during which tempi beyond these limits were not normally needed. Since the beat tracker is looking only for periods that match the foot-tap tempo (and not longer or shorter pulses in the rhythmic hierarchy) it makes sense to limit its search to the metronome standard.

Given this limitation, every possible millisecond period length between the two extremes can be covered by an array of 1200 beat theories. Each beat theory is represented by the structure shown in figure 3.17. A beat theory includes the number of points awarded to that period, the time it next will tick, and a boolean field indicating

```
typedef struct {

        int  points;      // # of points assigned to this theory

        int  expect;      // time of next expected hit

        bool onbeat;      // whether or not it was on the beat

} BeatTheory;
```

Figure 3.17   Beat theory

```
int Beat::ReduceOffset(long duration)
{
    int temp    = duration;
    int divisor = 2;                      // first try dividing by two
    while (temp > kBeatLong)              // while duration is too long
        temp = duration / divisor++;  // divide by progressive subharmonics
    return temp;                          // return a value in bounds
}
```

Figure 3.18   Subharmonic duration reduction

whether or not an incoming beat coincided with a tick of the theory's period.

When a new event arrives at the listener, the duration that elapsed since the previous event is reported to the beat tracker. The tracker then generates a number of possible beat period interpretations from that duration. The most important of these is the duration itself: any distance between two events is taken as a possible beat period. The only restriction to that assertion is that the duration must fall within the range of legal periods. If a duration is too long (longer than 1500 milliseconds) the routine ReduceOffset() will be invoked to bring it into range (figure 3.18).

ReduceOffset() examines each of the subharmonics of a duration in order until one is found that is short enough to count as a beat period. Remember that subharmonics are computed by dividing a value by successive integers. The first reduction, then, attempts to divide the IOI by two. If the interval was twice the beat period, the first subharmonic will be the correct duration. ReduceOffset() continually tests subharmonics against the upper limit of legal beat periods until one is found within the acceptable range. The legal subharmonic is then returned to the caller.

The caller of ReduceOffset() is the member function Eligible() (figure 3.19). Eligible() checks two conditions of candidate beat periods: first, it must be short enough to fall within the prescribed range; and second, it must not be within a critical bandwidth surrounding already existing candidates. Figure 3.19 shows how these conditions are handled. If a candidate is too long, it is handed off to ReduceOffset(). Once a legal candidate is returned, it is checked against all existing candidates in the offsets array.

```
int Beat::Eligible(long candidate, int* offsets, int numOffsets)

{

        if (candidate >= kBeatLong)    // if too long try subharmonics

                candidate = ReduceOffset(candidate);


        // if candidate is close to one already found

        for (int i=0; i<numOffsets; i++) {

                long diff = abs(candidate - offsets[i]);

                if (diff < offsets[i]/20)

                        return 0;        // declare it ineligible

        }

        return candidate;                // otherwise return legal candidate

}
```

Figure 3.19 Determine eligibility

Whenever the new IOI is within ±5% of an already generated candidate, the new interval is rejected and Eligible() returns zero.

The heart of the beat tracker is the algorithm that generates successive candidates to present to Eligible(). The first possible period to be considered is the incoming IOI itself. If it is within the legal range, the IOI itself is always kept as a candidate. The next is the previous IOI, if there is one. If the previous IOI is legal, the algorithm also checks the new IOI plus the previous one. This covers situations in which a beat is being articulated by two eighth notes, a quarter/eighth triplet, or some other division into two parts. Similarly, if the IOI two before the incoming event is legal, it is sent to Eligible() as well as its sum with the new event, or its sum with the prior event.

The goal is to generate a list of seven possible beat periods that could account for the incoming IOI. After the prior two events and combinations with them have been checked, the algorithm multiplies the new IOI by various factors in a search for more potential explanations. The list of factors {2.0, 0.5, 3.0, 1.5, .66, 4.0, 6.0, 1.33, .33, .75} is used for this purpose—the incoming IOI is multiplied by each of these factors and submitted to Eligible() until the candidate array is full.

Once all the candidate IOIs have been generated, the program looks in the array of beat theories to see if points have been awarded to any other theories near the candidate—in other words, if a recent candidate IOI has been close to this one. If so, the older theory is pulled toward the new one and points for the two of them are combined. It is this process that I call "multiple attractors," there may be several beat theories within the array that have some degree of activation. Whenever a new duration comes close to an existing theory, it adds activation to it and adapts the period to match the incoming information.

Figure 3.20 is a trace of the beat theories generated by the multiple attractors algorithm during a performance. The leftmost column is the input IOI—the time in milliseconds between the input event and the event before it. The columns to the right of the input, numbered 0 through 4, show the five leading beat theories after points have

	0	1	2	3	4	R	E
409	409[11]	818[6]	204[5]	1227[4]	613[3]	819	1228
412	410[22]	819[16]	205[10]	1228[8]	270[4]	1231	1641
402	409[33]	818[22]	1227[16]	204[15]	269[6]	1633	2042
396	408[44]	817[32]	1226[20]	203[20]	268[8]	2029	2437
218	407[50]	817[32]	1226[20]	203[20]	268[8]	2247	2436
201	407[63]	817[32]	202[27]	1226[20]	218[13]	2448	2855
410	408[74]	818[39]	202[33]	1227[26]	218[17]	2858	3266

Figure 3.20 Multiple attractors trace

been awarded for the input on the left. For example, after the first input (409) the leading beat period theories are 409 (the IOI itself), 818 (double the IOI length), 204 (half the IOI length), 1227 (triple the IOI), and 613 (1.5 times the IOI). The final two columns, labeled R and E, show the real time in milliseconds at which the event arrived and the predicted time of a subsequent event according to the leading beat theory. Therefore R + period[0] = E.

We can see how well the algorithm is doing by comparing the E listings with subsequent R times. For example, after the first IOI the beat theory is 409 milliseconds. 409 added to the arrival time of the event (819) yields a predicted arrival time of 1228 for the next pulse of this period. In fact, the next event arrives at time 1231 (as shown in the R column of the second row), 3 milliseconds late according to the 409 milliseconds theory. Therefore the activation for 409 is added to the weight according an incoming event and collected in the theory for 410 milliseconds, somewhat slower than the prior theory to match the delay in the incoming event relative to the expectation.

The input that generated the trace in figure 3.20 was a very simple sequence of four quarter notes followed by two eighth notes and two more quarter notes. The leading theory remained stable throughout, with a period moving between 407 and 410 milliseconds. The greatest difference between an expected beat and an actual arrival time was 13 milliseconds. This example indicates how the algorithm does with simple rhythms. The user is encouraged to experiment with the Attractors application on the CD-ROM to experience its behavior with more complex inputs. All of the source code for the application is found in the same folder for any who wish to modify the process.

3.3.2 Adaptive Oscillators

A pulse is essentially a form of oscillation, and beat tracking is equivalent to finding the period and phase of a very low frequency oscillator. Large and Kolen have incorporated these relationships into a system of adaptive oscillators that lock onto the frequency and phase of periodic impulses. These units gradually increase their level of activation until they reach a threshold level, at which point they "fire," their activation is reset to zero, and the process begins again. Because the oscillator fires when it reaches the threshold, changing the threshold level will vary the time between firings and effectively change their frequency. A driving signal can be used to reset the threshold level and thereby the frequency of the unit, causing the unit to lock to the frequency of the driver.

In the model of musical beat that we propose, the driving signal (a rhythmic pattern) perturbs both the phase and the intrinsic period of the driven oscillator, causing a (relatively) permanent change to the oscillator's behavior. In addition, the oscillator will adjust its phase and period only at certain points in the rhythmic pattern, effectively isolating a single periodic component of the incoming rhythm. (Large and Kolen 1999, 78)

The output of the oscillator as a function of time is defined as: $o(t) = 1 + \tanh[g(\cos 2pf(t) - 1)]$ (Toiviainen 1998).

Figure 3.21 lists the code for an oscillator unit as described by Large and Kolen. The Oscillator application is built from this routine and other source code found in the same folder on the CD-ROM. The first part of Large() updates the expected firing time for the oscilla-

```
void Oscillator::Large(bool pulse, long time)

{

  while (time > (expected+(period/2)))// move the expectation point

      expected += period;              // to within one period of onset

  phi = (float)(time-expected) / period;


  if (pulse) {                         // if this was an onset

      adapt      = gamma * (cos(twoPI*phi)-1.0);

      adapt      = 1.0 / cosh(adapt);

      adapt     *= adapt;

      adapt     *= sin(twoPI*phi);

      adapt     *= (period / twoPI);

      period    += (periodStrength*adapt);       // update period

      expected  += (phaseStrength *adapt);       // and phase

      phi        = (float)(time-expected) / period;

  }


  output = 1+tanh(gamma*(cos(twoPI*phi)-1.0)); // Equation 1

}
```

Figure 3.21 Large and Kolen adaptation

tor to bring it within one period of the current time. Then the variable
phi is computed as an indication of the phase of the oscillator. The
phase is important because it delineates the temporal receptive field
of the unit—that part of its period within which adaptation is max-
imized. "Each output pulse instantiates a temporal receptive field
for the oscillatory unit—a window of time during which the unit
'expects' to see a stimulus pulse. The unit responds to stimulus

pulses that occur within this field by adjusting its phase and period, and ignores stimulus pulses that occur outside this field" (Large 1999, 81). The part of Large() that is executed when a pulse arrives computes the adaptation for the unit. The adaptation strength is modified by the value of phi, keeping it high within the receptive field and attenuating it everywhere else.

Petri Toiviainen's Interactive MIDI Accompanist (IMA) uses a modification of the Large and Kolen oscillators to perform beat-tracking in real time (Toiviainen 1998). Toiviainen's application is an accompanist in that it can recognize a number of jazz standards and play the parts of a rhythm section, following the tempo of a solo-ist. The IMA introduces some significant departures from the Large and Kolen adaptation functions as a necessary consequence of the nature of the application (figure 3.22).

The first change has to do with the discontinuities introduced by the Large and Kolen adaptations. "To be able to synchronize the ac-companiment with a live musical performance, the system must pro-duce a continuous, monotonically increasing mapping from absolute time (expressed in seconds) to relative time (expressed in the number of beats elapsed since the beginning of the performance). In oscillator terminology, it must produce a continuous mapping from time to phase. . . . This is not the case with Large and Kolen's oscillator, as it adapts its phase abruptly and discontinuously at the time of each note onset" (Toiviainen 1998, 65).

The other problem from the point of view of Toiviainen's IMA is that the Large and Kolen adaptations consider every input impulse to be equally important. This works well enough for regularly spaced performances, but can go dramatically awry when ornaments such as a trill are added. Toiviainen's response was to design new adaptation functions for the Large and Kolen oscillator that take into account, among other things, the duration of events associated with an input impulse. "The main idea behind this approach is that all adaptation takes place gradually and a posteriori, instead of occurring at the time of the note onset. Consequently, notes of short duration do not give rise to any significant adaptation, even if they occur within the

```
void Oscillator::Toiviainen(bool pulse, long time)
{
    /* if just starting, initialize phi */
    if (lastPulseTime < 0) {
        phi = phi_at_pulse + phiVel_at_pulse *
                    ((float)(time-startTime) / 1000.0);
    } else {
        float deltaTime   = time - lastPulseTime;
        float varPhi      = (deltaTime/1000.0) * phiVel_at_pulse;
        float adaptLong   = GetAdaptLong(varPhi);   // get from table
        float adaptShort  = GetAdaptShort(varPhi);  // get from table
        phi = phi_at_pulse + varPhi + errFunc *
                    (etaLong*adaptLong + etaShort*adaptShort);
        if (pulse)                   // change tempo if on pulse
            phiVel_at_pulse = phiVel_at_pulse *
                        (1 + etaLong * errFunc * adaptShort);
    }


    if (pulse) {
        /* Equation 1 */
        output        = 1+tanh(gamma*(cos(twoPI*phi)-1.0));
        errFunc       = output * (output-2.0) * sin(twoPI*phi);
        phi_at_pulse = phi;
    }


    period = 1000.0 / phiVel_at_pulse;              // update period
}
```

Figure 3.22 Toiviainen adaptation

temporal receptive field. As a result, the field can be set rather wide even if the rhythm of the performance is complex, thus making it possible to follow fast tempo changes or intense rubato" (Toiviainen 1998, 66). Because the oscillator does not adapt at the onset of an event but rather some time after it has passed might seem to indicate that the response of the IMA adaptation would be slower. In practice the oscillator converges to a new beat quickly enough to keep up with a live performance and avoids sudden jumps of tempo with every update of the period.

Much of the strength of the IMA adaptation arises from the fact that it is the product of two components, called long- and short-term adaptation. "Both types of adaptation are necessary for the system to follow tempo changes and other timing deviations. A single timing deviation does not give rise to any permanently significant change in phase velocity. If, on the other hand, the oscillator finds it is, say, behind the beat at several successive note onsets, the cumulation of long-term adaptation gives rise to a permanent change in phase velocity" (Toiviainen 1998, 68).

The combination of long- and short-term adaptation means that the IMA oscillator retains a relatively stable firing frequency even through trills and other highly ametrical inputs. The program expects an initial estimate of the beat period to start off the oscillator: such an estimate can be obtained from the IOI between the first two events, for example, or from a "count-off" given by the performer on a foot pedal.

The Oscillator application on the CD-ROM implements a single adaptive oscillator that changes period and phase with the arrival of incoming MIDI events. The user can select either the Large and Kolen adaptation function or that of Toiviainen using radio buttons on the interface (figure 3.23). The interface also indicates both the length in milliseconds of the most recent inter-onset interval (IOI) and the period of the oscillator. In figure 3.23 the last performed event corresponded quite closely to the period predicted by the oscillator—the two values are within 11 milliseconds of one another.

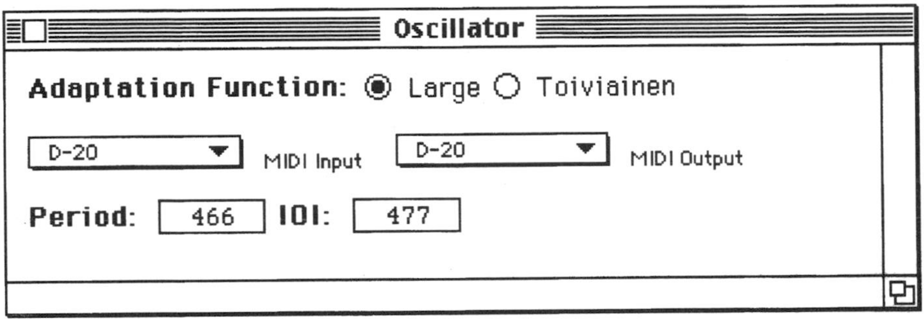

Figure 3.23 Oscillator interface

The example application reacts slowly to tempo changes and not at all to sudden shifts in speed. Both Large and Toiviainen use arrays of oscillators at different periods and choose the one with the greatest fidelity to the input. This makes their systems able to move between large variations in tempi and considerably more powerful than the limited example implemented here. The interested reader can modify the source code on the CD-ROM to multiply the number of adaptive oscillators.

3.3.3 Meter Induction

Beat tracking is the process of finding a regular pulse in a sequence of events. Meter in Western music is the organization of pulses into higher-level groups, whereby some pulses become regularly accented with respect to their neighbors. These higher-level groups typically occur in groups of two or three and are reflected in the time signatures of music notation. For example, a 2/4 meter indicates a metric group of two beats, in which the first is a strong beat and the second weak. A 3/4 meter indicates a strong beat followed by two weak ones. In a 4/4 meter, there is a strong beat at the beginning of the bar and on beat 3.

The problem of meter induction, then, is to find these higher-level groups as an organization of a series of undifferentiated beats. An important class of rule-based meter induction systems has arisen based on the model first proposed by Longuet-Higgins and Lee (1982). These models consist of a small set of rules that are used to confirm or revise a hypothesis about the ongoing beat period. The Longuet-Higgins and Lee algorithm used a set of five rules: INITIAL-IZE, STRETCH, UPDATE, CONFLATE, and CONFIRM. The INITIAL-IZE rule captures one of the main foundations of the approach: it takes the first IOI encountered as the beat period until proven otherwise by the remaining rules. Essentially the model assumes that the first period is the downbeat of a duple meter. It establishes increasingly higher-level metric periods built on this interval for as long as incoming events confirm the pulse. These higher-level periods extend to a range of about 5 seconds, after which pulses are no longer held to have metric significance.

The remaining rules of the system handle cases in which either the meter is triple and not duple, and/or the initial event is not a downbeat but an upbeat. The main structural cue that triggers the rules is an event with an IOI that is long relative to those of the events around it. That is, the model tries to place long notes on strong beats. In an article detailing his refinement of the rule set, Lee explains why long IOIs, and not only notes with long actual durations, are sufficient markers: "In musical terms, then, this means that—other things being equal—a long note is perceptually more salient than a short note, regardless of whether the absolute duration of the long note (measured from its time of onset to its time of offset) is greater than that of the short note. It seems reasonable to conclude that long notes and accented notes cue metrical structure in the same way: They tend to be heard as initiating higher-level metrical units than notes which are short or unaccented" (Lee 1985, 57). In other words, long IOIs can be taken as metrical markers whether or not the event filling the interval is long as well.

The Temperley and Sleator Serioso system (introduced in section 2.2.3) has a metric analysis component that, like the Longuet-Higgins and Lee model, uses long events as a marker for strong beats. Figure 3.24 lists the three preference rules of their metric component.

Event rule—prefer a structure that aligns beats with event onsets.

Length rule—prefer a structure that aligns strong beats with onsets of longer events.

Regularity rule—prefer beats at each level to be maximally evenly spaced.

Figure 3.24 Serioso metric preference rules

The Serioso rules can produce a metric interpretation of monophonic or polyphonic music and can parse information coming from a performed sequence of events. That is, the model does not depend on strict metronomic regularity (such as is produced by a quantized performance) to work.

Polyphony requires some additional interpretation of the rules. The event rule, for example, prefers beat locations that have the most event onsets. In other words, if all of the voices of a polyphonic context are arriving at one time point, that point makes a good beat. Further, it often occurs that a long note in one voice is obscured by intervening attacks in other voices. If a program tracks the MIDI stream coming from a keyboard performance, for example, all of the voices of the composition will arrive at the computer on the same channel and cannot be differentiated from each other. As in the Lee model cited above, Temperley considers long IOIs to be long events. That is, events are long whether or not the duration of the sounding note is long as well. "Intuitively, what we want is the IOI of a note within that line of the texture: we call this the *registral IOI*" (Temperley and Sleator 1999, 13).

There are published algorithms for separating the voices of a polyphonic composition (Marsden 1992) but the problem is notoriously difficult (as the Marsden article establishes) and will not be attempted here. Temperley adopts the simple heuristic of taking any note onset within nine semitones of a prior one to establish the registral IOI for that prior event. This breaks down, obviously, when two voices are operating within that span. "Taking all this into account, we propose a measure of an event's length that is used for the purpose of the length rule: the length of a note is the maximum of its duration and its registral IOI" (Temperley and Sleator 1999, 13).

Serioso's metric analysis is the structure that best satisfies all three rules after the evaluation of a composition as a whole. Though a complete analysis is required to arrive at a final parsing, Temperley's approach moves through the score from left to right and keeps track of the best solution at each step along the way (resembling Jackendoff's beam-search-like proposal [Jackendoff 1992]). At any given point the program is able to identify a maximal metric interpretation of the work to that moment, though the interpretation may change in light of further evidence later in the work. The process can therefore be used in real time as it only requires the information available as the piece is performed. It also accounts for "garden path" phenomena in which one way of hearing a passage is modified by the audition of subsequent events.

Serioso generates not only a tactus for the composition under analysis (beat tracking), but two metrical levels above the tactus and two below it. The upper and lower levels are found by evaluating tactus points much as events were evaluated to find the tactus itself. The tactus is called level 2, those above it are levels 3 and 4, and those below it levels 0 and 1. "Level 3 is generated in exactly the same way as level 2, with the added stipulation that every beat at level 3 must also be a beat at level 2, and exactly one or two level-2 beats must elapse between each pair of level-3 beats" (Temperley and Sleator 1999, 15).

There are two notable aspects of their method for generating additional metric levels: first, the method is essentially recursive, using the same rules for the tactus, its meter, and its subdivision. Second, their method searches for multiplications and divisions by two or three, just as the processes related to the Longuet-Higgins and Lee model do. The Serioso website lists the complete code of Temperley's system, including the metric analysis phase. The rules used in Longuet-Higgins-style models are clearly described by Desain and Honing (1999).

3.4 Max Externals

We have developed a number of algorithmic analysis programs using the C++ objects of the *Machine Musicianship* library. Many of the algorithmic composition techniques covered later in this text were written in the other language supported on the CD-ROM, namely Max. How can the examples written in one language be integrated with programs developed in the other? In many cases, the underlying algorithms can simply be ported: though it would be superfluous to implement the processes of this book in both environments, many of the programs discussed could be written equally well either way.

Another, more direct way of using C++ code in Max is to rewrite the objects involved as Max externals. Max itself is already object-oriented, or at least quite clearly designed using object-orientation as a model. The most straightforward approach would be to recast a C++ class as a Max object in which the C++ public methods become associated with particular messages sent to the Max object's inlet. As an example of this technique we will implement the Max external pcset.

The external takes a list of MIDI pitches as input and returns a pitch class vector such as those used by several of the harmonic analysis applications developed in chapters 2 and 3. This is not a particularly complicated process and could in fact be implemented quite easily in Max itself. We will write it as an external, however, to demonstrate the steps by which this is done.

David Zicarelli's manual *Writing External Objects for Max* is the essential guide to the process (1996). The CD-ROM uses Metrowerks CodeWarrior as the development environment, so I will briefly note the way that compiler is configured for the creation of Max externals.

The most important change from the other, stand-alone applications on the CD-ROM is that a Max external is compiled not as an application but as a shared library. (I will describe here the process of making a PowerPC external, but Zicarelli [1996] also explains how to compile the same code for a 68K external or a FAT version that will run on both processors).

CodeWarrior must be configured to produce a shared library instead of an application. To accomplish this one edits the Target settings of the CodeWarrior project. In the PPC Target panel, change the project type to Shared Library, the name to whatever the name of the Max external should be, the creator to max2 and the type to the string "????". This will make your external behave properly when called from Max, give it the correct name, and let the operating system know that it goes with Max (which will, for example, cause the external to be displayed on the desktop with the Max icon).

In writing an external, as with any computer program, we need first to decide what the functionality of the resulting object should be. To a large extent this depends on how the output of the object will be used and in what form the input is likely to arrive. What we certainly want to do is accept a list of MIDI note numbers and output twelve integers, with the first corresponding to the pitch class C, and where a value of one indicates the presence of a pitch class and a zero indicates its absence. Should the object output a list from one outlet, or have twelve separate outlets, one for each pitch class?

The answer depends on the most natural way to embed pcset in a patch. The external will be used primarily to send information to other objects that can perform analysis on pitch class sets, and so its output can best be cast as a list. If needed, Max provides an easy way to divide the list into twelve individual outlets with the unpack object (figure 3.25).

Writing a Max external is similar in many respects to designing a class in C++. Every Max external is associated with a data structure that maintains variables used by the object, which function much as private data members do in a C++ class. Figure 3.26 shows the data struct used by the pcset external. Every Max data struct has to begin

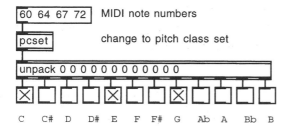

Figure 3.25 Unpacking the pitch classes of a pcset

```
typedef struct pcset

{

        struct object p_ob;        // used internally by Max

        long   p_args[MAXSIZE];    // MIDI note #s to be converted

        long   p_count;            // number of notes

        Atom   pcs[12];            // pitch classes array

        void*  p_out;              // outlet

} Pcset;
```

Figure 3.26 Pcset data structure

with a struct object field, as this is used by Max internally to manipulate the external. The subsequent fields are up to the programmer and arise from the calculations performed by the object. In pcset we need an array (p_args) in which to hold arguments, in this case MIDI note numbers. The variable p_count holds a count of the number of actual arguments currently recorded in the p_args array. Finally, the pcs array is a set of Max Atoms that will be sent as a list to the outlet p_out.

Max Atoms are themselves structures that can accommodate several types of data. Atoms have two fields, one to indicate the type, and the other to hold the data itself. We want all of our pitch class indicators to be integers, so internally there is no reason for the pcs

```
/* pcset_bang: governs the actual calculation of the pc array */

void pcset_bang(Pcset* x)

{

    register short i;


    EnterCallback();                    // needed for 68k compatibility


    for (i=0; i<x->p_count; i++) // add pitch class to array

        DoAtomPc(x, x->p_args[i]);


    outlet_list(x->p_out, 0L, 12, x->pcs);

    ExitCallback();                     // needed for 68k compatibility

}
```

Figure 3.27   Pcset bang method

array to be Atoms. Because we want to transmit lists from the outlet, however, we must conform to the Max standard for lists, which requires an array of Atoms. If we transmitted a list of integers instead of a list of Atoms, for example, unpack would not be able to separate the items as shown in figure 3.25.

The basic code for the pcset external is very simple. When the external is initialized, the pcs array is set to zero. The DoAtomPc() routine takes a MIDI note number modulo 12 and uses it as an argument into the array, setting that array member to one. In the bang method, then, DoAtomPc() is called repeatedly with all of the pitch classes in the input list, changing all of the appropriate array members to ones. The Max outlet_list() routine sends the list of twelve pcs to the outlet (figure 3.27).

The pcset_list method (figure 3.28) unpacks an input list of pitch classes and sends them one by one to the bang method. The

```
void pcset_list(Pcset* x, Symbol* s, short ac, Atom* av)
{
        register short i;
        long truncate;


        EnterCallback();          // needed for 68k compatibility
        if (ac > MAXSIZE-1)       // check to make sure buffer fits
                ac = MAXSIZE-1;
        for (i=0; i < ac; i++,av++) {
                if (av->a_type == A_LONG)      // save as long
                        SETLONG(x->p_args+i, av->a_w.w_long); else
                if (av->a_type == A_FLOAT) {
                        truncate = (long)av->a_w.w_float;
                        SETLONG(x->p_args+i, truncate);
                }
        }
        x->p_count = ac;          // save number of args
        pcset_bang(x);            // calculate and output pc array
        pcset_clear(x);           // reset to zero
        ExitCallback();           // needed for 68k compatibility
}
```

Figure 3.28 Pcset list method

```
void pcset_int(Pcset* x, long n)

{

    EnterCallback();

    SETLONG(x->p_args, n);          // copy inlet integer to args

    pcset_bang(x);                  // add to pcs array

    ExitCallback();

}
```

Figure 3.29 Pcset int method

input list can be either integer or floating point values—if they are floating, the routine truncates them to integer values before sending them on to bang.

A user may wish to send note numbers sequentially, instead of using a list, and have these incrementally build up a pitch-class set. To accommodate this usage, we need a method to respond to integer inputs and another that will set the pcs array to zero whenever a reset message is received. The integer method is even simpler than the list method, as all we need to do is call the bang method with a list of one item (figure 3.29).

Finally a simple method that resets all of the members of the pcs array to zero can be attached to a reset string sent to the inlet of the object. The pcset_clear method is already called within pcset_list to reset the array to zero after each incoming list has been processed and can simply be called by reset as well.

If one is accustomed to the decomposition of processes into interlocking methods, writing Max externals is a matter of learning some terminology and function calls unique to Max. As this simple example has demonstrated, C++ classes are particularly well suited to such implementation. The data members of the class need to be transferred to a Max object struct and member functions translated to Max methods. Though this simple demonstration has but limited utility, the technique of its construction can be applied to virtually all of the C++ classes written in this text.

4 Segments and Patterns

In the preceding chapters we have developed ways to analyze harmonic, melodic, and rhythmic material using both symbolic and sub-symbolic processes. Now we turn our attention to two of the primary organizing forces in the perception of music: the grouping of events and the recognition of patterns. As we shall see, these two processes are not only key components of machine analysis, but are fundamentally intertwined: "If all first-order elements were indiscriminately linked together, auditory shape recognition operations could not be performed. There must, therefore, be a set of mechanisms that enable us to form linkages between some elements and that inhibit us from forming linkages between others" (Deutsch 1999a, 299).

4.1 Segmentation

Segmentation is the process by which musical events are organized into groups. There are several reasons why segmentation is important: first, because we perceive music in groups at various levels and a machine musician should be able to form chunks analogous to the ones human listeners hear. Segments also offer a useful level of organization for the algorithmic categorization and analysis of music. The discovery of patterns within a musical stream, as we shall see in section 4.2, is greatly simplified when distinct and consistent segments can be used for comparison. We can also use segments to distinguish between levels of activity for harmonic or rhythmic processes: there may be small tempo fluctuations at the event level that occur within a larger structure of regular phrase lengths, for example.

4.1.1 Grouping Preference Rules

The publication of Lerdahl and Jackendoff's text, *A Generative Theory of Tonal Music* (GTTM) in 1983 was a watershed event for the development of music cognition. Much of the work developed since that point has been related in one way or another to the principles they laid out. One of the most novel elements of their approach was the treatment of rhythm:

They pointed out that rhythm in the tonal/metric music of the Western tradition consists of two independent elements: grouping— which is the manner in which music is segmented at a whole variety of levels, from groups of a few notes up to the large-scale form of the work—and meter—which is the regular alternation of strong and weak elements in the music. Two important points were made in this definition: first, although the two elements are theoretically independent of one another, the most stable arrangement involves a congruence between them such that strong points in the meter coincide with group boundaries. Second, the two domains deal respectively with time spans (grouping) and time points (meter): grouping structure is concerned with phenomena that extend over specified durations, whereas meter is concerned with theoretically durationless moments in time. (Clarke 1999, 478)

GTTM describes rule sets of two kinds: well-formedness rules define legal structures for the domain under analysis. Preference rules determine which of the legal structures are most likely to be heard by human listeners. We have already encountered preference rules in Temperley's Serioso analysis system (see sections 2.2.3 and 3.3.3). As Eric Clarke indicates, GTTM itself develops well-formedness and preference rules for two separate but interacting components: grouping and meter. In this section we will look at the grouping rules and ways in which these can be implemented for real-time analysis.

A common observation made of the rule set Lerdahl and Jackendoff introduced is that it is not algorithmic. That is, the set is defined in such a way that competing structures could be generated from rules that are both legal and incompatible with one another. The authors point out that "the reason that the rules fail to produce a definitive analysis is that we have not completely characterized what happens when two preference rules come into conflict" (Lerdahl and Jackendoff 1983, 54).

Moreover, GTTM is not a mechanism for evaluating music as it unfolds in time: "Instead of describing the listener's real-time mental processes, we will be concerned only with the final state of his understanding. In our view it would be fruitless to theorize about mental processing before understanding the organization to which the processing leads" (Lerdahl and Jackendoff 1983, 3–4). I see the relationship between organization and processing somewhat differently—I think one could easily produce an organization that would exhibit many structural characteristics in common with human understanding and yet be impossible to realize in real time. It would then be fruitless to theorize about processing if there is no way to generate the proposed structure from the experience of music. I do not claim that is the case with GTTM, which may be obvious since we are in the process of implementing it here. In any case, none of this represents a criticism of Lerdahl and Jackendoff's estimable theory; I am only noting that the theory does not immediately do what it was never designed to do. In fact, it is in my view a tribute to the flexibility of their theory that a real-time segmenter based on these principles works as well as it does.

There have been several efforts to implement parts of the GTTM rule set algorithmically. Donncha O Maidin presents a Pascal implementation of the grouping rules in (O Maidin 1992), though that work is not specifically designed for real-time use. Richard Ashley's LM melodic learning system similarly had a GTTM component for the segmentation of monophonic material: "On the first hearing of a melody, it parses the incoming perceptual stream (represented as an event-list) into time-spans, or 'trajectories,' by a production system using rules based on Lerdahl and Jackendoff's Grouping Preference

Rules" (Ashley 1989, 306). Because of its real-time orientation, the system on which I rely most heavily in this discussion is the one published by Stammen and Pennycook (1993).

The grouping well-formedness rules below (Lerdahl and Jackendoff 1983, 37–8) determine the structure of legal groups:

GWFR 1   Any contiguous sequence of pitch-events, drum beats, or the like can constitute a group, and only contiguous sequences can constitute a group.

The first well-formedness rule makes it easier to imagine this process occurring in real time, as it must for our purposes. If all groups are composed of contiguous sequences, then group boundaries may be formed as the events of the sequence arrive in succession. Even if a group boundary is not recognized as such for some number of events after its actual arrival, the bookkeeping and analytical apparatus is far less than would be needed if each new event could be a member of an arbitrarily large number of prior groups.

GWFR 2   A piece constitutes a group.

GWFR 3   A group may contain smaller groups.

GWFR 4   If a group G_1 contains part of a group G_2, it must contain all of G_2.

GWFR 5   If a group G_1 contains a smaller group G_2, then G_1 must be exhaustively partitioned into smaller groups.

GWFRs 2–5 establish that groups are hierarchical and impose restrictions on what kind of hierarchy they can form. In terms of real-time processing, these restrictions again make the task easier than it otherwise might be: if any group contains sub-groups, these are wholly contained within the larger group and serve to exhaustively partition it.

The rigidity of the hierarchy determined by the well-formedness rules is one of the more controversial aspects of Lerdahl and Jackendoff's theory (Kendall and Carterette 1990). Alternative constructions include a heterarchy or network representation (Narmour 1977) and musical schemata (Gjerdingen 1988). Our concern here, however, is with the production of terminal segments—the smallest elements of a Lerdahl and Jackendoff-style grouping hierarchy. Terminal segments could then form the lowest level of a full-blown GTTM structure, but might also become the atoms of other organizations, including the network and schema representations just cited.

Let us begin by defining a Segment class (figure 4.1). A Segment contains some number of Events and maintains information concerning which rules led to its formation. The ruleType array is indexed by the number of rules that can contribute to the assertion of a segment boundary. The Segment class as defined here can only represent the lowest level of a GTTM hierarchy—we have encoded no way to represent a segment composed of other segments. To make it fully hierarchical, we could add a type field to the object that would indicate whether it was a terminal Segment (containing Events) or higher-level (containing other Segments) and fill in the data arrays accordingly.

A group at McGill University led by Dale Stammen and Bruce Pennycook wrote a real-time segmenter based on GTTM as part of an interactive jazz analysis/performance system (1993). Their rules are grouped according to the amount of information required to apply them. Real-time rules, for example, are those that can be evaluated using only the information that has arrived up to the moment of computation. Three-note rules, by way of contrast, can only find a boundary one note after the boundary has already passed.

The first real-time rule is the simplest and is a derivation of GTTM's first grouping preference rule (43):

GPR 1 Strongly avoid groups containing a single event.
GPR 1, *alternative form*   Avoid analyses with very small groups—the smaller, the less preferable.

We can see the operation of the minimum size rule inside the AssertBoundary() method shown in figure 4.2, which is called whenever one of the other rules has detected a segment boundary. The argument number contains the length in events of the newly

```
class Segment {
public:

        enum RuleType { kAttackPoint = 0, kSlurRest, kRegisterChange,
                        kMaxSize, kGenerated, kNumRuleTypes };


private:
        Segment*           prev;
        Segment*           next;
        class EventBlock*  eventBlock;
        int                numEvents;
        int                segmentID;
        bool               rules[kNumRuleTypes];


public:
        Segment(int size);
        Segment(void);
        Segment& operator=(const Segment& rhs);
        ~Segment(void);


        Segment*     Prev(void) const { return prev; }
        Segment*     Next(void) const { return next; }


        void         CopyEvents(class Event* event, int size);
        class Event* FirstEvent(void);
        void         SetNumEvents(int newNumEvents)

                                    { numEvents = newNumEvents; }
        void         SetPrev(Segment* p) { prev      = p;                 }
```

Figure 4.1 Segment() class

```
void          SetNext(Segment* n) { next      = n;           }

void          SetSegmentID(int s) { segmentID = s;           }


void          AssertRuleType(RuleType r) { rules[r] = true;  }

void          IncNumEvents(void)          { ++numEvents;      }

class EventBlock* Events(void)   const   { return eventBlock; }

int           ID(void)           const   { return segmentID;  }

int           NumEvents(void)    const   { return numEvents;  }

bool          RuleOn(RuleType r) const   { return rules[r];   }
};
```

Figure 4.1 Continued

found segment. The first conditional of `AssertBoundary()` compares that value to `minEvents`. If the number of events played since the last segment boundary has not reached the minimum length, no boundary is asserted at this location. With `minEvents` set to three, for example, this means that no one- or two-note segments will be produced.

Here we see an example of the consequence of translating GTTM into a computer program—GPR1 says only that small groups should be strongly avoided, not that they cannot exist. The GTTM rule set is not algorithmic because the preference rules are an interlocking collection of suggestions rather than prescriptions. To make a computer program, however, we must decide the matter one way or another. The simplest solution is the one just described—set a threshold for the minimum number of events a segment must hold.

Lerdahl and Jackendoff's second grouping preference rule deals with the proximity of events in different parameters (45):

GPR 2 (Proximity) Consider a sequence of four notes $n_1n_2n_3n_4$. All else being equal, the transition n_2-n_3 may be heard as a group boundary if

```
/* AssertBoundary: assert a segment boundary because of the given rule
*/
void Segmenter::AssertBoundary(Event* event, Segment::RuleType ruleType,
                                        int number)
{
  register int i;

  if (number < minEvents)
      return;                       // reject segments that are too short

  if (newLength > 0) {          // already created this segment
      Segment* prior = currentSegment->Prev();
      prior->AssertRuleType(ruleType);    // just add rule type
      mac->DrawEvent(prior->Events()->Tail());
      return;
  }


  ++numSegments;                    // increase the number of segments
  if (numSegments > segments->NumSegments()) {
      int newSize = segments->NumSegments()+10;
      SegmentBlock* tmp = new SegmentBlock(newSize);
      for (i=0; i<numSegments-1; i++)
            *tmp->Member(i) = *segments->Member(i);
      delete segments;
      segments      = tmp;
      currentSegment = segments->Member(numSegments-2);
  }
```

Figure 4.2 AssertBoundary() method

```
Segment* nextSeg = currentSegment->Next();

int pastBoundary = eventsInSegment-number;

for (i=0; i<pastBoundary; i++) {    // point remaining events to new seg

    event->SetSegmentID(nextSeg->ID());

    event = event->Prev();

}

event->SetLastInSegment(true);      // make event show it is boundary


currentSegment->AssertRuleType(ruleType);

currentSegment->CopyEvents(thisSegStart, number);

for (i=0; i<number; i++)

    thisSegStart = thisSegStart->Next();


mac->DrawEvent(event);              // redraw event with rule names

currentSegment = nextSeg;

currentSegment->SetNumEvents(pastBoundary);

}
```

Figure 4.2 Continued

a. (Slur/Rest) the interval of time from the end of n_2 to the beginning of n_3 is greater than that from the end of n_1 to the beginning of n_2 and that from the end of n_3 to the beginning of n_4, or if
b. (Attack-Point) the interval of time between the attack points of n_2 and n_3 is greater than that between the attack points of n_1 and n_2 and that between the attack points of n_3 and n_4.

Let us examine the real-time issues involved in implementing GPR2 more closely. Both parts of the rule are written as a function of four notes, which implies that a segment boundary cannot be

n1   n2

Figure 4.3 Incomplete GPR 2b

asserted from these rules until two notes have passed beyond the location of the boundary. For the analysis and processing of music during performance, we would like to be able to segment and treat material more quickly. The solution developed by Stammen and Pennycook (1993) is to notice immediately the distinctive transitions that make up the first part of the preference rules and posit a provisional segment boundary when they are found. Once all of the evidence has arrived, two notes later, the provisional boundary may be confirmed or eliminated. Time-critical processing is executed on the basis of provisional boundaries, and analyses that occur over a longer span can wait for firmer segmentation.

Figure 4.3 demonstrates an incomplete occurrence of GPR2b (Attack-Point). We may consider that n_1 and n_2 correspond to the events so marked in the figure. To fully decide GPR2b we need three durations: the length of time between the attacks of n_1 and n_2, the length of time between the attacks of n_2 and n_3, and the length of time between the attacks of n_3 and n_4. When $(n_3-n_2) > (n_2-n_1)$ and $(n_3-n_2) > (n_4-n_3)$, GPR2b is true. Once the half note marked n_2 in figure 4.4 has sounded for longer than a quarter note with no subsequent attack, we already know that the first part of the conjunction is true because (n_3-n_2) will necessarily be longer than (n_2-n_1). We may then assert a provisional boundary at the attack of the next event n_3. When the attack of n_4 arrives, we will know whether the second part of the conjunction is also true $((n_3-n_2) > (n_4-n_3))$.

Figure 4.4 shows these two possibilities: 4.4 (left) is the case where the second half of the conjunction is true, leading to a segment boundary between n_2 and n_3 (indicated in the figure by a bar line). Figure 4.4 (right) shows an example where $(n_3-n_2) = (n_4-n_3)$, mean-

Figure 4.4 Possible continuations of GPR 2b

ing that the second half of the conjunction is false and GPR2b does not apply. The dotted line before n_3 represents the provisional boundary generated when the first part of the conjunction was true.

Positing provisional occurrences of a grouping rule makes it possible to recognize that an event is the beginning of a new segment at the moment it arrives. It even becomes possible to recognize that an event is the end of an ongoing segment while that event is still sounding. The price of such speed is, of course, that some events will be treated as segment boundaries when in fact they are not. Whether or not the trade-off is worthwhile depends entirely on what will be done with the provisional segments.

What happens if we wait until all the evidence is in? We still would not be in a terrible position with respect to real-time processing because we will know the outcome of the rule with the attack of the event following the first event in the segment. For example, we know in figure 4.4 whether GPR2b is true or false with the onset of n_4. In fact, we know the negation of the rule even without n_4: as soon as the duration $(n_3\text{-}n_2)$ has passed without finding the onset of n_4, we know GPR2b to be false.

Figure 4.5 lists the code for the full attack-point function. Notice the calculation of the search duration for long notes: the variable `longOnToOn` is set to the most recent duration plus 10%. Because we are dealing with actual performed durations and not quantized durations in a score, the 10% margin helps us avoid triggering the rule because of expressive variations. When we know we are looking at the duration $n_2\text{-}n_3$, the routine `LongNoteFound()` is scheduled to execute once `longOnToOn` has elapsed.

```
void Segmenter::AttackPoint(class Event* event)
{
  int index      = eventsInSegment-1;


  // first event of performance, no IOI
  if (event->IOI() == 0) return;
  OnToOns[index] = event->IOI();
  longOnToOn           = OnToOns[index];
  // make long IOI 10% greater than last one
  longOnToOn      += (longOnToOn/10);


  if (index > 0)                   // look for long n2-n3
      longNoteTask = scheduler->ScheduleTask(Now+longOnToOn, 0, 2,
                        0, LongNoteFound, this);


  if (eventsInSegment < 4) return;
  index      -= 2;
  long n1n2 = OnToOns[index++];
  long n2n3 = OnToOns[index++];
  long n3n4 = OnToOns[index];


  if ((n2n3>n1n2) && (n2n3>n3n4)) {        // GPR 2b
      AssertBoundary(event, Segment::kAttackPoint, eventsInSegment-2);
      newLength = 2;
  }
}
```

Figure 4.5 Attack-point function

The basic implementation of GPR2b is found on the line so commented. When we have all four durations, it is a simple matter of
comparison to see whether the inter-onset interval n2n3 is greater
than both n1n2 and n3n4. If it is, the attack-point rule fires and a
boundary is asserted between n2 and n3.

Figure 4.6 lists the GTTM grouping preference rule 3. The Segmenter application on the CD-ROM implements the first of these.
The others can be readily computed in the same way, as the only
difference between them and the RegisterChange function that implements GPR3a will be the intervals they measure. Dynamics are
encoded as the velocity value of the Notes in an event, for example,
and the articulation can be measured as the span of time between
the attack of an Event and its overall duration.

There remains the fundamental problem of combination and prio-
ritization that was signaled by the authors themselves: there are no
meta-rules that establish how to proceed when different preference

GPR 3 (Change) Consider a sequence of four notes $n_1 n_2 n_3 n_4$.
All else being equal, the transition n_2-n_3 may be heard as a
group boundary if

a. (Register) the transition n_2-n_3 involves a greater
   intervallic distance than both n_1-n_2 and n_3-n_4, or if

b. (Dynamics) the transition n_2-n_3 involves a change in
   dynamics and n_1-n_2 and n_3-n_4 do not, or if

c. (Articulation) the transition n_2-n_3 involves a change in
   articulation and n_1-n_2 and n_3-n_4 do not, or if

d. (Length) n_2 and n_3 are of different lengths and both pairs
   n_1, n_2 and n_3, n_4 do not differ in length [Lerdahl &
   Jackendoff 1983 p. 46].

Figure 4.6 Grouping preference rule 3

GPR 6 (Parallelism) Where two or more segments of the music
can be construed as parallel, they preferably form parallel
parts of groups [Lerdahl & Jackendoff 1983 p. 51].

Figure 4.7 Grouping preference rule 6

rules come into conflict. Beyond that, GPRs 4–7 are more problematic both in terms of algorithmic formulation and real-time performance. Consider GPR6 (figure 4.7).

There are two problems here from an algorithmic point of view: first,
how to determine that two musical segments are parallel, and second
how to ensure that they form parallel parts of groups. The parallelisms
that Lerdahl and Jackendoff use to illustrate the rule are similarities of
melodic and rhythmic contour. Exactly which similarities apply and
whether they must be present both melodically and rhythmically are
among the issues that are left to the judgment of the analyzer. The next
section is devoted to noticing such similarities algorithmically.

Even assuming we could develop a parallelism recognizer, however, let us note in passing a circular relationship that would become
more acute in combination with GPR6: pattern recognition, particularly in real time, relies on having consistent groups to compare. If
grouping depends on patterns that depend on groups, we find again
the kinds of control structure complications that were encountered
with the interplay between chords and keys. Here is another instance
of interacting processes that must collaborate to converge on a convincing structure.

The relevance of grouping preference rules for real-time segmentation depends, as usual, on the ends to which the discovered grouping
boundaries will be put. Similarly, the issues of control and arbitration
between competing rules can only be decided within the framework
of a particular application. GTTM itself does not offer any recommendations, but Ray Jackendoff suggested some ideas in his 1992 article,
"Musical Processing and Musical Affect." In particular he outlined a
parallel multiple-analysis model in which several structural candi-

dates would be developed simultaneously: "The idea behind this theory is that when the processor encounters a choice point among competing analyses, processing splits into simultaneous branches, each computing an analysis for one of the possibilities. When a particular branch drops below some threshold of plausibility, it is abandoned. Whatever branches remain at the end of the piece then contain viable structures for the piece as a whole" (Jackendoff 1992, 62). In computer science, such a strategy is referred to as *beam search*.

The multiplication of parallel theories is mitigated in the proposal by the stipulation of a *selection function*, which continually evaluates the emerging structures and indicates one of them as the most preferred. It is in the selection function that arbitration processes for competing preference rules would need to be worked out. With the addition of a selection function, real-time systems could use the most preferred analysis at any given point in the processing, even though that choice might be overridden by another at later moments of the performance. In fact much the same technique is used in the Serioso preference rule system of Temperley and Sleator.

Jackendoff's interest in devising a real-time mechanism for the preference rules lies primarily in the leverage it affords for theorizing about the listening process and its relationship to expectation:

The theory of musical processing sketched above makes possible a stronger notion of musical expectation or implication, or what might be called prospective hearing. The theory claims that the listener is using principles of musical grammar to assign multiple possible analyses to the fragment of music heard thus far. Among these principles, there are many that can project structure for parts of the music that have not yet been heard. For example, one of the principles of grouping (Grouping Preference Rule 5 in GTTM) creates a preference for symmetrical organization. When a single group is heard, this principle leads the processor to create a potential structure in which this group is balanced by a second group of the same length—that is, there is an "expectation" that the music will continue in a way that fills in a symmetrical structure. (Jackendoff 1992, 64–65)

It is precisely such expectations that would be most valuable for a machine musician to project, and the search for meaningful segments is an important part of generating them. Let us leave the grouping preference rules with some concluding observations: the GTTM rules must be adapted for application in a computer program. Some rules are readily usable as they stand while others present more difficulty, both in terms of formulation as well as application.

Figure 4.8 shows the interface of the Segmenter example on the CD-ROM. The interface and program design of the Segmenter are derived from code provided by Bruce Pennycook and Dale Stammen. I ported the code to C++ using the *Machine Musicianship* library. Incoming events appear in a piano-roll notation, with pitch number

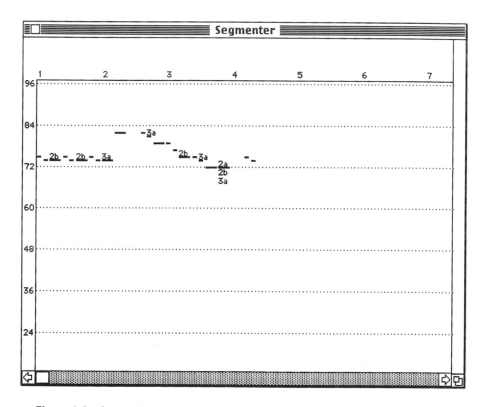

Figure 4.8 Segmenter interface

labeled along the y axis, and time advancing from left to right along the x axis. The input to the application that generated figure 4.8 was a performance of the opening of Mozart's *G Minor Symphony.* This work was used because it is also the musical material for the demonstration of GPRs 2 and 3 found on page 47 of GTTM. Since I have here implemented only GPRs 2a, 2b, and 3a, only those rules appear on the interface on the final event of the segment they define. Their placement in figure 4.8 corresponds to the illustration in figure 3.19 of GTTM (Lerdahl and Jackendoff 1983, 47).

The only differences arise from the way the rules are implemented—rule 3a fires on the 12th note, for example, because the program considers the unison to be an interval. Since the leap between notes 12 and 13 is larger than the half-step between 11 and 12, and larger than the unison between 13 and 14, rule 3a fires. Rules 2a and 2b do not fire on note 10, on the other hand, because of the prohibition against short segments. Since a boundary was just attached to note 9, a new one cannot be generated on note 10. Already in this short example we see that arbitration between conflicting rules is the primary hurdle to a fully developed GTTM segmenter.

4.1.2 Gestalt Segmentation

James Tenney and Larry Polansky's segmentation work is drawn from the tradition of Gestalt psychology, as indicated by the title of the article in which it is laid out: "Temporal Gestalt Perception in Music" (1980). Gestalt psychology is concerned with perceptual principles that ascribe a continuous cause to a series of discontinuous elements. One of these is the Law of Good Continuation: elements will be grouped together so as to form smoothly changing trajectories. A classic demonstration of Gestalt principles, particularly the law of good continuation, involves flashing discrete light sources in a particular time sequence. If a set of three light sources arranged in a line are flashed one after the other in a darkened room, viewers perceive the apparent motion of one light moving toward the final flash rather than three discrete events (which is what actually occurred). Other Gestalt principles include *proximity,* which holds that close elements are grouped together; *similarity,* that like elements give rise to groups; *common fate,* that elements changing the same way should be grouped; and the principle that we tend to group elements so as to form familiar configurations.

In Tenney and Polansky's work, the Gestalt principles of proximity and similarity are used as the basis for rules that govern grouping of *elements, clangs,* and *sequences.* "An element may be defined more precisely as a TG [temporal gestalt] which is not temporally divisible, in perception, into smaller TGs. A clang is a TG at the next higher level, consisting of a succession of two or more elements, and a succession of two or more clangs—heard as a TG at the *next* higher level—constitutes a sequence" (Tenney and Polansky 1980, 206–207). Essentially, an element corresponds to an Event in the hierarchical representation outlined in Chapter 2. A clang is then a group of Events, or a Segment. A sequence in Tenney and Polansky's work would be a collection of Segments in ours. Consequently, we are concerned for the moment primarily with the application of the rules to form clangs, or groups of elements.

The 1980 article formalized concepts that Tenney had been working with since the early 1960s, particularly the idea that Gestalt principles of proximity and similarity are two primary factors contributing to group formation in music perception. The rule related to proximity is defined as follows: "In a monophonic succession of elements, a clang will tend to be initiated in perception by any element which begins after a time-interval (from the beginning of the previous element, i.e., after a *delay-time*) which is *greater than those immediately preceding and following it,* 'other factors being equal' " (Tenney and Polansky 1980, 208 [italics in original]). The rule in this form, expressed with reference to time, is in fact identical to Lerdahl and Jackendoff's Grouping Preference Rule 2b (Attack-Point).

Lerdahl and Jackendoff note the resemblance in GTTM while considering the feasibility of implementing their rule system in a computer program. "Tenney and Polansky . . . state quantified rules of local detail, which are used by a computer program to predict grouping judgments. They point out, however, that their system does not comfortably account for vague or ambiguous grouping judgments, because of its numerical character, and they note the essential arbitrariness in the choice of numerical weights. And, although aware of the need for global rules such as those of symmetry and parallelism, they do not incorporate these rules into their system. It is our impression that they do not really confront the difficulty of how in principle one balances global against local considerations" (Lerdahl and Jackendoff 1983, 55). Though the problems of rule arbitration and the quantification of percepts such as parallelism remain, I believe that the number of algorithmic tools now at our disposal (many developed as an outgrowth of GTTM itself) makes a systematic and indeed computational investigation of the issues involved tractable. Let us continue, then, with a review of the Gestalt segmentation proposal.

Tenney and Polansky's similarity rule is a generalization of their proximity rule and corresponds closely or exactly to other Grouping Preference Rules: "In a monophonic succession of elements, a clang will tend to be initiated in perception by any element which differs from the previous element by an interval (in some parameter) which is *greater than those* (inter-element intervals) *immediately preceding and following it,* 'other factors being equal'" (Tenney and Polansky 1980, 209 [italics in original]). The similarity rule approximates GPR 3 (Change) in looking for intensifying discontinuities—that is, differences between neighbors in which the middle element changes more than the others.

Tenney and Polansky's temporal gestalt work was implemented in a computer program. This algorithmic orientation requires them to produce quite precise formulations of the objects and relationships described in their rules. The first manifestation of this precision is the definition of distance between two objects when those objects are quantified along several independent dimensions. In this case, the dimensions are pitch, duration, intensity (loudness), and, to some extent, timbre. Tenney and Polansky consider such objects as points in a multidimensional perceptual space. The problem, then, is how to measure the distance between two points. The two possibilities they consider are the Euclidean and city-block metrics.

"In the Euclidean metric, the distance between two points is always the square root of the sum of the squares of the distances (or intervals) between them in each individual dimension (in two dimensions, this is equivalent to the familiar Pythagorean formula for the hypotenuse of a right triangle). In the city-block metric, on the other hand, the distance is simply the sum of the absolute values of the distances (or intervals) in each dimension" (Tenney and Polansky 1980, 212).

The interval between two elements in any individual dimension is quantified by some measure appropriate to that parameter: pitch intervals are measured in semitones; durations are measured as a multiple of some quantization value (e.g., eighth-notes); and intensity in terms of dynamic-level differences printed in a score. The city-block distance between two elements is calculated by adding these parameter-specific intervals for all features under consideration. Figure 4.9 demonstrates the segmentation of the opening melodic line of Beethoven's *Fifth Symphony* arising from its intervals of pitch and duration (example taken from Tenney and Polansky [1980, 215]).

The segmentation rules used in figure 4.9 are quite simple and can be computed using a mechanism identical to the one introduced in the previous section. The "delay-time" and pitch intervals between consecutive Events can be found using the code shown in

Figure 4.9 Gestalt segmentation of Beethoven's *Symphony #5*

```
int TG::CityBlock(Event* event)

{

        int delay         = event->IOI();

        int pitchInterval = event->Notes(0)->Pitch();

        pitchInterval    -= event->Prev()->Notes(0)->Pitch();

        pitchInterval     = abs(pitchInterval);

        return (delay + pitchInterval);

}
```

Figure 4.10 City block measurement

figure 4.10. The delay-time is simply the IOI between one Event and the next, and the pitch interval is found by taking the absolute value of the first MIDI pitch number minus the second.

The problems with this from a real-time perspective are the ones we have come to expect: first, the delays in the Tenney and Polansky article are expressed in terms of some underlying quantized values, e.g., eighth notes. We will need to substitute ratios of some common base duration since the onset times of performed events have no quantized values attached (see a description of this process in section 2.4.2). The other problem is that segment boundaries are not found until one event beyond their occurrence, because we need to see that a given interval is larger than the ones both before and after it. This delay simply must be accepted if we wish to use the rules their article suggests.

The gestalt segmentation idea uses, in effect, the inverse of proximity and similarity to identify boundary lines between groups. In other words, when elements are not proximate and/or dissimilar, they tend to form the beginning and end of neighboring clangs. This concept is echoed in the literature of music theory, particularly in the work of Wallace Berry. In his text *Structural Functions in Music,* Berry states that musical structure "can be regarded as the confluence of shaped lines of element-succession which either agree (are complementary) in intensity direction or disagree (are mutually counteractive, or compensatory) in direction" (1987, 9). For Berry, the elements of music include tonality, texture, and rhythm. Elements are usually engaged in processes of intensification or relaxation, also called progression and recession, though sometimes they are in stasis. Tonality, for example, progresses as it modulates away from the home key and recesses as it returns.

Berry relates accentuation to grouping structure when he remarks that "the effort to understand accentual criteria in the experience of music is . . . the effort to enumerate factors which appear to contribute to and condition the perception of grouping by accentuation of certain impulses as metrically 'initiative'" (1987, 338). The criteria of accentuation he goes on to elaborate, then, can be read as a list of grouping markers. The accentuation criteria are grouped into three large classes ranked in order of importance. The first class of rules concern discontinuities between elements in which a superior value (accent) in some dimension follows a lesser value. For example, consider rule 1: Change to faster tempo. This criterion proposes that a noticeable shift to a faster tempo produces a structural accent that will be perceived as a group boundary. Interestingly, Berry considers that a shift to a slower tempo will less commonly produce such an effect. This is what he means by change to an accentually superior value: the first class of effects is brought about when an intensifying discontinuity takes place. Figure 4.11 lists all of the of class I accentuation criteria.

An examination of this list shows some criteria very similar to the ones we have already implemented (pronounced change of pitch, longer duration) and others that either require more information (more intense timbre) or operate on a higher hierarchical level (change to more intense texture). Berry's proposal is notable in the context of the current discussion both because he reinforces the identification of discontinuity as a grouping principle, and because some of the specific manifestations of the principle he identifies appear to be a useful expansion of the parameters we have examined so far. The

I.1. Change to faster tempo.

I.2. Pronounced change of pitch.

I.3. Approach by leaps in lines.

I.4. Longer duration (agogic accent).

I.5. Articulative stress.

I.6. Change to more intense timbre.

I.7. Change to denser or otherwise more intense texture.

I.8. Tonal or harmonic change of unusual degree or distance.

I.9. Dissonance.

Figure 4.11 Wallace Berry's accentuation criteria

most noticeable difference between this and the previous systems we examined is Berry's emphasis on "superior" values.

In his 1997 dissertation, Emilios Cambouropoulos reviews the gestalt origins of music segmentation and generalizes the proximity/similarity judgment into the Identity-Change Rule (ICR): "Amongst three successive objects boundaries may be introduced on either of the consecutive intervals formed by the objects if these intervals are different. If both intervals are identical no boundary is suggested" (Cambouropoulos 1997, 282). Another rule is added to handle the case of two successive identity changes: the Proximity Rule (PR) states "amongst three successive objects that form different intervals between them a boundary may be introduced on the larger interval, i.e., those two objects will tend to form a group that are closer together (or more similar to each other)" (Cambouropoulos 1997, 282).

Like Wallace Berry, Cambouropoulos regards accentuation and segmentation as two aspects of the same process. In fact, his work includes a technique for deriving one from the other: "In this paper it is maintained that local grouping and phenomenal accentuation structures are not independent components of a theory of musical rhythm but that they are in a *one-to-one* relation, i.e., accentuation

Figure 4.12 Smaller interval segmentation

structure can be derived from the grouping structure and the reverse''
(Cambouropoulos 1997, 285).

Berry's system puts particular emphasis on transitions to superior
values, and the proximity rules of both GTTM and Tenney and
Polansky similarly favor boundaries on large intervals. As Cambouropoulos points out, this bias excludes the recognition of a
boundary in a rhythmic sequence such as that shown in figure 4.12.
The ICR and PR rules are written in such a way that diminishing
intervals (i.e., changes to shorter, smaller, quieter values) will form
segment boundaries as well as intensifying ones. This orientation
produces a segment boundary in figure 4.12 at the location indicated
by the dashed line.

We have seen the Gestalt principles of proximity and similarity
cited by several researchers as the operative processes behind group
formation in music. The low-level distance metrics adopted by these
systems differ in detail but also show striking resemblances. My own
program Cypher noticed simultaneous discontinuities between several features of neighboring events as a way to detect segment boundaries, another way of expressing the same idea (Rowe 1993). The
Segmenter application on the CD-ROM can be used as the framework
for segmentation schemes along these lines, combining difference de-
tectors across several parameters simultaneously to arrive at low-
level grouping structures in real time.

4.2 Pattern Processing

Music is composed, to an important degree, of patterns that are repeated and transformed. Patterns occur in all of music's constituent
elements, including melody, rhythm, harmony, and texture. If com-

puter programs can be made to learn and identify musical patterns, they will be better equipped to analyze and contribute to musical discourse as it is understood by human practitioners. Pattern processing in music encompasses two goals: (1) learning to recognize sequential structures from repeated exposure, and (2) matching new input against these learned sequences. I will refer to processing directed toward the first goal as *pattern induction,* and that directed toward the second as *pattern matching.*

This usage follows the one suggested by Herbert Simon and Richard Sumner in their 1963 article "Pattern in Music," which proposed a formalism for describing musical patterns and a method for finding such patterns in music representations. Their study draws a direct parallel between musical patterns and the familiar letter-series sequences of intelligence tests, wherein the subject must continue a list of letters such as ABM CDM EFM. . . . "To perform successfully on a letter-series test, a person must do two things: (1) examine the partial sequence presented to him, and induct from it a pattern consistent with it; and (2) use the pattern to extrapolate the sequence, generating the successive symbols that belong to it. . . . We will call the first task *pattern induction,* the second task *sequence extrapolation*" (Simon and Sumner 1993, 103).

Patterns are so fundamental to our understanding of music that their identification can be part of many tasks, including indexing, analysis, and composition. Accordingly, much recent research has been concentrated in this area, and several working pattern systems are extant. Melodic similarities in particular have been a focal point of algorithmic development (Selfridge-Field 1998). Because they are designed for classifying large corpuses of existing material, many of these systems need not be concerned with causality or efficiency and so are not directly pertinent to real-time applications. Similarly, there is an extensive literature on pattern matching in computer science that documents algorithms generally intended for non-real-time search processes. We have, therefore, a large repertoire of sources, but must adapt them extensively to fit machine musicians.

In the most demanding real-time environment, both pattern induction and pattern matching would be carried out onstage. To achieve these goals, the program would need to notice sequences that have been repeated several times and find subsequent occurrences as they arise in the rest of the performance. Given that functionality, the program could report a match of the incipit of stored patterns and predict their continuation. That prediction might be used to deliberately harmonize or provide a counterpoint to the rest of the material as it is performed.

Carrying out both phases of pattern processing in real time consumes a great deal of processing power and so requires a stringent restriction of both the types of patterns treated and the number considered simultaneously. Another approach would be to conduct the induction phase on some corpus in advance, and then run the matching phase against the discovered patterns during the performance itself.

In either case, there must be some limits placed on the nature and length of the patterns considered—a brute force analysis of all patterns of all lengths is simply too computationally demanding for a real-time application, particularly one that is trying to accomplish other intensive processes at the same time. It is for this reason that we covered segmentation before pattern processing: if the elements returned from segmentation are grouped consistently, we may expect a measure of correspondence between template and candidate segments that is high enough for a program to recognize similar patterns.

4.2.1 Dynamic Programming

Joshua Bloch and Roger Dannenberg published a pattern matching technique derived from dynamic programming in "Real-time Computer Accompaniment of Keyboard Performances" (1985). I will refer to Bloch and Dannenberg in what follows because I make use of the description of the algorithm found there: the work is actually a polyphonic extension of a process first described by Dannenberg (1984). Computer accompaniment is another name for score following, a technique that tracks the progress of a human soloist's performance through a known score (see section 5.2). The tempo of the soloist's rendition can be calculated from the durations between successive matches, and that tempo drives the computer's performance of an accompaniment.

Imagine a representation of a solo musical line that consists of a sequence of pitch numbers, one for each note in the solo. Now imagine that same musical line being performed on a MIDI keyboard. With each note that is played, a new pitch number arrives at the computer. If the line is performed without error, the sequence of pitch numbers stored in the machine and the sequence arriving from the performer match exactly. Because errors often do occur, however, the goal of the Bloch and Dannenberg algorithm is to find the association between a soloist's performance and the score in memory that at any given moment has the greatest number of matched events.

A variable called the rating shows at any given moment the number of matches found between the performance (or candidate) and the stored score (or template). The rating is calculated using an integer matrix in which rows are associated with the template and columns with the candidate (table 4.1). When an item is matched, the rating for the corresponding matrix location is set to the maximum of two values: either the previous rating for that template location, or the rating of the previous candidate location plus one.

The matrix shown in table 4.1 illustrates how the values are updated as candidate elements are introduced. Time increases from left

Table 4.1 Rating Matrix

		candidate				
		9	1	8	2	7
template	9	<u>1</u>	1	1	1	1
	1	1	<u>2</u>	2	2	2
	8	1	2	<u>3</u>	3	3
	2	1	2	3	<u>4</u>	4
	7	1	2	3	4	<u>5</u>

to right across the figure. Labels at the top of the matrix indicate new candidate elements as they are introduced and the labels down the leftmost column represent the elements of the template pattern. The underlined values show which matches cause the rating value to be updated.

For example, when the candidate element 1 arrives, it matches the template element 1 at the second location in the pattern. At the location (1, 1) in the matrix, the rating is increased from one to two since incrementing the previous rating by one yields a value greater than the rating stored in the second location of the candidate prior to the match.

The MusicPattern class implements the Bloch and Dannenberg matcher. Figure 4.13 lists the heart of the algorithm. The matrix maxRating keeps track of the maximum number of matches found at any point in the performance, and the array matched shows which of the template pattern members have been found in the incoming material. Let us use the class to test some simple match conditions. We compare a template pattern of five elements { 9,1,8,2,7 } to four candidate patterns representing some common types of deviation: insertion, deletion, repetition, and transposition.

In the insertion test, the intruding element is not matched. Note in table 4.2 that the matrix entries under the candidate member 6 (the inserted element) are the same as those under the previous candidate. All other members are correctly identified as shown. In the implementation on the CD-ROM, the variable newMatch is set to −1 when the routine finds no match for an element under consideration, as happens with the insertion in this example. A negative value of newMatch, then, signals the insertion of an element that does not appear in the template at all.

The deletion test yields four matches (table 4.3). An array of integers, called matched, shows which elements of the template pattern have been found and which have not. At the end of this test, matched contains { 1, 1, 0, 1, 1 }, indicating that the third element was not found.

```
int MusicPattern::PatternMatcher(int start, int newElement)
{
   int rating   = start;
   int newMatch = -1;


   if (start < 1) return -1;


   for (int r=start; r<patternSize+1; r++) {
       int current = r-1;
       // initialization: current matrix element must be at least equal
       // to maxRating[r-1][1] since one more template item cannot reduce
       // # of matches, and at least equal to maxRating[r][0] because
       // that is the score attained by one less candidate element
       maxRating[r][1] = max(maxRating[r-1][1], maxRating[r][0]);


       // does the new element match the rth element of the template?
       if (newElement == element[current]) {
           // if first match and element was not matched before,
           if ((newMatch<0) && (matched[current]==0)){
               matched[current] = 1; // flag element as matched
               newMatch = current;   // save location of first match
               ++matches;            // increment number of matches
           }
           // found match, rating set to max of previous rating for
           // this element or the previous match plus one
           maxRating[r][1] = max(maxRating[r][1], 1+maxRating[r-1][0]);
           rating = maxRating[r][1];
```

Figure 4.13 PatternMatcher() listing

```
        }

    }


    return rating;

}
```

Figure 4.13 Continued

Table 4.2 Insertion Test

		candidate					
		9	1	6	8	2	7
template	9	1	1	1	1	1	1
	1	1	2	2	2	2	2
	8	1	2	2	3	3	3
	2	1	2	2	3	4	4
	7	1	2	2	3	4	5

Table 4.3 Deletion Test

		candidate			
		9	1	2	7
template	9	1	1	1	1
	1	1	2	2	2
	8	1	2	2	2
	2	1	2	3	3
	7	1	2	3	4

Table 4.4 Substitution Test

		candidate				
		9	1	6	2	7
template	9	<u>1</u>	1	1	1	1
	1	1	<u>2</u>	2	2	2
	8	1	2	2	2	2
	2	1	2	2	<u>3</u>	3
	7	1	2	2	3	<u>4</u>

Table 4.5 Repetition Test

		candidate				
		9	1	8	8	2	7
template	9	<u>1</u>	1	1	1	1	1
	1	1	<u>2</u>	2	2	2	2
	8	1	2	<u>3</u>	3	3	3
	2	1	2	3	3	<u>4</u>	4
	7	1	2	3	3	4	<u>5</u>

Substitution is accurately handled by a report of four matches (table 4.4) and a zero for the missing element in the corresponding matched array position. Further, newMatch contains −1 (no match) when the replaced element is encountered.

Repetition is much like insertion: the only difference is that the intruding element has already been seen. Because the matched array notes when an element has been matched, the algorithm correctly recognizes the second appearance of 8 in the candidate and does not increment the rating (table 4.5).

From the preceding tests we see that a very simple matching engine can handle the most common types of deviation from a pattern. The difficulty in musical pattern processing lies not in the matching algorithm, then, but in the preparation of patterns for presentation to the algorithm as well as in the maintenance of large numbers of remembered templates.

4.2.2 Intervallic Representation

The Bloch and Dannenberg algorithm uses an absolute representation of the pitch content of a score. That is, only a performance played at the encoded pitch level is recognized, and transpositions are not matched. In this respect the target task of their algorithm differs significantly from the pattern processing goals described in this chapter. We wish to identify repeated patterns in any transposition. Further, contours similar to a template should be identified as such with some metric to specify the degree of similarity. Processing melodic contour rather than exact tonal location also follows the evidence of human music cognition more closely. Humans can readily recall the shape of melodic material but cannot (unless they have perfect pitch) reproduce the melody at the original tonal location with much accuracy.

To that end, let us replace the absolute representation of pitch with an intervallic one. Actually, an intervallic representation will work with other aspects of music as well, such as rhythm. I refer to pitch in these examples because it is the simplest to demonstrate, but it should be understood that the techniques discussed are not exclusively applicable to that parameter.

Bharucha describes input representations for neural networks designed to recognize patterns through transposition: "When modeling the learning of musical sequences that are invariant across transposition, an invariant pitch-class representation is appropriate. . . . A complete invariant pitch-class representation would have 12 units corresponding to the 12 pitch-class intervals above the tonic, which may be referred to as Units 0 through 11 for tonic through leading tone, respectively" (Bharucha 1999, 416). This version of an invariant pitch-class representation requires identification of a tonic, information that we may or may not have in the pattern processing task.

Our discussion of sequential neural networks included a discussion of Bharucha's account of the architecture, which he terms temporal composites due to their integration of information that in performance was spread out through time. Neural networks are eminently well suited to pattern recognition and completion tasks, and the introduction of pitch invariance enables them to learn a number of useful harmonic categories: "A temporal composite of a pitch-class representation may be called a tonal composite, and a temporal composite of an invariant pitch class representation may be called a modal composite. Tonal composites that integrate information between chord changes represent the chords that have been either played or implied, and can account for aspects of the implication of harmony by melody. The corresponding modal composites represent chord functions. Tonal composites over longer durations represent keys, and modal composites represent modes" (Bharucha 1999, 422).

Bharucha's invariant pitch-class representation requires the designation of a tonic in the candidate patterns that are compared to the stored templates. We may wish to avoid designation of a tonic for any of a number of reasons: the music coming in may be tonally ambiguous or not tonal at all. Even assuming it is conventionally tonal, we may not have access to a process that can reliably identify a tonic in real time.

An alternative representation that avoids use of a tonic simply encodes intervals as the number of semitones separating a pitch from the one preceding it. Therefore the progression C4 to D4 would be represented by the sequence (60, 62) in an absolute representation, but as (+2) in an intervallic one. From this example we can see that one consequence of adopting an intervallic representation is that there is always one less element in the representation than there are pitches represented. The first pitch of a sequence is in essence always a match, since it serves only to establish the degree of transposition should all the following intervals match completely.

Other than this quirk, it would seem at first glance that the Bloch and Dannenberg algorithm would work just as well for intervals as for absolute pitches. This is largely true, but a second, less obvious

Figure 4.14 Effect of misplayed note on intervallic representation

consequence of having one value encode the distance between two pitches is that one misplayed note in a sequence will cause two values not to match. The problem can be seen clearly in figure 4.14.

Even though only one note differs between the two pitch sequences, two intervals are affected. A straight application of the earlier algorithm to these sequences would indicate that two deviations occurred, not one. Notice that adding together the first two intervals, however, will show that the third pitch is the same distance from the first in both examples. Examining four sums of candidate and template intervals, then, will accurately identify cases of insertion, deletion, substitution, and repetition. The routines listed in figure 4.15 implement a matching engine for these cases.

Let us run a second series of tests against the intervallic representation of the pattern shown in figure 4.16. We again will check each of the deviation types of insertion, deletion, substitution, repetition, and transposition (here referring to the reversal of two adjacent pitches in the pattern, not transposition to a different pitch location). The input sequences used for these tests are shown in figure 4.17.

Insertion, deletion, and substitution are correctly handled by the tests marked correspondingly in the code. Repetition is just a special case of insertion. Transposition is not recognized as such, but is seen by the program as a combination of deletion and insertion. Note that the first four intervals of the transposition example are the same as the deletion test. Accordingly, the program sees these intervals as representing a deletion. The appearance of the missing interval then is marked an insertion.

There are two other significant departures from the Bloch and Dannenberg algorithm in this code: first, the maxRating array has been

```
void IntervalMatch::UpdateMatched(int r)

{

    if (matched[r] == 0) {  // if element was not matched before,

        matched[r] = 1;      // flag current element as matched

        ++matches;           // increment number of matches

    }

}


int IntervalMatch::PatternMatcher(int rating, int newElement)

{

    if (rating < 0) return -1;


    int r = rating;

    if (newElement == element[r]) {

        UpdateMatched(r);                // match

        rating += 1;

    } else


    if (newElement == (element[r]+element[r+1])) {

        UpdateMatched(r+1);              // deletion

        rating += 2;

    } else


    if ((lastElement+newElement) == element[r]) {

        UpdateMatched(r);                // insertion

        rating += 1;

    } else
```

Figure 4.15 IntervalMatch matching engine

```
if ((lastElement+newElement) == (element[r]+element[r+1])) {

    UpdateMatched(r+1);                  // substitution

    rating += 2;

}


lastElement = newElement;

return rating;

}
```

Figure 4.15 Continued

-3   -2   2   2   1

Figure 4.16 Template pattern

eliminated. Bloch and Dannenberg are concerned with score following, and so want primarily to follow the advance of the match between the template and the candidate. In our pattern processing
goals, we are more interested in characterizing the degree of similarity between two patterns. This is captured by the matched array,
showing which template intervals have been found in the candidate,
the number of matches found, and the index number of the most
recent match. All of these parameters can be computed without the
added overhead of the matrix calculation from the previous program.

The second departure is that each incoming element is not
matched against the entire remainder of the sequence. To match
against the entire remainder was extreme in any event and clearly
would yield wrong results when used with large templates, since
elements far removed from the current context could be matched
with incorrect candidate elements. This implementation effectively

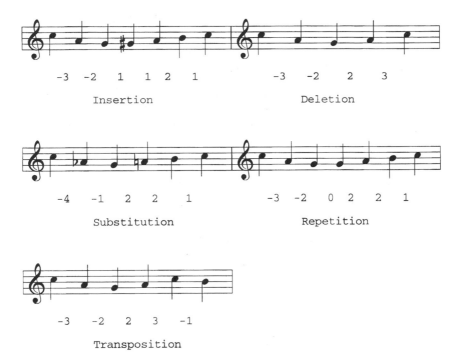

Figure 4.17 Intervallic matching tests

detects one element in advance because both the deletion and substitution tests compare input with the highest unmatched template element and its successor. The IntervalMatch application and its associated source code may be found on the CD-ROM.

Matching algorithms, like the other processes we have reviewed, must be considered with reference to some application. The IntervalMatch algorithm is one of a family of procedures that can be applied according to the nature of the task at hand. Adding the matched array and eliminating the matrix calculation from the Dannenberg algorithm speeds the work even as it discards information that may be useful for recognizing re-ordered patterns. For restricted kinds of material even exhaustive search may be tractable: traversing a tree that encodes each successive interval of a pattern at a deeper branching level could be accomplished in real time with a tree using less than one megabyte of memory (Dannenberg 1999). The IntervalMatch algorithm, then, should not be taken as a definitive solution, but as one choice among many, to be selected according to the requirements of the application and the computing resources available.

4.2.3 Segmentation and Matching

From the first two implementations we learned that the comparison algorithms necessary for monophonic pattern matching are relatively straightforward and can be adapted easily from the existing literature. The differences between score following (the primary application for which such algorithms have been developed) and the processing tasks that are our focus here, however, lead to significant departures from the published sources. First, as we have seen, our goal is to establish a measurement of the degree of similarity between two patterns while maintaining a point of correspondence between a template and candidate.

Measuring the degree of similarity brings this work into proximity with portions of David Cope's Experiments in Musical Intelligence (EMI). EMI is used to induce stylistic characteristics from a particular composer or corpus of works and to use these characteristics to synthesize new examples of the style. Cope writes in his book *Computers and Musical Style:* "If there is a discovery here, it is that one way of defining style is through pattern recognition and that musical style can be imitated if one can find what constitutes musical patterns. Further, comparisons of these patterns from work to work will reveal those patterns that are generic to a composer's style and those that are found in a single work only" (Cope 1991, xiv).

Accordingly, one of Cope's primary concerns is pattern induction. His software discovers *signatures*—patterns of melodic and rhythmic material found repeatedly in a particular composer's body of work. "A signature is a set of contiguous intervals (i.e., exempt from key differences) found in more than one work by the same composer. Signatures typically contain two to nine notes melodically and more if combined with harmonies. They are generally divorced from rhythm, though rhythmic ratios often remain intact. Signatures are work-independent. They do not sound as if they come from a certain work of a composer but rather from the style of a composer (or a group of composers)" (Cope 1991, 46). Signatures are saved together with information about the context in which they are typically used. For example, one pattern may be typically used at cadence points and another as a subsidiary melodic motive.

The matching algorithm described in *Computers and Musical Style* is a straightforward measurement of the distance between corresponding intervals in two lists. If the distance between the intervals is less than or equal to a tolerance setting, the intervals are judged to be the same. In other words, if one list has an entry of 2 semitones and the other an entry of 3 semitones, those intervals would be declared a match as long as the tolerance was set to 1 semitone or higher.

Cope's process (1992) matches intervals whose absolute value is within the prescribed tolerance. This amendment causes inversions of signatures to be recognized as the same: an interval of -2 semitones (down a major second) is judged to be a match with an interval of $+2$ semitones (up a major second). Other variables (or "tuners") of the matching process include motive-size, which controls the number of elements to be included in a motive; and interpolation, which governs the number of insertions that will be allowed in two motives judged similar.

A fundamental design decision of pattern induction is the choice of how much overlap between distinct segments to allow. "To illustrate, if the pattern ABCDEF is seen in the data, an order three model can store ABC, BCD, CDE, and DEF, capturing all possible segmentations of the data. Alternatively, a model can disallow overlapping segments and instead store only ABC and DEF" (Reis 1999).

An order three model is one that maintains only patterns with three members each. Table 4.6 illustrates the two overlap strategies Reis describes together with a third: partial overlap. Partial overlap makes it legal to repeat elements in different segments (e.g., both the first and second segments of the figure include the element C) but

Table 4.6 Segmentation Overlap

Pattern	ABCDEF			
Full Overlap	ABC	BCD	CDE	DEF
Partial Overlap	ABC	CDE	DEF	
No Overlap	ABC	DEF		

does not require that all possible partitions be produced, as full overlap does.

David Cope's matching engine uses full overlap and therefore is exhaustive in that scores are broken into patterns of motive-size length such that all possible contiguous patterns are generated. If motive-size were three, for example, each interval in the score would appear in three patterns—once as the first interval of a pattern, once as the second, and once as the last. All possible patterns of a given size in the compared scores are examined, using tolerance and interpolation to tune the degree of similarity allowed. The multiple-viewpoint music prediction system of Conklin and Witten similarly uses a full-overlap, exhaustive search paradigm (Witten, Manzara, and Conklin 1994).

This clearly constitutes pattern induction in our parlance, and yet is difficult to use in real time for the simple reason that it requires exhaustive search. For our purposes, matching all possible patterns of a given size is unacceptable because it will take too much time. Further, we wish to find patterns which presumably will be of several different sizes, meaning that we would need to exhaustively search many different pattern lengths simultaneously, making the algorithm that much further removed from real-time performance.

The great advantage of full overlap is that it will never miss a pattern due to faulty segmentation. A no-overlap system critically depends on the consistent grouping of events such that subsequent pattern matching will compare sequences that start at the same point in the figure. The other possibility is partial overlap: that is, the same event may be used in more than one segment when their boundaries are ambiguous (table 4.6). The rhythm analysis processes described by Rosenthal (1989), and Longuet-Higgins and Lee (1984) are both based on partial-overlap segments, as is the context modeling system described by Reis (1999). (I owe the categorization of degrees of overlap to Reis as well).

Context modeling involves extracting and accumulating a set of discrete sequences, or patterns, taken from the musical surface. Each stored pattern is then used as a context for the purposes of matching incoming musical data and generating appropriate expectations. For example, if the pattern ABCD has been stored in the model, the appearance of ABC in the data will trigger the expectation of D as the next event. Instead of absolute pitches, sequences of pitch intervals are stored in order to allow for matching transpositions. (Reis 1999)

Information theory is a way of measuring the amount of information present in a given sequence of symbols (Shannon and Weaver 1949). The information content of any given symbol within a sequence is a function of its predictability. For example, when processing sequences of letters in the English language, the letter "u" following the letter "q" imparts very little information because "u" after "q" is very predictable. "We quantify the information content in terms of *entropy*, a measure of the amount of order, redundancy, or predictability of a system. When applied to any communications situation, entropy measures the amount of information contained in a message; it is small when there is little information and large when there is a lot" (Witten et al. 1994, 70).

Context modeling, then, can be analyzed through information theory to measure the entropy of a signal with respect to predictions made from a stored set of patterns. Reis' context modeling technique uses a segmentation scheme, called *perceptually guided segmentation,* that is based on rules from music cognition similar to those discussed in section 4.1. Changes of melodic direction, large pitch leaps, and long note durations are among the perceptual cues the system uses to locate group boundaries. Because segmentation rules of this kind can yield conflicting placements of boundaries, Reis allows partial overlap of the segments to be analyzed rather than an arbitration scheme to decide which segment boundary is correct.

Here we see an advantage of using partial overlap: it does not involve the exhaustive search of full overlap, but will reserve competing segmentations of material when the best boundaries are unclear. A question arises, however, as to how much eliminating some of the segments that would be produced through full overlap might compromise the predictive power of the model. Reis investigated this question by comparing the predictive performances of segments asserted using perceptual guidelines to those of others shifted away from the perceptual segments's boundaries by one or more events.

"The idea behind segmentation shifting is fairly simple, and is based on two hypotheses: (1) There exist certain points of segmentation in a piece, named here *s-points,* which lead to a context model with better prediction performance. Other points, *o-points,* lead to context models with worse prediction performance. (2) The PGS [perceptually guided segmentation] strategy suggests segmentation that correspond to the s-points" (Reis 1999). Accordingly, PGS segments should have a better prediction performance than shifted ones that presumably fall on s-points only rarely, and only by chance.

Reis conducted his segmentation shifting experiment on short-term context models learned from a corpus of 100 Bach chorales. A short-term context model is one that develops patterns from a single composition, rather than from a style or oeuvre encompassing many works. The prediction entropy is a measure of the inaccuracy of a model.

All shift sizes produce segments that have less predictive power than the perceptually guided ones, confirming that the PGS strategy finds the most efficient patterns. Moreover, small shifts tend to be less accurate than larger ones. Reis conjectures that this occurs because small shifts are less likely to randomly shift the segment onto another s-point. The exceptions to this regularity are segments shifted by one event. Reis notes: "It is often unclear whether discontinuous events, such as longer notes, should be included in the end of the previous segment, or at the beginning of a new one. Thus, a shift of one note can sometimes correct for this, and prediction performance degradation is less drastic" (Reis 1999).

Ben Reis's segmentation shifting work establishes empirically two important principles for real-time pattern processing: first, that a partial or no overlap regime can produce the most relevant segments for context modeling; and second, that the use of perceptual cues derived from music cognition research is effective in establishing the proper segmentation.

4.2.4 Pattern Processors

Pierre-Yves Rolland and his group at the Laboratoire Formes et Intelligence Artificielle (LAFORIA) in Paris have developed techniques to apply pattern processing to the analysis of jazz improvisations. Much of their work has been devoted to the discovery of a collection of motifs similar to those first presented in Thomas Owens' doctoral dissertation on the improvisations of Charlie Parker (1974). "Our aim is to investigate the possibility [of developing] a system able to perform motive-oriented analyses such as Owens's, with performances comparable to musicologists's, and within minutes instead of years" (Rolland and Ganascia 1996, 241).

In designing their system, Rolland's group distinguishes between two phases of a motive induction process: (1) factor matching, which aligns sequence segments and organizes them into a similarity graph, and (2) categorization, which clusters groups of similar sequence segments encoded in the graph, yielding patterns. This algorithm, named FlExPat (from *Fl*exible *Ex*traction of *Pat*terns), has been implemented in a system called Imprology. Central to the process is a similarity judgment: the FlExPat algorithm calculates the similarity between two sequence segments according to a comparison of multiple perspectives on their content.

Given two sequence segments, the comparison model first aligns them using a set of allowed pairing types (APTs). Alignment associates (possibly empty) groups of elements from one sequence with (possibly empty) groups of elements from the other. Allowed pairing types correspond to the typical sequence mismatches discussed in section 4.2.1: for example, the standard set of APTs is { Insertion, Deletion, Replacement }. Other pairing types accommodate more complex alignments, such as those that occur when an element of one pattern is ornamented in the other. Swaps, fragmentations, and consolidations are among the APTs FlExPat uses to handle such cases.

Moreover, FlExPat associates a contribution function with each pairing type that assigns a numerical rating to the contribution of any pair to the similarity of two sequences as a whole. The contribution functions can be changed to give more or less weight to a particular perspective on the material under examination. For example, one perspective might favor the rhythmic similarities between two sequences while another emphasizes their melodic pairs.

The factor matching phase produces a similarity graph that represents the relations between all couples of sequence segments. The contribution functions for aligned pairs are computed to yield an overall similarity rating for all sequences connected by the graph. Categorization is accomplished by the "star center" algorithm that groups the most prototypical occurrence of a pattern together with its variants (the prototype appears at the center of a cluster in the graph resembling a star, hence the name).

Rolland's pattern extraction process is unique in that it can group sequences from a corpus into different categories according to the matching priorities set by a user (through the contribution functions). Though the extraction itself does not work in real time, FlExPat could be used to organize pattern libraries for matching in performance.

Figure 4.18 shows a collection of three patterns from Charlie Parker blues solos found to be similar by FlExPat. Though similar to the motives identified in Owens's study, this sequence was "discovered" by FlExPat and does not appear in the musicologist's compendium.

I have developed a number of segmentation and pattern processing algorithms over the years (Rowe 1993). The Pattern Processor application on the CD-ROM combines several of them, most notably

Figure 4.18 Charlie Parker motives from FlExPat

those documented in 1995 (Rowe and Li). That work itself relied heavily on the Timewarp application described by Pennycook et al. (1993).

Timewarp was built on the Dynamic TimeWarp (DTW) algorithm first developed for discrete word recognition (Sankoff and Kruskal 1983). The DTW can be visualized as a graph, where the horizontal axis represents members of the candidate pattern and the vertical axis members of the template. A local distance measure is computed for each grid point based on feature classifications of the two patterns. Pennycook and Stammen used an intervallic representation of pitch content and suggested duration ratios for rhythm, defined as the ratio of a note's duration divided by the previous note's duration.

In order to recognize [an] unknown fragment, the candidate's feature template is compared to a database of reference templates. The DTW compares the unknown candidate with each template in the database and assigns a distance value that indicates the degree of similarity between the candidate and reference templates. The Recognizer matches the candidate with the reference template that results in the lowest distance measure. When several close matches occur, an Evaluator is used to select the best match. If the best match distance is higher than a pre-defined threshold, the candidate's template is

considered to be unique and can be added to the database of refer-
ence templates. (Stammen 1999, 92)

The Pattern Processor application on the CD-ROM, following Pennycook and Stammen, uses a similar procedure. The first step is to
segment the material using the Segmenter process introduced in section 4.1. Segments then generate patterns, which consist in this case
of melodic intervals. Though the example concentrates on melody,
the same approach might be used to treat chord roots from a progression of tonal harmonies or sequences of rhythmic durations. Timewarp combines time differences with other parametric intervals to
yield a single distance metric, within which there is no way to identify whether intervallic or temporal differences are the source of the
deviation. The Pattern Processor framework can be used to coordinate separate matches for pitch and rhythm (for example), allowing
similar harmonic material to be recognized even when presented in
vastly varying rhythmic guises, and vice versa (Rowe and Li 1995).

The Pattern Processor algorithm proceeds as follows: (1) incoming
MIDI data is treated by segmentation rules and segment boundaries
are flagged; (2) ongoing segments are compared to two key patterns,
one with an upwardly moving contour and the other moving down-
ward; (3) the distance between the candidate and the key patterns is
used to direct the search to a group of patterns that are equally as
distant from the keys as is the candidate; (4) additional comparisons
are made between the candidate and the collection of patterns found
at the same distance from the keys; and (5) reports are issued concerning the proximity of the candidate to the stored patterns.

When a new segment boundary is found, the most recent pattern
is either added to the list at the appropriate distance location, or the
instance count for an existing pattern is incremented if the most recent one was a close match. The Pattern Processor is able to discover
previously unknown melodic patterns presented repeatedly in a
stream of MIDI data and to flag ongoing new occurrences of these
patterns as the input continues. Such capabilities can be used in
composition and performance to give special treatment to salient

patterns that have been remembered from previous passes with the system or that are introduced onstage during the course of improvisation.

4.3 Auditory Models

Auditory inputs to interactive systems receive a digitized audio stream rather than the idealized representation of notes that is MIDI. As was discussed in section 2.2, MIDI captures the physical actions of fingers on a keyboard, not acoustic reality. The leverage that we have been able to obtain from analyzing MIDI input comes from the reasonably direct correspondence between such physical actions and the sounding output, at least as far as keyboard instruments are concerned. Keyboard instruments, such as the piano, are essentially percussive. That is, sound is produced by striking a vibrating medium (the string) with an object (the hammer). Nothing can be done to change the resulting sound from that point on aside from damping the string in some way (e.g., by releasing a sustain pedal). Therefore most of the information produced with a piano is retained by simply recording the keystrokes, and the MIDI mapping between finger actions and aural events works well enough.

MIDI also is capable of a relatively direct representation of the notation in a musical score, at least when augmented with timing information. Extensive libraries of MIDI-encoded musical scores exist because of this correspondence. A musical score, however, shares some of MIDI's limitations with respect to the actual sound of music, the auditory information that arrives at listeners' ears. Listening to the complex sound arising from a symphony orchestra, for example, or the Art Ensemble of Chicago is an experience quite removed from the notion of a conglomeration of individual and identifiable notes. "There seems to be a general consensus on the notion of discrete elements (e.g., notes, sound events or objects) as the primitives of music. It forms the basis of a vast amount of music-theoretical work and research in the psychology of music, but a detailed discussion and argument for this assumption is missing from the literature" (Honing 1993, 226).

As Eric Scheirer points out, representations built on notes generally reflect a bottom-up approach to the information involved. That is, notes are gathered into phrases, phrases into groups of phrases, and so on, until a higher level is reached that somehow encompasses a global understanding of the work. "We know from existing experimental data that this upward data-flow model is false in particular cases. For example, frequency contours in melodies can lead to a percept of accent structure . . . which in turn leads to the belief that the accented notes are louder than the unaccented. Thus, the high-level process of melodic understanding impacts the 'lower-level' process of determining the loudnesses of notes" (Scheirer 1996, 318). As in the case of the missing fundamental (section 2.2), our minds interpret sounds, including the sounds of music, according to genetic predispositions and our own prior experience. The auditory modeling research I will sketch now moves toward a formalization of those aspects of experience.

4.3.1 Auditory Input and Self-Organizing Maps
Both musical scores and MIDI represent music as a sequence of discrete notes defined by pitch and quantized on and off times. Performed music does not conform to these conventions, however. The sound reaching a listener's ears is a continuous, unquantized stream of pressure changes that are interpreted according to the low-level features of the sound itself and the high-level expectations that the listener has acquired (either genetically or through experience). Because of this difference, many researchers are basing their analysis on an untreated audio stream rather than a more structured representation such as MIDI.

Using audio signals as input to a real-time system avoids the distortions of discretization even as it introduces other kinds of problems. It can be difficult and computationally costly to get timing and pitch information from an audio stream in real time that is as accurate as MIDI information. At the same time, the sheer mass of information available explodes, particularly concerning timbre, and this explosion can itself be problematic. One way to think of MIDI is as an extreme form of data reduction. Without such a reduction, much more of the real-time resources of a system are devoted to gathering, storing, and analyzing an image of a human musician's performance.

Some of the work of the Machine Listening Group at the M.I.T. Media Lab is based on modeling the musical perceptions of untrained listeners rather than those of musicians. The motivation for this orientation combines several observations: first, non-musicians cognitively structure what they hear in ways that differ markedly from the concepts used by musicians: "Non-musicians cannot recognize intervals, do not make categorical decisions about pitch, do not understand the functional properties which theoreticians impute to chords and tones, do not recognize common musical structures, and might not even maintain octave similarity" (Martin, Scheirer, and Vercoe 1998). Another reason is that multimedia systems are currently unable to perform even those tasks of musical discrimination that untrained listeners can, so that using the non-musician's abilities as a point of departure may more readily produce tools with widespread application.

A well-known tool for real-time sound analysis is the Fast Fourier Transform (FFT), a method for computing the spectral content of a sound. The accuracy of the FFT is constrained, however, when the transform must be performed in real time. Because it changes the representation of information from the time domain to the frequency domain, there is a trade-off in precision between the length of time analyzed and the number of distinct partials present in the transformation. Simply put, analyses of short durations (good temporal resolution) will show energy in broad spectral regions (poor frequency resolution), while analyses of long durations (poor temporal resolution) will produce finer-grained spectral information.

A spectrogram plots the evolution of the spectral energy of a sound through time. One version represents time along the x axis, frequency along the y axis, and intensity by the shading of the line at a particular point on the graph. "This kind of 'spectrogram' is often seen still in texts and in legal proceedings, yet it does not represent what the cochlea reports: it has linearly spaced filter bins (y-axis) with the same bandwidth at all frequencies, while the cochlea has near logarithmic spacing of hair cell frequencies with roughly proportional bandwidths (constant ratio to the center frequency). The FFT gives poor frequency resolution in the lower octaves, and too much in the upper, and since its bandwidths are constant it entirely misses the 'beating' that can make up for a missing fundamental" (Vercoe 1997, 313).

To skirt the problems of the FFT and model much more closely the function of the ear itself, Vercoe developed an auditory model based on constant-Q filters and auto-correlation that is able to perform beat tracking from an audio signal. The first step divides the audio signal into 96 filter bands, with 12 bands per octave spread across 8 octaves. These bands are scaled according to the Fletcher-Munson curves to approximate human loudness sensitivity (Handel 1989). Once scaled, the process detects note onsets by tracking positive changes in each filter channel. These positive difference spectra are elongated with recursive filters to extend their influence over time and added together to provide a single energy estimation. A version of narrowed auto-correlation is then performed on the summed energy to recognize regularities in the signal and predict their continuation: "As the expectations move into current time, they are confirmed by the arrival of new peaks in the auditory analysis; if the acoustic source fails to inject new energy, the expectations will atrophy over the same short-term memory interval" (Vercoe 1997). This algorithm, realized with Vercoe's widespread Csound audio processing language, can perform beat tracking on an acoustic signal without recourse to any intervening note-level representation.

Marc Leman has developed a system that can learn to identify tonal centers from an analysis of acoustic input (1995). It is a central premise of his system that it proceeds from an auditory model rather than from some predefined representational abstraction: "Many computer models of music cognition . . . have thus far been based on symbol representations. They point to the objects in the world without re-

flecting any of the physical properties of the object" (Leman and Carreras 1997, 162).

Leman's analysis systems send an audio signal through a number
of steps that produce increasingly specific cognitive "images" of the
input. They are divided into two parts: a perception module and a
cognition module. The perception module is an auditory model of
the output of the human ear. Leman has used three kinds of auditory
models in his work, including (1) a simple acoustical representation;
(2) one based on the work of Ernst Terhardt (Terhardt, Stoll, and
Seewann 1982) that computes virtual pitches from a summation of
subharmonics; and (3) another derived from work described by Van
Immerseel and Martens (1992) that models the temporal aspects of
auditory nerve cell firings. Shepard tones (Shepard 1964) are used
as input to the models, eliminating the effect of tone height.

The input part of the simple acoustical model (SAM) is organized
in essentially the same way as the pitch class sets we introduced
in chapter 2. Because the representation models Shepard tones, all
pitches are reduced to a single octave in which height has been eliminated from the percept and only the tone chroma (pitch class) remains. The analytic part of SAM, then, outputs vectors of integers
where a one indicates the presence of a pitch class and a zero its
absence. The synthetic part calculates *tone completion images* from
input patterns of this type. Tone completion images are computed
from the sum of subharmonics of the pitches in the chord, following
the tradition of virtual pitch extractors discussed in section 2.3. Subharmonics are weighted according to the table in table 4.7.

A C-major triad, for example, would assign a weight of 1.83 to the
pitch class C, since the chord contains intervals of an octave (1.00),
fifth (0.50), and major third (0.33) relative to that pitch class. The C♯
pitch class, in comparison, would get a weight of 0.1 since only the
minor third above C♯ (E) is present in the input chord.

The heart of the Van Immerseel and Martens perception module
(VAM) is a set of 20 asymmetric bandpass filters distributed through
the range 220–7075 Hz at distances of one critical band. After some
additional processing, the "auditory nerve image" is output, a

Table 4.7 SAM Virtual Pitch Weightings

SUBHARMONIC	WEIGHT
Octave	1.00
Perfect Fifth	0.50
Major Third	0.33
Minor Seventh	0.25
Major Second	0.20
Minor Third	0.10

vector of 20 elements corresponding to these filter channels that is updated at a sampling rate of 2500 samples per second (one every 0.4 milliseconds).

The VAM has two stages. The first is an auditory front end that uses the 20 overlapping bandpass filters to change sounds into neural firing patterns. The second is a periodicity analysis of the firing patterns output by the filters, a process reminiscent of Barry Vercoe's audio beat tracking algorithm described above. "For each neural firing pattern that comes out of one of the 20 auditory channels, a periodicity analysis is done by means of a short-term-autocorrelation analysis using delays of 0.4 ms. The analysis is applied to frames of 30 ms." (Leman and Carreras 1997, 149).

The periodicity analysis outputs a *completion image,* formed from the sum of the 20 channels, from which the frequency content of the audio input may be calculated. Leman is less concerned with particular frequencies than he is with the pattern arising from the analysis, however. Accordingly, completion images are integrated into *context images* that "give an account of the context-dependencies among perceived musical pitch patterns over a time period of about 3 seconds" (Leman and Carreras 1997, 150).

The cognition module of Leman's system is based on a Kohonen self-organizing map (Kohonen 1984). Kohonen nets learn to cluster inputs into categories through unsupervised learning. The neural networks reviewed in section 3.1 use supervised learning to guide the development of connection weights. Another important class of networks is based on unsupervised learning in which sets of training inputs are presented to the network without "correct answers" attached. Unsupervised learning applies to cases where the target output patterns are unknown, or to see whether the traditional categories of a discipline emerge from the system without any external direction.

The version of Leman's systems that combines the simple auditory model (SAM) as a perception module with a Kohonen self-organizing map (SOM) as a cognition module is called SAMSOM, from the acronyms of the two parts. SAMSOM was used to analyze a training set of 115 chords (table 4.8). We inherit from music theory ways of thinking about the categories that organize such a collection. The goal of categorizing them with SAMSOM is to see whether matching categories arise from the nature of the auditory system (as represented by SAM) and the inherent similarities between the chords themselves.

The form of unsupervised learning used in a Kohonen network is called competitive learning. The architecture of the network consists

Table 4.8   SAMSOM Training Set

NUMBER	TYPE
12	major triads
12	minor triads
12	diminished triads
4	augmented triads
12	major seventh chords
12	minor seventh chords
12	dominant seventh chords
12	half dim. seventh chords
12	augmented seventh chords
12	minor/major seventh chords
3	diminished seventh chords

of two layers, an input layer and the Kohonen layer. The input layer contains one node for each component of the input patterns. In SAMSOM, then, the input layer contains 12 nodes, one for each pitch class. Each unit in the input layer is connected to all units in the Kohonen layer, and an initial random weight is associated with each connection. When an input pattern is presented, it is multiplied by the weights on each connection and fed to the Kohonen layer. There the unit that is most activated by the input is able to participate in learning, hence the name "competitive learning." In fact, the most highly activated node is referred to as the "winning" node.

The Kohonen layer is organized as a two-dimensional array. Following the example of the cerebral cortex, the winning node and units in the neighborhood benefit from learning. A neighborhood comprises all the nodes within a certain number of rows or columns around the winner in the grid. "As the training process progresses, the neighborhood size decreases until its size is zero, and only the winning node is modified each time an input pattern is presented to the network. Also, the learning rate or the amount each link value can be modified continuously decreases during training. Training stops after the training set has been presented to the network a predetermined number of times" (Rogers 1997, 136).

At the end of training, a topology of characteristic neurons has emerged as a classification of the input set. The characteristic neuron (CN) for an input is the unit in the Kohonen layer most activated by that input. The CNs for the training set become clustered during learning according to the similarities of their represented inputs. In the CN-map produced by SAMSOM, for example, the characteristic neurons for C major and A-minor 7th are near one another. These two chords are closely related from the standpoint of music theory, as well, because all of the pitch classes of C major are subsumed in A-minor 7th. All other major/relative minor 7th combinations presented to the model become similarly clustered.

Aside from the identification of closely related chords (which Leman shows goes well beyond the simple example just cited [1995]), the SAMSOM output map shows an association between tonal centers that are related by the cycle of fifths. The response region of an input is that part of the Kohonen layer activated by the input. Considering the set of major chord inputs, the response regions of the SAMSOM map most highly correlated to C major (for example) are G major and F major—those a perfect fifth away from C. The correlation between G major and F major is much lower.

Leman refers to the product of the SAMSOM model as "images out of time," meaning that the inputs make no reference to the timing of their presentation. We may also consider it "out of time" because the calculation it performs is complex enough to take it well out of the realm of real time. When such a Kohonen network has been trained, however, subsequent inputs are classified according to the learned associations of the training set. Thus a trained network can be used, even in real time, as a classifier of novel inputs.

The main reason that auditory input to and output from interactive systems have been used less than MIDI I/O is that they required more sophisticated (and more expensive) hardware. Even personal computers have now become so powerful, however, that extensive treatment and synthesis of digital audio can be performed with no additional hardware at all. With the physical and financial limitations to the technology largely eliminated, the focus shifts to deriving structure from an audio stream that will multiply the possibilities for interaction. Though the techniques of unsupervised learning are not appropriate for use onstage, the work of Leman and others has demonstrated that it can be applied before performance to derive structural categories for the interpretation of audio signals in real time.

5 Compositional Techniques

Through four chapters we have concentrated on methods of algorithmic music analysis and how these can be executed during live performance. Now we change focus to the compositional processes that can be shaped in response to information about the ongoing musical context. Algorithmic composition is an ancient and extended craft whose many manifestations cannot be explored here, just as those of algorithmic analysis were not. To limit the scope of the discussion, we will be concerned first of all with techniques that can be realized in real time because we want to run them onstage. Beyond that, all of the algorithms will be interactive in some way—that is, they will change their behavior in response to user input, musical or otherwise.

Algorithmic composition differs markedly from algorithmic analysis in several respects. First, the range of techniques included in the activity called composition varies much more widely than does that of analysis. One can imagine a twentieth-century composer using numbers chosen from listings in a telephone book to organize pitch relationships. It is difficult to envisage how an analyst could use telephone listings to devise an account of pitch relationships unless it were the specific passage from the very same phone book used to explain a piece made reading from it. In other words, though there could be a general-purpose telephone-book pitch generator (which is not to say that there should be), there could hardly be a general-purpose telephone-book pitch analyzer.

Much of the algorithmic analysis developed in this book relates to research in music cognition concerning the processes of human listening. A similarly extensive literature for the cognition of composition simply does not exist. Part of the reason for that may stem from the phenomenon just discussed—that composers may be engaging in quite different activities when they work. Another reason is that it is much harder to test what is going on cognitively during composition. Analysis, like listening, is easier to model computationally in a general sense than is composition. The result of an analysis is a written, rational document that may be examined for formal constructions amenable to implementation in a computer program. It is not, however, the inverse transform of an act of composition. At the end of an analysis we are not back at the composer's thoughts.

In his novel *Amsterdam,* Ian McEwan describes the thoughts of a fictional composer as he walks, looking for ideas for a large-scale orchestral work: "It came as a gift; a large grey bird flew up with a loud alarm call as he approached. As it gained height and wheeled away over the valley it gave out a piping sound on three notes which he recognised as the inversion of a line he had already scored for a piccolo. How elegant, how simple. Turning the sequence round opened up the idea of a plain and beautiful song in common time which he could almost hear. But not quite. An image came to him of a set of unfolding steps, sliding and descending—from the trap door of a loft, or from the door of a light plane. One note lay over and suggested the next. He heard it, he had it, then it was gone" (McEwan 1998, 84).

Such a stream of thought seems familiar to me, at least, as a composer, even though I rarely compose songs in common time. Because of the fleeting and unconscious quality of much compositional work, I cannot reduce the entirety of composition to a set of rules or even to a list of parameters and a training set. I can, however, imagine using processes to make music and even imagine how different processes might be appropriate to different musical situations. It is in that spirit, then, that we will explore algorithmic composition—as a collection of possibilities that can be employed within the aesthetic context of a composition or improvisation.

5.1 Generation Techniques

In my book *Interactive Music Systems,* I identified three classes of compositional algorithms that are particularly suited to interaction: sequencing, generation, and transformation (1993). Sequencing involves the use of prerecorded material that is played back more or less as recorded, but with control over start and stop points, looping, playback tempo, and so on. The Max seq and mt objects are paradigm examples of the sequenced approach. One can apply the same kind of thought to recordings of audio data rather than MIDI sequences. Transformation techniques, which were discussed extensively in *Interactive Music Systems* in connection with my program, Cypher, take input arriving from an external source, apply one or several transformations to it, and output the varied material as a counterpoint to the original. Generation techniques extract seed material from some stored repertoire and apply processes to adapt, extend, or embellish it.

Simon and Sumner's 1963 article "Pattern in Music" has already been cited in connection with pattern processing techniques (section 4.2), particularly with reference to their term, "pattern induction." The other part of their article dealt with a process they called "sequence extrapolation." Sequence extrapolation can be considered a type of compositional process, in fact an example of a generation technique. Essentially Simon and Sumner describe patterns as extractions from an alphabet according to a set of rules. The most straightforward rule is the NEXT operator, which simply chooses the next element from a given alphabet. They generalize this operation to the function "$N^k(s) = N(N^{k-1}(s))$, for $k = 2. \ldots$ Thus N^2 means 'NEXT of NEXT,' N^3, 'NEXT of NEXT of NEXT,' and so on" [Simon and Sumner 1993, 93].

The system introduced by Deutsch and Feroe (1981) similarly describes pitch patterns in terms of operations on an alphabet. In fact, the operations they use are virtually identical to those of Simon and Sumner. If we notate an alphabet as follows: $x = [e(1), e(2), e(3), \ldots$

```
s[e(k)]   = e(k)      ; same

n[e(k)]   = e(k+1)    ; next

n.i[e(k)] = e(k+i)    ; multiple next

p[e(k)]   = e(k-1)    ; previous

p.i[e(k)] = e(k-i)    ; multiple previous
```

Figure 5.1 Elementary operators from Deutsch and Feroe

e(n)], we see that each element of the alphabet is given an index that corresponds to its place in the sequence (here 1, 2, 3, . . . n). Then the operators are ways of selecting a new element from the alphabet. For example, the operator same is defined as: s[e(k)] = e(k). In other words, the same operation applied to any element of an alphabet produces that same element again. Figure 5.1 shows the complete list of elementary operators.

Similarly, Eugene Narmour's implication-realization model defines a number of operations for the elaboration of structural pitches on several hierarchical levels (Narmour 1999).

5.1.1 Selection Principles

We will not develop the alphabet operator idea as an analytic system here, but rather as a method of composition. The pattern-oriented systems just discussed consider musical material as the product of operations on an underlying alphabet of elements. This same methodology forms the basis of a number of compositional algorithms, whether interactive or not (Loy 1989). The composer Gottfried Michael Koenig developed similar ideas in a series of algorithmic composition programs beginning in the 1960s, including Project 1, Project 2, and the Sound Synthesis Project (SSP). Beginning from a background of serialism, Koenig designed a number of selection principles by which elements from a stored pool were chosen and combined. The most clearly serial of these was series, which would randomly choose elements from a collection without repeating any until all had been output. The Max object urn performs the same operation and in fact can be used compositionally in much the same way that Koenig's selection principles are. (See section 7.2 for a patch using urn by Amnon Wolman.)

Composer/programmer Paul Berg, who worked with Koenig at the Institute of Sonology in the Netherlands for many years, has incorporated a number of selection principles (both Koenig's and his own) in the Algorithmic Composition Toolbox (AC Toolbox), written for the Apple Macintosh in Common Lisp (Berg 1998). The Toolbox is a collection of algorithmic techniques for producing compositions. The choice, combination, and application of the tools is left up to the user, providing an environment in which many different styles and manifestations of compositional ideas can be realized.

In the AC Toolbox, a *section* is a collection of one or more notes. Sections are always defined with respect to a basic pulse duration. One can think of the pulse (called the clock) as the default resolution of an underlying quantization grid. Since rhythms are defined as floating point multiples of the clock value, however, there is no enforced quantization. A rhythm of 1.3 times the clock pulse will produce an event that falls between two adjacent ticks, for example. A *data section* is one in which each parameter is calculated without reference to the others. Pitch and rhythm, e.g., may be controlled as independent qualities of the material. A data section is defined by specifying values or functions for its clock (pulse), pitch, rhythm, dynamic, and channel (figure 5.2).

The length of a section can be defined by indicating either the number of notes that should be generated or the span of time that the material must fill. The data section defined in figure 5.2 has a clock pulse of 100 milliseconds and contains fifteen notes. Each note has a duration of one clock tick (100 ms), a velocity of mezzoforte, and will be played on channel one. The entire section, then, would cover a span of 1500 milliseconds (1.5 seconds). The pitches are determined by applying a tool called multiple-bandwidths.

The multiple-bandwidths tool produces all values between pairs of low and high bounds supplied by the user, inclusively. The

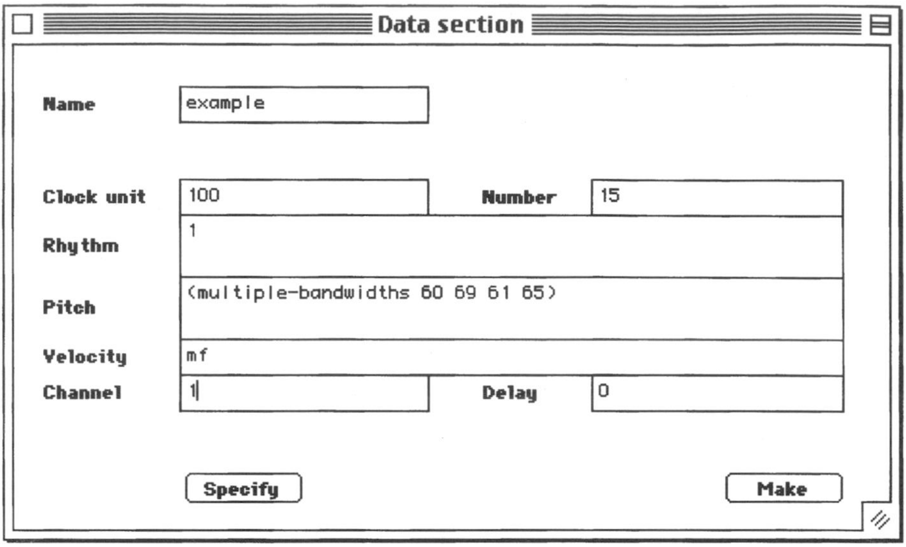

Figure 5.2 Data section dialog box

expression in figure 5.2, then, will generate the following list of values: (60 61 62 63 64 65 66 67 68 69 61 62 63 64 65). Multiple-bandwidths is used to produce a collection of stored elements that Berg calls *stockpiles.* Stockpiles are sets of values from which selections can be made to generate sequences. They are similar to the alphabets of Simon and Sumner, and Deutsch and Feroe, except that elements of a stockpile may be repeated while those in an alphabet typically are not. Stockpiles might be interpreted as pitches, durations, or dynamics. They can be formed initially by listing the elements of the set, by combining existing stockpiles, or by applying a generation rule (such as multiple-bandwidths).

Figure 5.3 lists a C++ version of the AC Toolbox multiple-bandwidths generator. Much of the code in it is necessary purely because C++ is not Lisp. (Notice that even the name must change because C++ thinks the hyphen is a minus sign). The arguments to the Lisp version of multiple-bandwidths are simply pairs of low and high bounds. This works because Lisp can see when the list of pairs comes

```
int* ToolBox::multiple_bandwidths(int pairs, ...)
{
      register int i;
      va_list args;                           // variable argument list
      va_start(args, pairs);
      int* bounds = new int[pairs*2];         // allocate bounds array
      for (i=0; i<pairs*2; i++)
            bounds[i] = va_arg(args, int);// read bounds from arguments
      va_end(args);


      int length = 0;
      for (i=0; i<pairs*2; i+=2)               // calculate length of output
            length += ((abs(bounds[i]-bounds[i+1]))+1);


      int* list = new int[length];             // allocate output list
      int index = 0;                           // address into output list
      for (i=0; i<pairs*2; i+=2)
            for (int j=bounds[i]; j<bounds[i+1]; j++)
                  list[index++] = j;           // generate and store values


      delete [] bounds;                        // clean up bounds array
      return list;                             // return generated list
}
```

Figure 5.3 multiple_bandwidths()

to an end. In C++, on the other hand, we must first specify how many pairs will be coming. The argument definition (int pairs, ...) indicates that the first argument will hold the number of subsequent low/high pairs required, followed by the pairs themselves. The ellipsis (...) is the language's way of indicating that an unknown number of arguments will be used to invoke this function. In this formulation we assume that the caller will know how many pairs follow as arguments: another approach would be to assign an unambiguous marker to the end of the list such that when multiple_bandwidths encountered the marker it would stop processing boundary pairs.

There are four macros, defined in the header <stdarg.h>, that handle variable argument lists in C and C++. The first, va_list, is used to declare a pointer to variable length arguments. Any use of variable arguments must include at least one typed argument, here the integer pairs. The macro va_start(args, pairs) initializes the arguments pointer and indicates how many bytes are used by the first argument in the stack. Subsequent calls of the form va_arg(args, <type>) will return a value of the type required from the argument stack and advance the pointer accordingly. Finally, va_end completes the argument list processing.

Once we have the bounds pairs collected, we can compute the length of the output list required. Then it becomes a simple matter of filling the list with the successive values requested. Note that in this technique, it becomes the responsibility of the process invoking multiple_bandwidths to eventually release the memory allocated for the stockpile—in Lisp this would be done automatically by garbage collection.

Selection principles become viable once we have a stockpile of values from which to choose. One of G.M. Koenig's most valuable principles, carried forward in the AC Toolbox, is the *tendency mask*. A tendency mask is a set of dynamic boundary points between which elements will be selected at random. In a process similar to the invocation of multiple-bandwidths, a tendency mask can be generated by specifying lists of upper and lower bounds. Unlike multiple-

Figure 5.4 Tendency mask generator

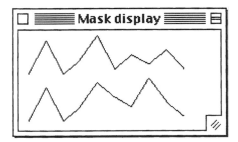

Figure 5.5 Tendency mask

bandwidths, however, there need not be an equal number of upper and lower bounds.

Figure 5.4 shows a dialog box that is used to generate a tendency mask. The mask is given a name and some number of upper and lower bounds. The upper and lower values are scaled to occupy the same duration, such that if there are more top or bottom values, the corresponding boundary line will change direction more often. Figure 5.5 shows a display of the mask generated by clicking on the

Make button of figure 5.4. Though it does not occur in this example, there is in fact no restriction on the relationship between upper and lower boundary values. In particular, the upper bounds need not be greater than the lower. A tendency mask could well have the top and bottom boundary lines cross several times throughout the duration of the mask.

The use of a tendency mask, once defined, depends on the number of events that are to be generated. If, for example, we were to request 100 events from the tendency mask defined in figure 5.4, the top and bottom boundary values would be distributed evenly across the generated events, i.e., a new value would be encountered every 10 events. Tendency masks are actually a kind of breakpoint envelope, in which the values given are points of articulation within a constantly changing line.

Figure 5.6 lists the member function GetValue(), which returns a number from the tendency mask at the current index position. First

```
int TendencyMask::GetValue(int index)
{
        int upper = CalculateUpperBound(index);    // get upper bound
        int lower = CalculateLowerBound(index);    // get lower bound
        int range = upper-lower;                   // find range
        if (range == 0)                            // avoid division by 0
            return lower;
        int value = rand()%range;                  // generate random value
        if (range < 0)                             // if range is negative
            value = -value;                        // make value negative
        return (value + lower);                    // add to lower
}
```

Figure 5.6 GetValue()

the actual upper and lower bounds corresponding to the index argument are calculated. Then a random number is chosen that falls within the absolute value of the difference between the upper and lower bounds. (We may consider the random number the absolute value because the modulo operation simply returns the remainder after division by the argument—the remainder will be positive whether the division was by either a positive or negative number.) If the range is equal to zero we simply return the lower value (since upper and lower are the same), thereby avoiding a division by zero in the modulo operation. If the range is in fact negative, the random value is made negative as well. Finally the lower boundary value is added to the random number and the result is returned.

Figure 5.7 shows the output of the tendency mask defined in figure 5.4 applied to a stockpile of pitch values covering all semitones between C2 and the C6 (where C4 = middle C). Though there is random movement on a note-to-note basis, the overall shape of the pitch sequence follows the outline of the mask shown in figure 5.5. The tendency mask selection principle offers a way to produce variants of a constant structural gesture. Each realization of the mask is different due to the random selection, but they all will express the same

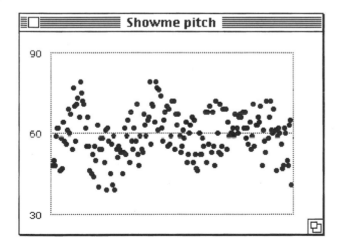

Figure 5.7 Tendency mask output

underlying shape. The similarity of each realization will be further determined by the consistency of the stockpile referenced by the mask. If the same mask is used to output values from two unrelated stockpiles, for example, the relationship between the realizations will be more distant. The Toolbox routines on the CD-ROM make it possible to generate stockpiles with `multiple_bandwidths` and reference them with a tendency mask. The AC Toolbox itself is the best environment for exploring these ideas, however, and is available for free download from the internet.

5.2 Score Following and Algorithmic Signal Processing

Score following is a pattern matching technique that traces the progress of a live performer through the composition she is playing. The technology of score following has been developed for over a decade and documented thoroughly elsewhere (Dannenberg 1989). The examples Cort Lippe contributed to the CD-ROM companion to my book *Interactive Music Systems* (1993) documented score following techniques implemented in Max. Rather than review the mechanics of score following again, I will here concentrate on the compositional opportunities the technique engenders.

Miller Puckette is universally known as the father of Max. Less widely recognized is the impact of Philippe Manoury and his compositions on the development and sophistication of Max, particularly with respect to its signal processing version. It was while working with Philippe Manoury and Thierry Lancino on interactive compositions for traditional instruments and live signal processing on the 4X machine at IRCAM that Puckette first developed and refined the Max language. The combination of score following and algorithmic digital signal processing as implemented in Max at IRCAM traces back to this work, perhaps most influentially from Manoury's composition *Jupiter,* written in 1986–7.

The computational engine of the signal processing performed in these pieces has gone through several generations since the date of *Jupiter*'s composition. The original configuration required a 4X machine, the summit of IRCAM's di Giugno-designed digital signal processing hardware series (Baisnée et al. 1986). An extremely powerful and original device, the 4X was powerfully expensive as well, beyond the reach of most every computer music studio in the world save IRCAM. The successor to the 4X became the IRCAM Signal Processing Workstation (ISPW), a dedicated sound processor built as a peripheral to the NeXT machine (Lindemann et al. 1991). When multiple ISPW cards were used the configuration was roughly equivalent to a 4X machine but at a much lower price. At that point, the technology became affordable for many institutions and a significant number of them acquired systems and began producing music. As all hardware cycles must, however, this one came to an end when production of both the NeXT machine and the i860 chip, heart of its DSP engine, ceased.

Currently, the move to a third generation of interactive digital signal processing systems is underway, with several packages already available that can support to varying degrees the computation necessary to perform works composed in the 4X/ISPW tradition. The most notable characteristic of these projects is that they are comprised almost entirely of software. The speed of central processing units, including those found on personal computers, has become so fast that they have the power to analyze and produce audio in real time even while attending to other tasks, such as disk I/O and user input. The beauty of this development is that it effectively ends the grip of hardware cycles, even though the sheer DSP horsepower available will in many cases be less in the short term. Maintaining and developing software packages as sophisticated as these bring their own set of problems, to be sure, but these are negligible when compared to the intractability of trying to keep old machines running that are no longer manufactured.

The three projects most immediately relevant are Miller Puckette's Pd, David Zicarelli's msp, and IRCAM's jMax. One of the things to which the name of Puckette's Pd system refers is the fact that it exists in the public domain. We therefore have access to the source code and can examine the algorithmic workings of the objects involved directly. Msp comprises digital signal processing extensions to the well-known MIDI version of Max, and is itself largely a port of Pd objects to the

Macintosh. jMax is IRCAM's latest iteration of the idea with a front end written in Java and is available from the IRCAM website.

Beyond the heartening prospect of avoiding a hardware port every five years or so, these packages really complete the price trajectory of this technology: now composers and researchers have the hardware necessary for real-time DSP simply by purchasing a personal computer. There remains only a relatively inexpensive additional purchase necessary for the software—and in the case of Pd, the software is free.

DSP software provides the technology to synthesize a response in score-following applications. If the instrument played by the soloist is not a MIDI device, the other technological problem is to accurately represent the music being played in real time.

5.2.1 Pitch Tracking

Pitch tracking attempts to find the fundamental pitch of notes in a monophonic audio signal. One purpose of this exercise is to allow instruments other than keyboards and mallet percussion to function accurately as sources of MIDI, thereby interfacing with commercial synthesizers and software packages. Pitch-to-MIDI converters are devices built for this task.

MIDI keyboards can use very simple sensors under the keys and have no reason to analyze the acoustic sound of a piano, for example. All of the performance information is present in the attack and can be adequately represented from the key-strike alone. Analogous devices have been built for other instruments—that is, physical monitors that track fingerings, bow position, or other manipulations rather than the acoustic sound itself. The IRCAM flute incorporated such a physical extension in the form of optical sensors that tracked the movement of the Boehm mechanism on the instrument. In cases where one fingering might produce more than one pitch, additional signal processing of the acoustic signal on the 4X decided between them (Baisnée et al. 1986).

In his article, "Cybernetic Issues in Interactive Performance Systems," Jeff Pressing develops the idea of dimensionality of control as a way of evaluating the interaction between a player and a performance system (1990). He outlines the control dimensions, or degrees of freedom, available to performers of traditional and computer-based instruments. A cellist, for example, has available roughly four degrees of freedom: bow force, bow velocity, bow distance from the bridge, and finger position on the fingerboard. Each one of these control dimensions affords the player some degree of control over various parameters of the sound: bow force controls dynamic, for example, while the finger position on the fingerboard is primarily responsible for pitch. A physically based sensing mechanism should be able to capture information corresponding to the available degrees of freedom. The hypercello developed for Tod Machover's composition, *Begin Again Again . . .* , for example, tracked all four of the dimensions outlined by Pressing and output the orientation of the cellist's bowing wrist as well.

Though the physical interface solution may be the best one for detecting pitch and performance gestures, it suffers a number of limitations. First of all, physical sensors often interfere with the normal sound production capacities of the instrument. Many instruments so equipped make no sound of their own or must be amplified to be heard, just as MIDI master keyboards only control the sound of a separate synthesizer. Second, even when working flawlessly, simple pitch detection takes us exactly as far as the MIDI standard does and no farther. We certainly do not want to step back from the standard of precision set by MIDI, but rather seek ways to augment pitch and velocity with additional information describing the evolution of a sound's timbre over time. At the end of chapter 6 we will review some research that explores these possibilities.

5.2.2 *Jupiter*

Jupiter was the first of four interactive works Philippe Manoury and Miller Puckette realized at IRCAM that together form the cycle *Sonus Ex Machina: Jupiter* for flute and 4X (1987); *Pluton* for piano and 4X (1988); *La Partition du Ciel et de l'Enfer* for flute, two pianos, 4X and orchestra (1989); and *Neptune* for three percussion and 4X (1991). The titles of the compositions reveal the technological platform of their initial realization: the redoubtable 4X machine designed and built by Giuseppe di Giugnio and his team at IRCAM in the 1980s. Since their initial composition they have graduated to the relevant successive hardware configurations: first the IRCAM Signal Processing Workstation (ISPW) and currently jMax/Pd.

The non-technical references of the titles are not to planets but rather to the sons of Saturn (Jupiter, Neptune, and Pluto) who divided the world between them on their father's death: Jupiter ruled over heaven, Pluto over hell, and Neptune over the seas (Odiard 1995, 41). *La Partition du Ciel et de l'Enfer,* then, refers to the fact that the processes in the piece are derived from those of both *Jupiter* (le ciel) and *Pluton* (l'enfer). Though the entire cycle is a monumental exploration of new musical and technical ground, here we will make some observations concerning the implementation of compositional ideas in *Jupiter* alone.

The form of *Jupiter* is divided into fourteen sections (figure 5.8). The construction is strongly symmetrical, in that every section save the third is paired with at least one complement. In fact, every section but the first is tied to exactly one other one. The first is coupled not only with section IV, but with the final section (XIV), as well. (Section XIII was eventually omitted from the work.) The relationship between coupled sections assumes one of four types: (1) elaboration of an initial melodic cell, (2) detection/interpolation, (3) ostinati, and (4) spectral envelopes.

The melodic cell tying together sections I, IV, and XIV is based on the name of Larry Beauregard, the talented flutist for whom the piece

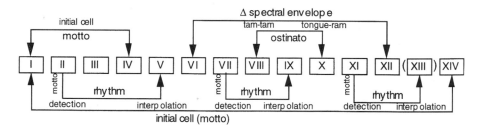

Figure 5.8 *Jupiter* formal plan (Odiard 1995)

Figure 5.9 *Jupiter* melodic plan (Odiard 1995)

Figure 5.10 *Jupiter* opening

was written but who died before it could be completed. There are eight pitches in the cell that correspond to the name as shown in figure 5.9 (Odiard 1995, 54). Figure 5.10 shows how the cell is animated rhythmically during the flute opening of the piece.

The detection/interpolation sectional pairs are based on the recognition and elaboration of sequences of durations. The processing is typical of Manoury's disposition toward algorithms as a compositional device: "A process which can be perceived as such, that is to say whose future course may be anticipated, destroys itself of its own accord. It should reveal without being revealed, as if it were the secret artisan of a universe whose forms we perceive, but whose mechanisms we fail to grasp" (1984, 149–150).

The Max process that implements the required interpolation is divided into several sub-patches. The recording of the interpolated material itself is accomplished using explode, Miller Puckette's multi-channel MIDI recording/playback object.

Figure 5.11 demonstrates one sub-process from the interpolation patch, PlaybackLoop (note that this example, like all of the examples in this book, has been modified to focus on the algorithms under discussion and is therefore somewhat different from the one actually used in *Jupiter*).

All of the *Jupiter* patches make extensive use of the Max send/receive mechanism, and PlaybackLoop is no exception. There are

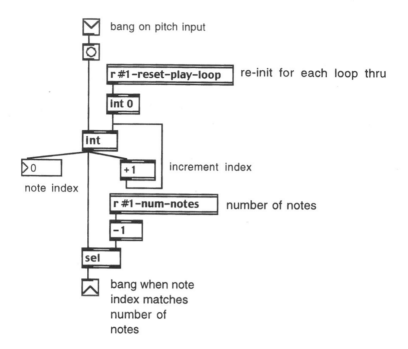

Figure 5.11 PlaybackLoop

two receivers present, one which resets the note index to zero, and another that resets the number of notes to be played in a loop. The main function of the patch is to increment a note count with each incoming pitch. The inlet receives the pitches from an explode object that has recorded the material to be repeated. Whenever a new pitch arrives at the inlet of PlaybackLoop, it bangs out the number stored in the int object in the center of the patch. Initially the int holds zero, but each time a value is output it adds one to itself, incrementing the pitch count. The select object at the bottom of the patch performs the rest of the processing. When the note index from the int matches the number of notes in the loop, select sends a bang to the outlet of PlaybackLoop.

Figure 5.12 demonstrates another sub-patch from the interpolation process: NumberOfPlaybacks. At the top of the patch is a receive object that starts the patch when a playback message is received. Note

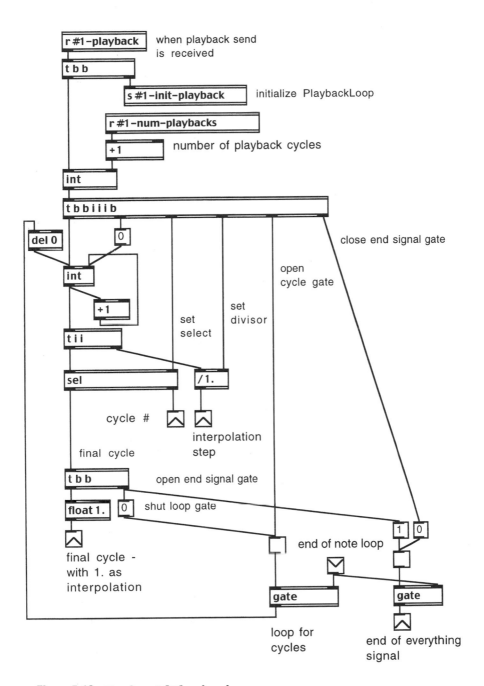

Figure 5.12 NumberOfPlaybacks

that this triggers an init-playback message that sets the loop counter of PlaybackLoop to zero. NumberOfPlaybacks itself performs a number of functions, keyed to the number of playback cycles requested on invocation. The int object below the large trigger keeps track of the number of cycles through playback that have been performed. At each increment, the cycle number is divided by the total number of cycles requested. This produces a floating point value between 0 and 1 that is used to control the interpolation between sequence playbacks in the interpolation control patch (figure 5.13).

The rest of NumberOfPlaybacks is itself a control structure that keeps track of when the requested number of cycles has been generated. When all loops have finished, the gate at the bottom of the patch that controls subsequent loops is closed and the gate governing the transmission of a "finished" bang is opened. The only input to the patch is the bangs coming from PlaybackLoop. These bangs are used to increment the cycle count and update the interpolation fac-

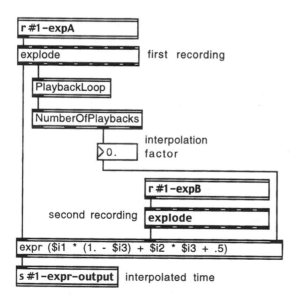

Figure 5.13 Interpolation control

tor, unless all requested loops have been produced. Then the interpolation is set to 1.0 (the end of interpolation) and a `bang` is sent through the rightmost outlet of `NumberOfLoops`, signaling the end of the process.

Figure 5.13 shows how the `PlaybackLoop` and `NumberOfPlaybacks` patches are tied together. Two `explode` objects are used to record the two sequences. As they play back, the interpolation factor generated by `NumberOfPlaybacks` is sent into the right inlet of an expression that calculates a duration interpolated between the output of the two sequences.

5.2.3 Spectral Analysis and Control of Interaction

We have noted the limitations of MIDI as an input representation. Just as extreme are its limitations with respect to the control of synthesis. The limited bandwidth restricts the range of real-time control that can be exercised over external synthesis equipment. Commercial synthesis gear itself has suffered from a "me-too" approach to sound generation, leading virtually all devices to become some variety of sound sampler, playing back pale imitations of traditional instruments.

Consequently, the advantages of digital audio as an input representation are echoed and even multiplied when composers are able to design their own synthesis processes and control these at a much finer grain than can be accomplished through MIDI. The composers Cort Lippe and Zack Settel have made extensive use of these possibilities using the same underlying signal processing environments as those used to realize *Jupiter,* both in their own compositions and together as The Convolution Brothers.

Their approach is interactive in that the synthesis methods are directed by an analysis of the performance of a human player. As Settel writes in his program note for *Hok Pwah*—a composition for voice, percussion, and live electronics—one intention of the work is "to extend the role of the duet, giving the two soloists an extremely large instrumental and timbral range *nonetheless based on* (or *controlled by*) their instrumental technique" (Settel 1993).

To accomplish such control, specialized objects of the DSP Max environment are used to analyze a digital audio signal emanating from the performance of a human musician. (DSP Max refers to a family of implementations, including the IRCAM version of Max with which *Jupiter* was realized; Cycling '74's msp; Miller Puckette's pd; and IRCAM's jMax). One such object is jack~. "The jack~ object detects up to twenty peaks in a given signal for each FFT analysis window, and outputs frequency/amplitude pairs. The jack~ object attempts to maintain continuity between analysis windows by keeping the same voice allocation for common frequencies in adjacent windows. (When controlling a bank of twenty oscillators with the twenty frequency/amplitude pairs, this attempt at maintaining continuity helps to keep the oscillators from jumping to extremely different frequencies when the spectrum of the input changes)" (Lippe 1997, 1).

Figure 5.14 shows the jack~ object in a simple patch that demonstrates one aspect of its analysis: the leftmost outlet returns a MIDI note number corresponding to the pitch of the input. In figure 5.14, the split object restricts the range of pitch-tracking to the notes of the piano keyboard, bounded by 21 (low A on the piano) and 108 (high C). Finally a send object broadcasts the detected pitch number to all parts of the patch that require it.

The second outlet of jack~ transmits a bang when the analysis has detected a note onset. As shown in figure 5.15, this can be used to compute inter-onset intervals between events by feeding it to both inlets of a timer object, a simple way to measure the time elapsed between successive bangs.

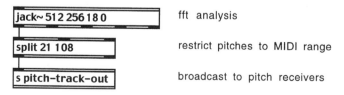

Figure 5.14 jack~ pitch tracking

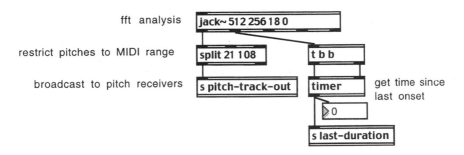

fft analysis

restrict pitches to MIDI range

broadcast to pitch receivers

get time since
last onset

Figure 5.15 jack~ IOI measurement

These patch fragments are taken from the program written by Cort Lippe for his composition *Music for Piano and Computer* (1996), one of a number of his works for soloist and interactive digital signal processing. As indicated in the citation, jack~ is used in this composition not only for pitch tracking, but to control a bank of twenty oscillators as well. The input signal to the analysis is the sound of the live piano. The traditional approach to analysis/resynthesis uses sine-wave oscillators to recreate individual partials of the analyzed sound. Lippe follows tradition for part of the piece, but replaces the sine waves in the oscillator lookup tables with other sounds during other sections. In fact, at some points the resynthesis sounds are determined algorithmically by the piano performance— for example, by switching oscillator tables according to the performer's dynamic.

Zack Settel has written a large number of analysis processes contained in the Jimmies library distributed by IRCAM. In keeping with Max design philosophy, these processes are small units that can be plugged together to create more individual and sophisticated forms of audio tracking. Figure 5.16 shows the patch for calculating the root-mean-square (RMS) amplitude of a digital audio signal. The RMS amplitude is computed just as the name suggests: values from the signal are squared and their mean is taken. The square root of the mean provides a measure of the energy in the signal.

The object zerocross~, another building block, returns a rough estimation of the amount of noise in a signal by counting the

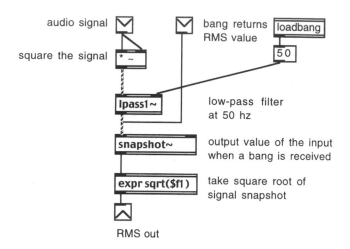

Figure 5.16 RMS amplitude computation

frequency of zero crossings. In *Punjar,* Settel uses zerocross~ together with the RMS computation to detect vocal qualities such as sibilance as a control parameter for synthesis.

Figure 5.17 shows part of the analysis process of *Punjar.* Audio arriving at the top of the patch is sent to the RMS~ computation (figure 5.16) and zerocross~. If the RMS amplitude falls below 0.02, the send variable t_rest, representing a rest (silence), is set to true. When the amplitude is above the threshold, a gate is opened and the output of zerocross~ passes through to a comparison operator (>). The combination of the comparison and the change object will cause a one or zero to be sent to select whenever the zerocross~ output moves across a threshold of 50. That is, when zerocross~ goes from below 50 to above it, a one will be sent to select, and when zerocross~ goes from above 50 to below, a zero is sent. Once the threshold is crossed, no other messages are sent until it is crossed again.

Settel uses movement up over the noise threshold of 50 as evidence of a sibilant sound (e.g., "s", "sh", or "v"). Such positive changes go to the send variable t_zero, used to broadcast noise information to the rest of the patch. In this way the vocal quality of the singer's

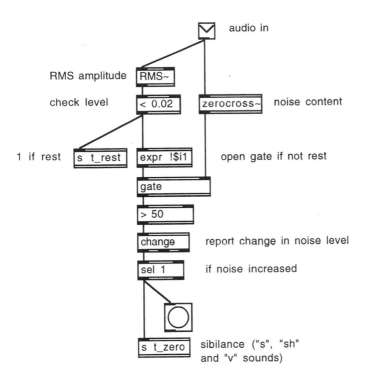

Figure 5.17 Rest and sibilance detection

performance can be used to affect the synthesis and processing of the electronic part.

The Japanese composer Takayuki Rai has used compositional algorithms and real-time signal processing in a number of works including *Four Inventions* for piano and a signal processing computer (1988/rev.1996); *Seven Refractions* for flute and a signal processing computer (1995); and *Kinetic Figuration* for MIDI piano, VP-1 synthesizer, and the ISPW (1994). *Kinetic Figuration* presents the pianist with twelve Cells, collections of musical material that can be ordered by the player during performance. A DSP-Max patch written by the composer processes both the MIDI information coming from the keyboard as well as the sound of the piano itself. "Most of the Cells have function notes or function keys notated in the upper

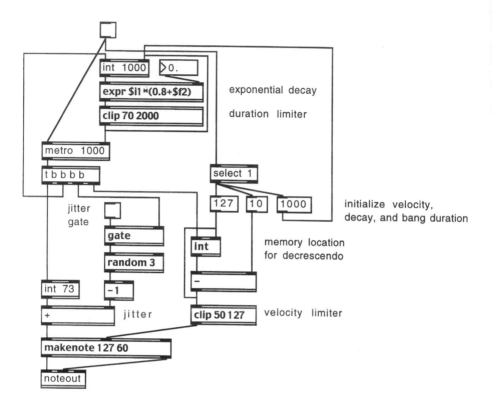

Figure 5.18 Accel path

area of the score. By playing these indicated notes, a pianist, as if he/she gives input data to [a] computer via a normal computer keyboard, can control the entire computer system; chang[ing] parameters, mov[ing] out from the current Cell to the next, and so on" (Rai 1998).

Figure 5.18 demonstrates one of the compositional processes Rai developed for *Kinetic Figuration*. Note the two clip objects labeled "duration limiter" and "velocity limiter." Both of these complete feedback loops that control the velocity and timing of the patch's output. The velocity limiter, for example, comes after a subtraction object that continually subtracts 10 from the last velocity used. When the example patch is turned on, the integer object maintaining the velocity is initialized to 127. Whenever the velocity is banged out from the int, 10 is subtracted from it and the remainder stored back in the memory. The velocity is set to 127 for the first note and decreases with each attack by 10s until it reaches 57. Because the remainder is passed through the clip object, there it will pin until the patch is stopped and started again.

The duration between bangs coming from the metro undergoes a similar modification through feedback. The expression object continually reduces the number of milliseconds input to the right inlet of the metro until it reaches 70. In the example patch, both of these parameters stick at their target value until the toggle at the top is stopped and started again. In Takayuki Rai's version, all of the relevant parameters (velocity decay, acceleration rate, number of notes output, etc.) are controlled through inlets to a subpatch. The CD-ROM includes both the reduced version shown above and an accel subpatch following the composer's original.

5.2.4 Rhythmic Effects in Improvisation

Composers at IRCAM have used signal processing combined with score following as a compositional paradigm for some decades. Musicians at other centers around the world followed suit, beginning with the commercialization of the ISPW in the late 1980s. Another approach to algorithmic signal processing developed in roughly the same time frame, often using the same equipment: rather than tying the control of signal processing techniques to the progression of a human musician through a fixed score, these systems change the processing of external sounds as a function of a developing improvisation.

Though we have focused on the IRCAM tradition of signal processors, many practitioners have used other commercially available gear. Several manufacturers make effects and signal processing devices available at a relatively low cost that can be controlled in real time with MIDI messages. The composer/singer Dafna Naphtali has worked for years with the Eventide family of signal processors in improvisational performances. An important part of her Max patch coordinates control of the signal processing with a pulse that is computed during performance. The approach is similar in spirit to the beat-tracking applications discussed in chapter 3, but differs in that the only durations input to the process are already stipulated to be beat events. Once all inputs are defined as pulses, beat tracking becomes a simple matter of measuring their duration.

The subpatch Roundup takes a floating point input and rounds it to the nearest integer. If the floating point value falls precisely between two integers it will be rounded up (hence the name). The patch makes use of the fact that an integer number box will truncate a floating point input (that is, throw away the fractional part).

As shown in figure 5.19, an incoming value of 3.5 is truncated to 3 by the integer number box. The truncated 3 is used as one part of an integer sum and as the right inlet in a modulo operation. The floating point input is multiplied by two and fed to the other inlet of the modulo box. Continuing the example shown, 3.5 multiplied by 2 is 7. The remainder of 7 divided by three is one, shown as the output of the modulo operation. This added to the integer part of the input gives 4.

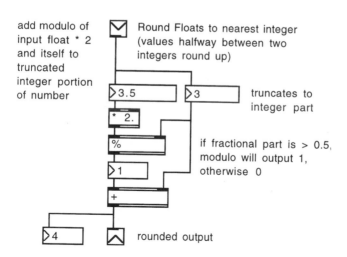

Figure 5.19 Roundup

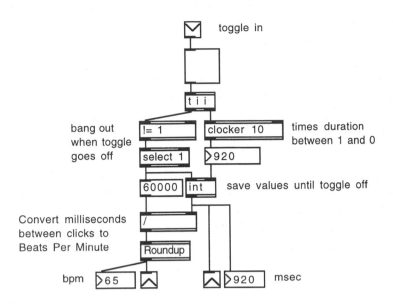

Figure 5.20 Clicktime

Clicktime (figure 5.20) reports the time in milliseconds and beats per minute between two clicks on the mouse. The timing is performed by a `clocker` object that times the duration between receiving a one and a zero at its left inlet. The beats per minute equivalent is found through dividing 60000 by the millisecond duration (60000 is equal to 1000 milliseconds * 60 seconds in a minute). When a zero is received at Clicktime's inlet, it turns off the `clocker` and bangs out the millisecond and beats-per-minute versions of the duration since the previous click.

Note that because one action (a mouse-click) is used to turn the toggle on and off, only the durations between every other click will result in the computation of new output values. That is, if the user regularly clicks the mouse, every other click will update the bpm value reported from Clicktime. Naphtali uses Clicktime as a control structure for sending parameter values to the Eventide signal processor in real time. She has developed an extensive library of presets appropriate to both standard Eventide effects and custom processes.

Clicktime and other controls allow her to quickly change and manipulate such effects in completely improvised performances.

The Center for New Music and Audio Technologies (CNMAT) has developed many systems for interactive improvisation, often expressed through algorithmic signal processing or synthesis. Their work has an extensive rhythmic component based on research first carried out by Jeff Bilmes at the MIT Media Laboratory. Bilmes built an engine for the analysis and synthesis of expressive timing variations on the observation that musicians maintain independent, very fine-grained subdivisions of the beat pulse as a reference for the placement of events in time. "When we listen to or perform music, we often perceive a high frequency pulse, frequently a binary, trinary, or quaternary subdivision of the musical tactus. What does it mean to perceive this pulse, or as I will call it, tatum? The tatum is the high frequency pulse or clock that we keep in mind when perceiving or performing music. The tatum is the lowest level of the metric musical hierarchy. We use it to judge the placement of all musical events" (Bilmes 1993, 21–22).

Tatums are very small units of time that can be used to measure the amount of temporal deviation present or desired in any performed event. The name tatum has multiple connotations: first, it is an abbreviation of "temporal atom," referring to its function as an indivisible unit of time. In addition, it honors the great improviser, Art Tatum, as well.

A central tenet of the tatum approach is that expressive timing variation in many musical styles (including jazz, African, and Latin music) is not convincingly modeled by tempo variation alone. Rather than defining expression as a change in the tempo of an underlying pulse, the deviation of a given event from a fixed pulse is used. When modeling the performance of an ensemble, each member of the ensemble has her own deviation profile. This means that some performers might be ahead of or behind the beat, while others play more strictly in time. Such a conceptualization corresponds more closely to the way musicians think about their temporal relationships during performance than does the idea that they all are varying their tempi independently.

In his thesis, Bilmes demonstrated tools for deriving, analyzing, and synthesizing temporal deviations present in the multiple layers of drums he recorded in a performance by the Cuban percussion ensemble, Los Muñequitos de Matanzas (1993). His work has become a foundation of the CNMAT Rhythm Engine (CRE), used to organize the rhythmic activity in several interactive environments.

One such environment used the CRE to store, transform, and combine rhythmic patterns related to those of North Indian classical music. Rhythm in this tradition is based on *tal* theory, a way of organizing drum patterns within beat cycles of a certain length, such as the 16-beat *tin tal* or 12-beat *jap tal*. "A particular *tal* is characterized not only by its number of beats, but also by traditional *thekas,* fixed patterns that would normally be played on a tabla drum to delineate the rhythmic structure of the *tal* in the most straightforward way" (Wright and Wessel 1998).

The system organizes a collection of rhythmic subsequences in a database. Each subsequence identifies one "reference tatum," the point that is anchored to a rhythmic grid when the subsequence is timescaled and scheduled to be played. Normally the reference tatum is the first event of the subsequence, but could come sometime later if the pattern includes pickup notes. Subsequences can undergo several forms of transformation before they are played, the most important of which is timescaling. That is, a subsequence can be sped up or slowed down by some multiple, as well as adjusted to match the tempo of an ongoing performance.

Subsequences record the placement of events in time. Usually an event is a note or drum stroke, but it can represent some other type of action as well: for example, the system can position "start record" and "stop record" messages within a rhythmic pattern. In this way, material from the live performance can be sampled at precisely controlled moments within the rhythmic structure: "We think of the notes before the 'start record' as a musical stimulus, and then use the recording feature to capture a co-improviser's response to this stimulus" (Wright and Wessel 1998).

Subsequences can be initiated as repeating or one-time cells. Each time through the *tal,* the CRE scheduler combines ongoing cell repetitions with newly scheduled one-time cells. Filtering and modification of the subsequence outputs are applied just before the sounds are played, providing real-time access to their timbral and dynamic presentation. One kind of modification affects the performance of overlapping events: if a repeating cell and a one-time cell both schedule an event on the same tatum, one of several strategies can be executed before that tatum is played. For example, one of the competing event sounds may be chosen and the other dropped, with the surviving sound played louder. Alternatively, the two competitors may be performed as a flam, with one slightly ahead of the other.

The CNMAT website maintains several articles describing the use of the Rhythm Engine in real-time improvisation, as well as a link to Jeff Bilmes's thesis describing the theoretical foundation of tatums (Bilmes 1993). As the North Indian example demonstrates, this way of thinking about time offers a powerful and flexible structure for organizing the temporal relationships of many different styles of improvised music.

5.3   Standard MIDI Files

Standard MIDI Files (SMF) are an extension to the MIDI standard that were developed to allow applications to interchange complete musical scores. Accordingly they include much more extensive information about the music encoded than does the simple stream of MIDI note messages that might be generated from such a file. One could input a Standard MIDI File to the applications we have developed simply by routing the output of a sequencer that has read the file to an IAC Bus, and then reading from the bus in the same manner demonstrated with Max in section 2.2.2. It would be preferable to build in a Standard MIDI File reader, however, to gain access to the additional information those files can provide. This section, then, presents an SMF reader that outputs `EventBlocks` suitable for analysis by the listening objects.

There are three formats of Standard MIDI Files: Format 0 encodes sequences with one track and is best suited for monophonic music. Format 1 supports multi-voiced sequences, where each voice is recorded on a separate track. Format 2 files allow each track to be temporally independent. The application described here (and the corresponding code on the CD-ROM) deals with format 0 files only.

Each note event in an SMF has five fields: (1) a delta time, (2) note on/note off status, (3) channel number, (4) MIDI note number, and (5) MIDI velocity. Four of these five (status, channel, note, and velocity) are sent in normal MIDI channel voice messages. The only information that SMF adds at the note level, then, is the delta time. "Delta time indicates the time delay between the onsets of discrete MIDI events in a serial stream of data. Delta times are encoded either as pulses per quarter note (PPQN) or as SMPTE time code" (Hewlett et al. 1997, 48). Given either PPQN or SMPTE values, we may compute for each event the absolute onset time in milliseconds. Since the additional information is available, however, we may be well served to maintain it in our representation.

· Analytical applications generally have little use for SMPTE times. PPQN, however, can be used to calculate the position of an event in terms of bars, beats, and ticks, where ticks are the number of pulses per quarter note (usually there are 480 PPQN). The work of beat and meter induction (section 3.2), then, becomes superfluous. We already know which events fall on the beat and where the beats fall in a metric structure. This assumes, of course, that the sequence being read has already been quantized. If it has not, the events in the file will have an arbitrary relationship to the grid of bars and beats, and no information gain will result from dealing with an SMF as opposed to a MIDI stream output from it. In fact the quantization process described in section 3.2.1 could be used on an unquantized MIDI stream to produce a quantized Standard MIDI File by calculating the appropriate PPQN values for each event.

Parsing a Standard MIDI File is simply a matter of reading the events as specified by the standard and repackaging the information in the *Machine Musicianship* library representation. Rather than labor over the details here, I refer the reader to the SMF Reader application on the CD-ROM, which opens MIDI files and reads them into an `EventBlock`. The application then simply plays the file back from the `EventBlock`, though clearly at that point the information could be sent to any of the analysis routines as well.

6 Algorithmic Expression and Music Cognition

The traditional creation of Western music moves from the score written by a composer through a performer's interpretation to the understanding of a listener. We have considered algorithmic tools for composition and analysis, informed by the cognition of listening. In this chapter we will review proposals for algorithmic performance, particularly those that deal with expression. Before addressing that work, let us pause to think more closely about the cross-fertilization between music cognition and machine musicianship.

6.1 Music Cognition and Machine Musicianship

Music cognition occupies a position at the intersection of music theory, cognitive science, and artificial intelligence. Artificial intelligence in particular is concerned with the emulation of human reasoning in computer programs. In cognitive science, the viability of proposed human mental processes is often tested by implementing such programs. This repertoire of software, then, offers a rich library of tools for the exploration of machine musicianship.

In this study, I assume a substrate of knowledge and understanding underlying our musical behavior, generally. A common objection to the idea of machine listening is that different people experience music differently, and therefore encoding a particular version of musical understanding enforces one type of experience at the expense of others. I am sympathetic to that argument and, in fact, believe it to be true at higher levels. I also believe, however, that such differences of experience rest on a much simpler and relatively uncontroversial layer of perceptions and concepts available to every listener—every listener, that is, within a given musical culture. Though the techniques described in this book specifically address Western music, there are, in my opinion, cognitive foundations underlying the experience of music in other cultures that overlap Western norms to some extent.

Different people may have very different experiences and opinions of a novel they have read. Nonetheless, they will agree that certain characters populated the novel, participated in certain events, and reacted by taking certain actions. If we can develop programs capable of making plausible inferences about the obvious, we will have a platform on which more individual and sophisticated musical processes can be built.

That said, this text remains agnostic concerning the question of whether a program is capable of musical "reasoning" in the same way that humans are. Researchers in music cognition carry an additional burden in the design of musically capable programs—they must ensure that the output of the algorithm correlates significantly with the behavior of human subjects performing the same task. While we are concerned with emulating human performance as well, we do not face the methodological requirement of reproducing the experimental data produced by human subjects.

There are essentially two reasons why the recreation of experimental data from music cognition is not the standard of verification for algorithms described in this text: the first and most important is that it would simultaneously expand the scope considerably, and eliminate much work in computer music that was never written to address the music cognition literature in the first place.

The second reason is that matching the performance of human subjects and writing programs that work well musically are not always the same thing. People are much more musical than programs, but it is not hard to find musical tasks that machines can do better, or at least more quickly. (Try to write down the root and type of any chord you hear within 10 milliseconds.) The point of the exercise is to design tools that can help people make better music. Given that orientation, there would be no point in changing a program that performs well simply because it does not go about the work in the same way that humans do. Deep Blue doesn't play chess the way people do, but plays better than almost all of them. Certainly no one would suggest that Deep Blue should be made to play worse if it then would better match the data from experiments on human chess players.

Machine musicianship as I consider it in these pages is a form of weak AI: weak in that I claim no necessary isomorphism to the human cognitive processes behind the competencies being emulated. It would be wonderful, certainly, if these programs could shed any light on the psychology of music and some of them may serve as platforms from which to launch such inquiry. It certainly works in the other direction, however: because of their meticulous attention to the details of human musicianship, music cognition and music theory are the most abundant sources of ideas I know for programming computers to be more musical.

Artificial intelligence has been an important partner in the development of musically aware computer programs as well. Every new wave of AI technology, in fact, seems to engender an application offering possibilities for some aspect of music composition, analysis, or performance. Ebcioglu's expert system for harmonizing chorales in the style of J.S. Bach (1992), Bharucha and Todd's modeling of tonal perception with neural networks (1989), and Cope's use of augmented transition networks for composition (1991) are only some of the more celebrated instances of this phenomenon. From the point of view of artificial intelligence research, such applications are attractive because of music's rich capacity to support a wide variety of models. Musical problems can be stated with the rigidity and precision of a building-blocks world, or may be approached with more tolerance for ambiguity, multiple perspectives, and learning. From the point of view of algorithmic composition and performance, artificial intelligence is of central importance because it directly addresses the modeling of human cognition.

6.1.1 Expert Systems

An AI technique that has been widely and successfully applied to algorithmic composition is the *expert system* (Ebcioglu 1992; Schwanauer 1988). These programs maintain a knowledge base of assertions concerning the compositional task at hand and use some variation of generate-and-test with backtracking to find solutions to problems that are consistent with the given knowledge base. Let us sketch the architecture of a generic expert system: Given a complete specification of some goal state (the problem), partial solutions are generated using collections of condition-action pairs (productions) that look for certain conditions in the problem and the solution as it has been constructed so far. If those conditions are satisfied, the action part of the rule fires, causing some change to be made in the solution.

This process constitutes the generation part of a generate-and-test cycle. Tests are made by comparing a solution against some number of constraints. Solutions that do not satisfy the constraints are rejected. In a final phase of the process, heuristics are applied to direct the search for solutions in the most promising directions and to assign merit values to solutions that have successfully passed the test phase. Successive steps in a sequence of operations are concatenated in this manner. If at any step a partial solution cannot be found, the system backtracks to the previous step and selects an alternative solution in an effort to find a successful candidate at the previously insoluble next step.

Kemal Ebcioglu implemented such a cycle as the heart of his system for harmonizing chorales in the style of J.S. Bach:

The condition-action pairs are called the generate section, the constraints are called the test section, and the heuristics are called the recommendations section of the knowledge base. Each step of the program is executed as follows. . . : All possible assignments to the n'th element of the partial solution are sequentially generated via the production rules. If a candidate assignment does not comply with the constraints, it is thrown away; otherwise its worth is computed by summing the weights of the heuristics that it makes true, and it is saved in a list, along with its worth. When there are no more assignments to be generated for solution element n, the resulting list is sorted according to the worth of each candidate. The program then attempts to continue with the best assignment to element n, and then,

if a dead-end is later encountered and a backtracking return is made
to this point, with the next best assignment, etc., as defined by the
sorted list. (Ebcioglu 1992, 304)

In this review I am primarily concerned with those techniques that
can improve the real-time musicianship of interactive programs.
From this point of view, the generic expert systems architecture is
appealing as long as the move to backtracking in the face of insoluble
positions is eliminated. Decisions in an interactive setting most often
cannot be retracted, since generally they are executed as soon as they
are made. Therefore reversing a prior decision when a dead end is
reached, as in backtracking, is impossible. As a corollary, an interactive system must have some default way of declaring a winner when
the normal generate-and-test cycle does not complete successfully.
If backtracking is not available to break an impasse, some other mechanism for moving on must be devised.

Generate-and-test cycles, on the other hand, can certainly be used
in interactive situations as long as the cycles can be executed quickly
enough. The choice of a particular solution must be made assuming
that the current state cannot be altered by backtracking through previous decision nodes. The importance of fast and effective heuristics
in such a strategy is then magnified with respect to the non-real-time
case.

Part of my program Cypher operates using techniques similar to
generate-and-test. Cypher has been described in detail elsewhere
(Rowe 1993), and will be summarized and implemented again here
in section 7.4. For the purposes of this discussion the following outline should suffice: Cypher is composed of two large components: a
listener and a player. The listener examines MIDI data arriving from
some source and characterizes a number of musical features found
there. It passes messages relaying the result of its analysis to the
player. The user of the program can configure the player to respond
to those messages in various ways. For example, the listener could
pass a message asserting that the input is "a loud C-minor chord in
the high register." (Actually Cypher transmits classifications of six
features for each incoming event).

The user of the program sets up some number of listener-to-player links that function as condition-action pairs, in which a message sent from the listener constitutes a state to be examined by the condition part. Actions are algorithmic transformations of the MIDI material being input to the program. To continue the previous example, a user could assert that when loud, high, C-minor chords are heard, that material should be inverted, slowed down, and arpeggiated. This process corresponds in a rough way to the generate section of an expert system such as the one described by Ebcioglu earlier. The comparison is very limited, however, in that Cypher only generates one solution. There are no competing versions to be ranked according to heuristics.

The solution can be modified, however, by the test part of a generate-and-test cycle. The test section uses a second instance of the same listener process found in the generate section. Here, the listener describes the features found in the material the program is about to play after completing the actions designated by the generation productions. I call this test section the critic, since it acts as an internal arbiter of the music the program will produce. The critic includes an independent list of condition-action pairs. These productions look at the analysis of the incipient output and make changes to the output if necessary. Roughly, then, the condition parts of the critic condition-action pairs constitute the test in a generic generate-and-test system. In this case, however, solutions that fail the test are not rejected, but are modified by the actions. For example, a critic production might specify that if the program is about to output fast, loud, dense chords in the low register, that material should first be thinned out, slowed down, and made softer.

The important points to notice here are two: first, much of the mechanics of expert systems (with the important exception of backtracking) can be adapted for use in real-time interactive applications. Second, real-time analysis processes will permit the conditions and actions of expert systems to be stated using common musical expressions about such elements as density, register, dynamic, and the like.

6.2 Knowledge Representation

A central issue for both artificial intelligence and cognitive science is that of knowledge representation. Symbolic systems in particular rely on the organization of knowledge about things and relationships in the world to build a framework within which reasoning processes can function. Even sub-symbolic systems make assumptions about some frame of reference in the kinds of inputs they accept and the way their outputs are interpreted.

6.2.1 Schemata

An important representation for all of these fields, and for music cognition in particular, is the schema, or frame. Albert Bregman defines schema as "a control structure in the human brain that is sensitive to some frequently occurring pattern, either in the environment, in ourselves, or in how the two interact" (Bregman 1990, 401). Programs modeling some aspect of cognition frequently make use of a formal version of the schema, typically interpreted as a collection of interrelated fields that is activated when a certain pattern of activity is encountered. For example, Marc Leman describes the output of the self-organizing maps used in his system (section 4.3) as schemata. The title of his book, *Music and Schema Theory* reflects the importance of the concept to his model (1995).

Schemata are important both as a way of organizing the response to a situation and as a compact representation of knowledge in memory. Many of the structures and processes we have already developed may be considered from a schematic viewpoint. Irene Deliège and her colleagues suggest that the structures of the Generative Theory of Tonal Music, for example, are schemata for the organization of tonal material in memory: "The same underlying structure could be related by a listener to many different surface structures. The capacity to abstract an appropriate underlying structure in listening to a given piece could thus be held to represent the most highly developed mode of musical listening" (Deliège et al. 1996, 121). The application of such schemata to different compositions could indeed underlie many of the differences found between musicians and non-musicians in performing musical tasks. For example, the superior performance of trained musicians in memorizing and reproducing previously unknown material could well be a product of their ability to relate the novel material to structures already in mind.

The Deliège article goes on to suggest an alternative structure for musical memory, namely a cue-abstraction mechanism (mécanisme d'extraction d'indices). Cues are small groups or patterns within a larger musical texture that exhibit certain salient attributes. These attributes could include striking characteristics of melody, harmony, rhythm, gesture, and so on. Their recognition acts as a grouping trigger such that the arrival of a new cue spurs the creation of a grouping boundary.

In this way, longer structures (motives, phrases, etc.) may be labeled and encoded in memory by means of cues that alone are stored in immediate memory and enable access to the entire structure. The cues can then be used as signposts; they embody invariant characteristics of the musical material and take on the function of referential entities enabling constant evaluation of new material. Thus the cue provides the basis for grouping and for the chaining together (concatenation) of groups at different hierarchical levels of listening; concatenation of groups will continue for as long as a particular cue continues to be recognized. When a new and contrasting cue is perceived, it establishes the boundaries of the higher level grouping—periods or sections of the piece—and can initiate a new grouping. In other words, grouping can be seen to make use of two principles; the principle of "sameness," which determines the length of the concatenated groups, and that of "difference," which establishes their boundaries (Deliège et al. 1996, 122–123).

We may consider a cue to be a particular kind of pattern (see section 4.2). A pattern becomes a cue when it exhibits attributes that are particularly striking for the context in which they occur. An algorithmic cue finder, particularly during performance, would be a challenging undertaking, but at a minimum would require some reference to the style of the music in which the cues are embedded. In section 8.1 we will review a proposal for automatic style recognition. Certain cue attributes could be tied to the recognition of styles such that when a given style is active, the presence of the associated attributes would mark a pattern as a cue.

None of the segmentation techniques we built in section 4.1 make use of the recognition of distinctive patterns as suggested by the cue-abstraction proposal. Using cues in segmentation would lead to a circularity that must be dealt with in control structures governing the two. That is, we use calculated segments as the starting point of the pattern recognition procedures outlined in section 4.2. Ongoing segments are matched against stored patterns that have been assigned boundaries by the same grouping process. Once we use the recognition of patterns as boundary markers, we encounter a feedback problem in which cues determine groups that determine cues. Though cue abstraction may be a very powerful addition to the segmentation techniques currently in use, the resonance between groups and cues would need to be closely controlled in the real-time case.

Another kind of schema models progressions of tension and relaxation through time:

Research on musical expressivity and on musical semantics, carried out by Francès (1958) and Imberty (1979, 1981) showed the essential part played by musical tension and relaxation schemas; these schemas are extracted from the musical piece and then assimilated to kinetic and emotional schemas of tension and relaxation, which accumulate all of the affective experience of the listener. Therefore, it seems reasonable to consider that the most important part of musical expressivity might be determined firstly by the specific way each composer organises the musical tension and relaxation in time, and secondly by the kinds of musical tension and relaxation the listener manages to abstract. (Bigand 1993, 123–124)

Bigand proposes algorithmic means of determining the tension and relaxation of musical segments, particularly as these are manifested by melodic, harmonic, and rhythmic processes. For example,

Table 6.1 Bigand Tonal Weights

TONAL FUNCTION	WEIGHT
Tonic	7
Dominant	6
Third	5
Other	4

he outlines a system that assigns particular melodic pitches a weight according to their tonal function (table 6.1). Pitches that are not part of the prevailing tonality would be assigned three or two points depending on whether the tonality of which they are members is closely or distantly related to the current key. The tonal function weight is further modified by other multipliers for note duration and metric position. The result is a tension/relaxation curve induced by a given segment that approximates those recorded from human subjects.

Here we see the outlines of a way to describe the emotional expression created by a piece of music. Emotion in music has been a subject of intense interest for writers in such diverse fields as philosophy, music theory, and music criticism for centuries. It is particularly problematic for algorithmic modeling because it seems so keenly personal and variable, even for the same listener on different hearings. At the same time, an account of the listening experience that makes no reference to emotion at all seems seriously incomplete—for many listeners, an emotional response is the most important aspect of why they listen to music in the first place. John Sloboda opens his classic text *The Musical Mind* with the assertion that "the reason that most of us take part in musical activity, be it composing, performing, or listening, is that music is capable of arousing in us deep and significant emotions" (Sloboda 1985, 1).

Like Jackendoff's sketch of an algorithmic listening system, Bigand's tonal weights are devised partly to provide a method for evaluating the affective course of a piece of music. I will not pursue the algorithmic analysis of emotional responses in this text, though many of the analytic tools we have developed could help describe the affective dynamic of a work when cast in those terms. (The work that has been published in this area is still developing. For one of the most refined examples, see Antonio Camurri's EyesWeb project; see also section 9.3.) For the moment let us consider the other crucial part of Bigand's tension/relaxation schemata, which is that they are formulated with explicit reference to temporal development.

6.2.2 Scripts and Plans

Schemata that have a particular trajectory in time are often called scripts, or plans. Schank and Abelson's *Scripts, Plans, Goals and Understanding: An Inquiry into Human Knowledge Structures* provides a particularly succinct overview of these structures and the kinds of processing they make possible (1977). The temporal element is of course critical for music because music is an art that exists in time. Schemata, as we have seen, are collections of information and processes that are invoked by the appearance of particular configurations of elements. Scripts add to this concept sequencing events: for example, the script of a birthday party might include a number of actions, some with a determined order and some that can change. That is, the guests will arrive near the beginning and leave near the end, but the cake may be eaten before the presents are opened or the other way around.

In his book *A Classic Turn of Phrase,* Robert Gjerdingen argues for the psychological and music theoretic reality of schemata. His use of schemata is tied to parallel developments in cognitive science, but is also explicitly related to certain traditions in music theory: "With respect to the harmonic and voice-leading aspects of classical music, an early proponent of a type of schema theory was the great Austrian theorist Heinrich Schenker" (1988, 23). Beyond Schenkerian analysis, Leonard Meyer's discussions of form, process, and archetypes, and Eugene Narmour's style forms, style structures, and idiostructures all relate to Gjerdingen's concept of musical schemata. In other work, Dowling credits schemata with guiding the perception of overlapping melodies in his influential studies of the process (Dowling and Harwood 1986). Stephen McAdams's sketch of information flow during music listening gives a prominent position to mental schemata as capturing the listener's accumulated knowledge of music and guiding her attention while hearing a particular piece (1987).

Gjerdingen's book examines in some detail the "changing-note archetype" described in the work of Leonard Meyer, in particular the variety with scale degrees moving from 1–7 and then 4–3 in a melodic line. Considering this archetype as a network of related schemata requires elaborating the features, implications, and processes typically associated with the archetype in actual works of music. "A defensible definition of the schema underlying these cadences would require that the norms and interrelationships of meter, harmony, rhythmic groupings, voice leading, melody, and texture all be specified" (Gjerdingen 1988, 34).

Organizing knowledge into schemata is a music theoretic undertaking of considerable scope. Gjerdingen's 300-page work covers one variant of the changing-note archetype. Transferring the work to computer programs would pose a comparably daunting task. We may be encouraged, however, by the fact that much work on representing and manipulating frames and schemata has already been accomplished in the field of artificial intelligence (Bobrow and Winograd 1977). A number of knowledge representation languages have been produced that simplify the collection of concepts into semantic networks or schemata—Antonio Camurri's HARP system for musical reasoning is built on a variant of one of these, KL-ONE. In chapter 9 we will review one of Camurri's knowledge bases more closely.

6.3 Learning

A remarkable property of most interactive music systems is that they do not learn. They are endowed by their programmers with certain methods for generating music and (perhaps) analyzing the music with which they play. Once the program appears onstage, or even in the rehearsal hall, it has largely reached a level of performance that will change little until the concert is over. Exceptions to this generalization are programs such as Barry Vercoe's Synthetic Performer, which learns in rehearsal the interpretation that a particular human player brings to a piece of chamber music (Vercoe 1984).

Steven Tanimoto defines learning as "an improvement in information-processing ability that results from information-processing activity" (Tanimoto 1990, 312). Learning therefore involves change in the functioning of a system due to the operation of the system itself. Tanimoto's definition makes learning a positive change—the system is not held to have learned if its performance degrades. Critical to identifying learning, then, is a specification of what "improvement" means for a particular system. The field of machine learning is a broad and active one, and I will not undertake any overview here. Rather, let us consider the issues involved in using machine learning techniques in an interactive system.

"Each learning model specifies the learner, the learning domain, the source of information, the hypothesis space, what background knowledge is available and how it can be used, and finally, the criterion of success" (Richter et al. 1998, 1). Here again we find reference to an improvement metric as a way to quantify learning. One of the most widely used learning models is the neural network, which we have already considered in some detail. The key induction network introduced in section 3.1, for example, used information from music theory both as the source of knowledge about chord functions and as the criterion of success, and the network was considered successful if it produced key identifications in agreement with music theory. Another criterion of success might be agreement with the results of music cognition experiments. As in the case of representation, successful learning can only be judged within the context of a specific problem.

We can distinguish two basic learning phases that we might wish a machine musician to undergo: first, learning as preparation for performance; and second, learning during performance. Several interactive programs have incorporated learning as preparation for performance—Vercoe's Synthetic Performer is one example. Others include the CNMAT systems that use neural network components (Lee and Wessel 1992) and the NetNeg program described in section 6.4. There have been relatively few cases of learning during performance (though these do exist, for example in the work of David Rosenboom [1992]).

Neural networks, though fast enough for real-time use after training, generally take too much time during the learning phase to be of much use onstage. Pattern induction as covered in section 4 can be seen as a form of learning since the program learns new material from repeated exposure. The form of learning we will consider now—learning during performance—involves the use of genetic algorithms.

6.3.1 Genetic Algorithms

Genetic algorithms (GAs) simulate the evolution of chromosomes in an ecology as a learning paradigm. Derived from work pioneered by John Holland and his associates at the University of Michigan in the 1960s, genetic algorithms have become a powerful tool for developing novel solutions to complex and poorly defined problems (Mitchell 1996). The concepts and processes of genetics are modified to produce an environment of algorithmic development. A "chromosome" in a genetic algorithm is a potential solution to some problem. Such chromosomes are normally encoded as a bit string. Chromosomes are evaluated by a fitness function that determines how well the candidate solution solves the problem at hand. "The minimal requirements for using a GA are that the solutions must map to a string of symbols (preferably bits), and that there be some way of determining how good one solution is at solving the problem, relative to the other solutions in the population" (Biles 1994, 131).

A genetic algorithm evolves its chromosomes by selecting the fittest ones and mating them to produce a new population. Two chro-

```
Parent  A         Parent  B

  0010              1001


Child  1          Child  2

  0001              1010
```

Figure 6.1 Bit-string crossover

mosomes are mated by taking parts of the bit strings of each and combining them to make a new string. The methods of combining chromosomes follow biology: two of the most important mating functions are *crossover* and *mutation*. In crossover, a chromosome locus is chosen at random. Bits before the locus in parent A are concatenated with bits after the locus in parent B to form one offspring, and the post-locus bits of A are concatenated with the pre-locus bits of B to form another. Figure 6.1 shows the offspring created from two four-bit parents with crossover at locus 2.

Mutation randomly flips bits in one chromosome. That is, a single bit position in a chromosome is chosen at random and the value there is inverted (a zero becomes a one, and vice versa).

A fitness function gauges the success of a solution relative to other solutions (chromosomes). A famous genetic algorithm was developed by W. Daniel Hillis to evolve sorting algorithms (1992). In that case the fitness of a chromosome was a measure of whether or not it could correctly sort a list of 16 items. The sorting algorithm is a well-known optimization problem in computer science, described extensively by Donald Knuth in the third volume of his classic text *The Art of Computer Programming* (1973). One of Knuth's solutions is a sorting network, a parallel process in which pairs of elements in the list are compared and swapped if they are found to be out of order. Such networks are correct if they are guaranteed to produce a sorted list at the end of all comparisons. They are minimal if they produce a correct result with the fewest number of comparisons.

After several years of work, the minimal network found as of 1969 used 60 comparisons.

The first version of Hillis's sort algorithm GA evolved a sorting network that used 65 comparisons. Because the fitness function was testing only for correctness, and not minimality, it is already remarkable that such an efficient network evolved. The reason the GA did not produce even more efficient networks, rivaling those produced by human researchers, was that its fitness was tested against a random sample of unsorted lists (the complete set of such lists being a universe too large to use). Once the GA arrived at a network that worked, it was not challenged often enough by the test patterns (the ecology) to be pressured to change.

The second version of the GA therefore co-evolved the sort algorithms together with the tests used to determine their fitness. The analogy Hillis had in mind was host-parasite or predator-prey coevolution in which two organisms evolve in relationship to each other. In this case the sorting networks were a kind of host and the test samples a parasite. "Both populations evolved under a GA. The fitness of a [sorting] network was now determined by the parasite located at the network's grid location. The network's fitness was the percentage of test cases in the parasite that it sorted correctly. The fitness of the parasite was the percentage of its test cases that stumped the network (i.e., that the network sorted incorrectly)" (Mitchell 1996, 26). No longer would the networks stop evolving at the point of being able to solve a test of average difficulty. Now as the networks improved, the problems they were given to solve would also become harder. The GA with coevolution produced a network with 61 steps—only one step behind the best human solution.

The fitness function for the sorting network GA is clear: for a chromosome to be considered fit, it must represent a correct network. The ecology within which the chromosomes evolve exerts pressure on them to sort correctly. In an artistic application of GAs, however, we might expect a very different sort of ecology—one in which the aesthetic preferences of an observer determine the fitness of a solution.

Karl Sims has written a drawing program that causes images to evolve according to the ecology of the viewer (1991):

In a typical run of the program, the first image is generated at random (but Sims can feed in a real image, such as a picture of a face, if he wishes). Then the program makes nineteen independent changes (mutations) in the initial image-generating rule, so as to cover the VDU-screen with twenty images: the first, plus its nineteen ("asexually" reproduced) offspring. At this point, the human uses the computer mouse to choose either one image to be mutated, or two images to be "mated" (through crossover). The result is another screenful of twenty images, of which all but one (or two) are newly generated by random mutations or crossovers. The process is then repeated, for as many generations as one wants. (Boden 1994, 110–111)

Working with Sims's program is absorbing and leads to novel and interesting images that are related in a perceptible but indirect way to the choices of the user. The observer determines the creation of the work by providing the environment in which evolution of the images proceeds.

In the domain of music, John Biles has written a genetic algorithm called GenJam that improvises jazz solo lines (1994; 1998). Here it is the preference of a listener that determines the fitness of chromosomes: at the end of each generation a human partner rates the output of the GA to guide its evolution at the next step.

Biles uses what he calls "GenJam Normal Form" (GJNF) to represent the pitch and rhythm information of a solo melodic line. GJNF uses one chromosome to encode the material of one measure. Each measure is assumed to be four beats long and each beat can be articulated by two eighth notes. With these assumptions, a chromosome in GJNF consists of a string of eight symbols, one for each eighth note position within a measure. In this case the symbols are not bits, but addresses into a table that contains a scale consonant with the chord being played in the corresponding measure.

For example, Biles uses a hexatonic minor scale without the sixth degree to accompany minor seventh chords. The chord progression

Table 6.2 GenJam Fm7 Scale Map

INDEX	1	2	3	4	5	6	7	8	9	10	11	12	13	14
PITCH	C	E♭	F	G	A♭	B♭	C	E♭	F	G	A♭	B♭	C	E♭

Figure 6.2 Output from scale map against Fm7

for a tune being learned is read from a file prior to running the GA. A preprocessor then constructs scale tables for each measure according to the given harmonic structure. The scale used to accompany an Fm7 chord might consist of 14 pitches arranged as shown in table 6.2.

Note that these are not pitch classes but rather pitches in a particular octave. A GenJam chromosome with the sequence of symbols { 9 10 11 12 13 11 10 9 }, then, would perform the musical fragment shown in figure 6.2 when played against an Fm7 chord (this example is taken from Biles [1998, 233]).

Indices into the table begin with one because the locus symbol zero has a special meaning: whenever the program encounters a zero in a chromosome it generates a rest in the output by sending a note off command to the MIDI pitch most recently sounded. A locus symbol of 15 also has a special meaning, in that when 15 is encountered no MIDI messages at all are sent, effectively holding the most recently sounded pitch (or continuing a rest).

GenJam makes four kinds of mutations to measure chromosomes:

1. *reverse*   replace a chromosome with its retrograde
2. *rotate*   rotate symbols from 1 to 7 positions to the right

3. *invert*   reverse direction of symbol intervals

4. *transpose*   add or subtract random amount from symbols

Biles developed this set of what he calls "musically meaningful mutations," notably without the use of crossover or single-point mutation. Beyond the mutations to measure chromosomes, moreover, there is an additional set of four phrase mutations:

1. *reverse*   play the four measure chromosomes in reverse order

2. *rotate*   rotate the measures from 1 to 3 positions to the right

3. *repeat*   repeat a random measure, replacing the follower

4. *sequence*   repeat the human's last measure 2 or 3 times and fill

A phrase is a sequence of four measures. The phrase mutations therefore operate one level up the rhythmic hierarchy from measure mutations. The set of phrase mutations listed here comes from Biles's interactive version of GenJam that is able to "trade fours" with a human partner (Biles 1998). That accounts for the fourth form of mutation, in which material from the human's phrase is used to form the response of the GA.

Interactive Genjam forms chromosome representations of the improvisation of a human partner in real time. During the performance, a quantization window continually advances by eighth-note durations. As MIDI pitches arrive, they are matched against the scale maps for each measure to find the closest index. The last index found during a given quantization window becomes the scale map symbol for that locus. Previous indices found within the same window are simply discarded.

Trading fours is a jazz improvisation style in which one soloist will improvise four bars, answered by another who plays the next four. Interactive GenJam trades fours, then, by building a set of four measure chromosomes from the human performance as its partner plays. During the last 30 milliseconds of the human's four, GenJam performs the mutations listed above on the collected material. The mutated phrase is then played out over the course of the following four measures.

This version of the algorithm in fact does not evolve phrases based on a fitness evaluation. The human player has no foot pedal or other virtual gong with which to reduce the fitness of phrases judged to be poor. Other implementations of GenJam have used a fitness estimation, however, either issued by a human observer as in Karl Sim's drawing GA, or even derived from the reaction of an audience of listeners.

John Biles's GenJam is interesting both because of the ingenuity with which it adapts genetic algorithms for jazz improvisation and because it uses a learning algorithm during the performance itself. The applications to which GAs could be put as part of an interactive system are legion—GenJam is to some extent an aural equivalent of Sims' drawing program, and there are many other ways to interpret chromosome strings as control parameters of compositional algorithms. GAs might be used, for example, to evolve interpolation functions such as those found in Philippe Manoury's *Jupiter* or tendency mask settings for the AC Toolbox. Learning could be carried out before the performance allowing the composer to exert pressure on the GA according to the nature of the composition.

The CD-ROM includes a genetic algorithm application that simply evolves bit strings with as many bits as possible set to one. I use such a simple example because the fitness function involved is particularly straightforward. The use of this process for other applications involves a redesign of the interpretation of the bit strings and an associated fitness function—much of the evolutionary mechanism (crossover, mutation) can remain as written. Beyond this example, genetic algorithms (like neural networks) are well documented on the internet and many working environments can be found with a simple keyword search.

Figure 6.3 shows the definition of the genetic algorithm class. Most of the member functions follow the preceding discussion: the function `Fitness()`, for example, is a routine that determines the fitness of a particular chromosome. `SelectParent()` will choose a parent for the next generation of offspring according to how highly it is rated by `Fitness()`.

```
class GA {
private:

        typedef struct {              // used for sorting chromosomes

                int fitness;

                int ID;

                int odds;

        } SortRecord;


        int             bitLength;       // number of bits in string

        SortRecord*     sort;            // array of sort records

        int             populationSize;  // # of chromosomes in population

        Chromosome** population;         // current population

        Chromosome** newPopulation;      // next generation


public.

        GA(void);

        ~GA(void);

        void            Generation(void);


private:

        int             Fitness(Chromosome* x);

        void            Mutate(Chromosome* x);

        Chromosome* SelectParent(Chromosome** population);

        Chromosome* SelectParent(Chromosome** population,

                                        Chromosome* noCopy);

        void        SortPopulation(void);
};
```

Figure 6.3 Genetic Algorithm class definition

```
class Chromosome {
private:

    int         bitVector;          // string of bits

    int         bitLength;          // length of bit string

    float       crossoverRate;      // percentage of crossover (0..1)

    float       mutationRate;       // percentage of mutation   (0..1)

    int         fitness;            // fitness rating


public:

    Chromosome(int bitLength);


    int         BitVector(void) const { return bitVector; }

    int         Fitness(void)    const { return fitness;   }

    void        Mutate(void);

    void        SetFitness(int f)    { fitness = f; }
};
```

Figure 6.4 Chromosome class definition

   The Chromosome class is shown in figure 6.4. The data and
functions are again related directly to the preceding discussion of
GAs: each Chromosome maintains its own fitness rating, as well as
floating point rates of crossover and mutation. Finally figure 6.5
shows how each new generation is spawned. First the fitness of each
chromosome in the current population is evaluated. A new population is generated from the fittest parents using crossover, and offspring are mutated according to their mutation rate. The GA
application on the CD-ROM uses this code to evolve a population of
bit strings with as many ones as possible from an initially random
collection.

```
void GA::Generation(void)
{
    for (int i=0; i<populationSize; i++) {
        Chromosome* x = population[i];
        x->SetFitness(Fitness(x));
    }


    newPopulation = new Ptr[populationSize];
    i = 0;
    while (i < populationSize) {
        Chromosome* dad = SelectParent(population);
        Chromosome* mom = SelectParent(population, dad);
        Chromosome* son      = new Chromosome(dad, mom);
        Chromosome* daughter = new Chromosome(dad, mom);
        Mutate(son);
        Mutate(daughter);
        newPopulation[i++] = son;
        if (i < populationSize)
            newPopulation[i++] = daughter;
    }
}
```

Figure 6.5 Generation function

6.3.2 Artificial Agent Societies

A burgeoning field of research within artificial intelligence involves the design and implementation of autonomous software agents. The explosive growth of the internet and of the information the internet makes available gives rise to a demand for independent entities that can search through the wide universe of available resources and return those that will benefit a client, human or otherwise. The paradigmatic example of such an agent is one that goes off to book the most desirable (in terms of cost and speed) transportation between two points. It may be that the agent looking for the ticket encounters other software agents representing airlines or travel agencies and then needs to negotiate with them in order to arrive at the best solution.

In *Interactive Music Systems* (1993) I described simple listening processes as agents, and larger operations involving several such analyzers as agencies. This usage borrowed from Marvin Minsky's book, *The Society of Mind* [Minsky 1986] and corresponded to ideas in that text that inspired the control structure of my program, Cypher. Since then, the field of software agents has grown remarkably, and with it the uses to which the term agent has been put: "ultimately terms and notions become increasingly watered, so that the same term may refer to a very concrete technology or to almost every entity within DAI [Distributed Artificial Intelligence]. A prominent example constitutes the term 'agent' which may denominate everything from a computational 'neurone' up to a complex expert system" (Ossowski 1999, 31).

Sascha Ossowski's own use of the term agent shows interesting similarities to the description of an interactive music system: "Agents are conceived as situated systems, being in continuous interaction with the outside world. Consequently, the basic architecture of such an agent is then made up of three components: sensors, which transmit data to a cognition component, which communicates action commands to effectors" (Ossowski 1999, 36). Interactive music systems similarly receive information from sensors, perform calculations based on that information, and send commands to synthesizers or other sound processors (effectors) in response.

NetNeg is a hybrid artificial intelligence model for producing first species counterpoint in real time (Goldman et al. 1999). NetNeg is interesting for our purposes for several reasons: first, because it is deliberately designed to work in real time using information as it becomes available: "dealing with the problem of creating music in real time opens up the possibility of building real time interactive applications that combine the activities of a musician and a computer" (Goldman et al. 1999, 71). This orientation means that the system is not permitted to backtrack during the production of counterpoint: previous solutions are assumed already to have been played as they were generated.

Second, NetNeg is an example of a hybrid system combining symbolic and sub-symbolic components. One subsystem is a sequential neural network that learns to produce new melodies; a second subsystem consists of two agents, one responsible for the behavior of each voice. One of the central problems of Multiagent Systems (MAS) is the design of control structures in which agents with their own, sometimes conflicting, agendas can develop a form of cooperation that will allow them to accomplish tasks collectively that none of them could achieve independently. Control structures are further complicated in NetNeg by the subsymbolic component, another source of information that must be coordinated with the agents to generate satisfactory counterpoint.

The scheme used in NetNeg sends separate output vectors from the sequential net to each of the voice agents.

On the one hand, each agent has to act according to its voice's aesthetic criteria; and on the other hand, it has to regard the other voice-agent such that both together will result in a two-part counterpoint. Both agents have to negotiate over all the other possible combinations to obtain a globally superior result. Thus, they influence the context with their agreement. Given this new context and the initial

values of the plan units, the network will predict another output vec-
tor. This process continues sequentially until the melodies are com-
pleted. (Goldman et al. 1999, 78)

NetNeg can compose convincing examples of two-part counterpoint. More importantly, the performance of the system as a whole
is better than can be achieved by either subsystem alone. The design
of NetNeg demonstrates that real-time hybrid systems can work in a
live context and that the flexibility arising from a combination of
several strategies, both symbolic and sub-symbolic, improves the
musical quality of the results.

Goto and Muraoka report a parallel agent-based program that can
find the beat in an acoustic representation of popular music recordings in real time (1994). The agents in their beat-tracking system
(BTS) simultaneously examine multiple theories of the current beat
period and calculate their reliability. At any given point the most
reliable hypothesis is broadcast from the BTS as the current beat.
(This strategy is, in some respects, similar to my multiple attractors
algorithm, described in chapter 3).

The input to BTS is an acoustic signal from a CD player. After
digitization the basic unit of calculation is a buffer of 256 samples,
referred to within the system as one time frame. A fast fourier transform (FFT) is performed on four frames at a time, providing a window size of 1024 samples. With each new calculation of the FFT the
earliest frame from the last FFT is removed and one new frame
added, giving a time resolution of 256 samples. The main purpose
of the FFT is to find note onsets and to isolate the bass drum and
snare drum components of the sound.

Bass and snare drum sounds are important because BTS uses regularities of drum playing in popular music to locate the beat. "Multiple agents interpret the results of the Frequency Analysis stage and
maintain their own hypotheses, each of which consists of next beat
time predicted, its beat type, its reliability, and current IBI [inter-
beat-interval]" (Goto and Muraoka 1994, 368). Different agents employ different strategies to look for the beat: one technique compares

Figure 6.6 Cindy dancing to the BTS

the detected bass and snare onsets to stored drum patterns and reports beat information from the pattern that best matches the input. BTS tracks the beat of its target music style remarkably well, to the point that animated dancers can synchronize with the beat of arbitrary compact disc recordings of popular music in real time (figure 6.6).

The BTS in 1994 could locate the tactus, or quarter-note beat level. An extension reported in 1997 finds not only the quarter-note level but also higher-level pulses including the half-bar and the bar (assuming 4 beats to a bar). Detecting the higher levels involves recognizing strong and weak beats of a meter, not simply a multiplication of the quarter-note pulse by two or four. Besides metric structure, the 1997 program employs music knowledge to find the pulse of drumless performances as well. Though this brings the work closer to MIDI-based beat trackers, the authors note the difficulty in attempting a direct translation: "Musical knowledge that is useful for analyzing musical scores or MIDI signals, however, cannot immediately be applied to raw audio signals because of the difficulty of obtaining MIDI-like representations of those signals" (Goto and Muraoka 1997a, 136).

The heuristic employed to approximate MIDI information is to notice chord changes in the input and mark their onsets as more likely beat locations. The chord changes are found without identifying the names of the chords or indeed of any of their constituent pitches. In this the program is similar to a musically untrained listener who can sense changes in harmony without knowing which chords make up a progression. BTS uses the prevailing beat theory to delineate quarter-note and eighth-note beat "strips." The expectation of the beat agents, then, acts as a top-down attentional device, focusing sensitivity for chord changes on particular temporal spans.

FFT data within each strip is used to calculate a histogram of salient frequencies. To detect chord changes, BTS compares the histograms of adjacent strips and assigns a chord change probability to the transition between them according to the magnitude of their differences (figure 6.7). This information directs the assignment of metric structure, using the following "quarter-note-level knowledge: Chords are more likely to change at the beginnings of measures than at other positions. In other words, the quarter-note chord

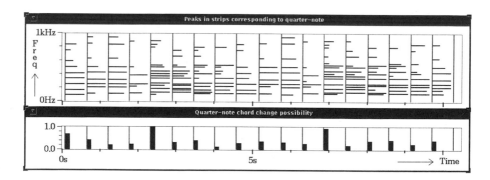

Figure 6.7 FFT strips indicating chord boundaries

change possibility tends to be higher on a strong beat than on a weak beat and higher on the strong beat at the beginning of a measure than on the other strong beat in the measure" (Goto and Muraoka 1997a, 138).

Musical knowledge about chords, then, helps not only to confirm the placement of beat boundaries, but to identify those beats that are more salient and therefore likely to be the strong beats of the measure.

The agent architecture of BTS comprises, in the 1997 version, twelve agents grouped into six agent-pairs. The two agents in a pair maintain rival hypotheses that predict beats one half inter-beat interval away from each other. The heightened sensitivity of one agent in a pair around the expected arrival of its beat serves to inhibit the sensitivity of the other. The six pairs differ from each other in their parameter settings, which direct each of them to evaluate distinct aspects of the audio analyses. Besides the FFT itself, the audio analysis conducts auto-correlations and cross-correlations of onset times in several frequency bins. The frequencies examined and the settings of the correlations, then, are the parameters used to differentiate agent theories.

Each agent computes its own reliability based on the accuracy of its predictions and the input of the chord-change heuristic. The most reliable agent's theory at any given point is taken as the output of the system as a whole. In a quantitative evaluation system they developed, Goto and Muraoka found that the BTS "correctly tracked beats at the quarter-note level in 35 of the 40 songs (87.5%) and correctly recognized the half-note level in 34 of the 35 songs (97.1%) in which the correct beat times were obtained" (1997b, 13).

BTS and NetNeg both demonstrate the power of artificial agent systems to reconcile the sometimes conflicting information arising from a variety of analysis processes. That this arbitration and control can be executed in real time promises more consistent and effective ways to manage similar complexities in interactive performance systems.

6.4 Expressive Performance

The realization by a sequencer of a strictly quantized score sounds lifeless, as anyone who has more than a passing acquaintance with sequencers knows. Human musicians make temporal, dynamic, and timbral deviations from the written score to express an interpretation of the music. Some of this deviation results from different levels of technique and the simple foibles of human musculature, but research of the last few decades has shown that much variation is intentional and carefully controlled by skilled performers (Palmer 1989). To some degree expression varies with the temperament of the player, but it is largely determined by the structure of the composition being performed: "Thus the expressive changes that accompany changes in performance tempo are based on structural properties of the music, and can be characterized as the transformation of latent expressive possibilities into manifest expressive features in accordance with the dictates of tempo and musical structure" (Clarke 1988, 12).

Eric Clarke showed that the performed timing of notes is affected by their metric position (1985). Three interacting principles lead to the deviation: (1) the stronger the metric position occupied by a note, the more likely it is to be held longer, and, conversely, the weaker the metric position of a note, the more likely it is to be shortened; (2) notes that complete musical groups are lengthened (at several levels of grouping); and (3) the note *before* a structurally prominent note is often lengthened. "This demonstrates that the relative duration of a note is a property that emerges from the interaction of a number of features that include its symbolic representation, its metrical position and position within a group, and its melodic and harmonic significance" (Clarke 1985, 214).

Clarke's work measured the influence of musical structure on expression. A study carried out at the University of Padova focused on the impact of a player's expressive intentions. The group had performers play short excerpts while trying to realize various expressive qualities: light, heavy, soft, hard, bright, and dark. Then listeners were asked to characterize the performances and a comparison was made between the performer's intention and the listener's experience. Factor analysis demonstrated that the variations indicated by the listeners closely matched the expressive intent and could be largely explained by two independent variables. "The first factor (bright vs. dark) seemed to be closely correlated to the tempo, while the second factor (soft vs. hard) was connected to the amplitude envelope of the notes, and particularly to the attack time" (Canazza et al. 1997, 115).

Such evidently controllable and rule-oriented relationships between structure, intention, and expression has led a number of researchers to design algorithms that can add expression to a quantized score. As we have noticed in other areas, both symbolic and subsymbolic processes have been explored in the search for algorithmic expression. In the case of the Padova group, the information gathered from the factor analysis was used to design a system that could automatically vary synthesis parameters to produce expressive intentions from the original group of adjectives: light, heavy, soft, etc. (Canazza et al. 1998).

6.4.1 Rule-Based Systems

One of the most highly developed expressive performance systems has been implemented over a period of years by Johan Sundberg and his colleagues at the Swedish Royal Institute of Technology (KTH) in Stockholm (Sundberg, Friberg, and Frydén 1991; Friberg 1991). The KTH program takes an entire score as input and outputs a MIDI representation with expression added as determined by a rule set. "The music score is written into a Macintosh microcomputer, which controls a synthesizer over MIDI. Expressive deviations are automatically generated by a set of ordered, context dependent performance rules. These rules can be said explicitly and exhaustively to describe all the expressive deviations that are present in the computer generated performance" (Sundberg, Friberg, and Frydén 1991, 163).

The KTH system is an instance of analysis/synthesis in that an expert performer (Lars Frydén, a professional violinist) suggested

rules based on his experience and commented on their effect in simulated performances. The rules affect duration, sound level, sound
level envelope, vibrato, and pitch deviations. There are two primary
categories of rules: "Some rules appear to help the listener to *identify
pitch* and *duration categories.* Rules serving this purpose will be referred to as *differentiation* rules. Other rules seem to help the listener
to *group tones* which form melodic Gestalts of various lengths. These
rules will be referred to as *grouping rules*" (Sundberg, Friberg, and
Frydén 1991, 165).

Each rule is applied independently over the entire performance
before the next one is considered. Clearly this eliminates the system
as designed from real-time application. Many of the rules can be directly adapted to onstage use, however. Consider the first duration
differentiation rule: "*DDC 1A The shorter, the shorter* shortens short
notes and lengthens long notes depending on their absolute nominal
duration" (Sundberg, Friberg, and Frydén 1991, 166). Because it depends only on the absolute duration of the note, DDC 1A can easily
be applied in real time if the duration of a note to be output is known
at the time that it is attacked. Let us look at a simple expression
function that can apply DDC 1A to the output of a compositional
algorithm.

This implementation of DDC1A follows the chart published by
Sundberg, Friberg, and Frydén (1991, 166). The data described in the
chart actually does not lengthen long notes, it just doesn't shorten
them. In figure 6.8 we look for progressively longer durations and
perform the corresponding reduction when the duration of the note
we are handling is less than the current threshold. Because we return
from the function whenever the duration is found to be within the
currently considered bound, we ensure that the same note will never
be modified twice.

In the KTH rule set, DDC1A not only modifies the articulation of
the affected notes but changes the effective beat duration as well.
That is because the span of time subtracted from the target notes is
not replaced by a pause. Any reduction of the note durations then
shortens the length of the beat containing them as well. We may add

```
Expression::DDC1A(Note* n)

{

    if (n->duration <  50) return;     // very short durations unchanged

    if (n->duration < 150) {           //  50-150 shortened by 2 ms

        n->duration -= 2;

        return;

    }

    if (n->duration < 200) {           // 150-200 shortened by 5 ms

        n->duration -= 5;

        return;

    }

    if (n->duration < 500) {           // 200-500 shortened by 3 ms

        n->duration -= 3;

        return;

    }

}
```

Figure 6.8 Expression Rule DDC1A

this effect to the implementation in figure 6.8 by shortening the IOI of the following Event, as shown in figure 6.9.

The KTH system references a quantity control that functions as a kind of volume knob, determining how pronounced the effect of each rule on the output of the system should be. The effect could be written into a rule like DDC1A by adding a floating point quantity parameter and using that to multiply all of the constant adjustments coded into the routines of figures 6.8 and 6.9.

The second duration differentiation rule, DDC1B, can also easily be applied in real time, again assuming that the duration of the note to be output is known at attack time: "*DDC 1B The shorter, the softer*

```
Expression::DDC1A(Note* n)

{

  if (n->duration  <   50) return;    // very short durations unchanged

  if (n->duration >= 500) return;    // long durations unchanged


  Event* prev = n->Event()->Prev();

  if (n->duration < 150) {             //  50-150 shortened by 2 ms

    n->duration -= 2;

    prev->SetIOI(prev->IOI()-2);

    return;

  }

  if (n->duration < 200) {             // 150-200 shortened by 5 ms

    n->duration -= 5;

    prev->SetIOI(prev->IOI()-5);

    return;

  }

  if (n->duration < 500) {             // 200-500 shortened by 3 ms

    n->duration -= 3;

    prev->SetIOI(prev->IOI()-3);

    return;

  }

}
```

Figure 6.9 Reduction with beat shortening

reduces the sound level of notes in proportion to their inverted duration" (Sundberg, Friberg, and Frydén 1991, 166). DDC1A and 1B taken together serve to deemphasize short notes, particularly in contrast to long notes that may succeed them. When they are applied they tend to make short notes leading to a long one sound like anticipations of the longer event. The Expression application on the CD-ROM is an implementation of DDC1A and DDC1B together with a simple compositional algorithm that makes it possible to hear a performance of the output with or without the effect of the rules.

The model of musical expression developed by Neil Todd relies on the observation that phrases are often articulated by a crescendo/decrescendo shape. Todd expresses this principle as follows: "*Proposition:* (a) a group is phrased by a crescendo/decrescendo shape; (b) the particular shape is a function of structural importance; (c) musical dynamics is coupled to tempo" (1992, 3542). His approach is thoroughly computational and therefore requires that he be able to formally declare the relationship between groups and functions of expression. One important principle of the system is that tempo and dynamic fluctuations within a phrase will be correlated. That is, as the performance gets louder it gets faster, and as it gets softer it gets slower.

This correspondence between speed and loudness is connected to Todd's view of musical expression as an outgrowth of human kinematics: "The model of musical dynamics presented in this paper was based on two basic principles. First, that musical expression has its origins in simple motor actions and that the performance and perception of tempo/musical dynamics is based on an internal sense of motion. Second, that this internal movement is organized in a hierarchical manner corresponding to how the grouping or phrase structure is organized in the performer's memory" (Todd 1992, 3549).

Todd's model of musical expression produces some strikingly effective results and can be easily applied to the output of compositional algorithms that meet certain conditions. In particular, algorithms must generate entire phrases, or at least have planned their projected duration and structural role. Given these two parameters, a Todd performance module can shape the dynamics and speed of the nascent output.

6.4.2 Learning Expression

The KTH expressive performance rule set was developed through an analysis-by-synthesis process much like the knowledge acquisition development of an expert system. Neil Todd's model is a mathematical formulation of certain observations about tension, relaxation, and kinematics. Beyond these symbolic formulations, several research projects have developed methods capable of learning expression from examples.

Roberto Bresin's neural networks were developed initially to see whether the symbolic rules in the KTH system could be learned (1998). To this end artificial neural network (ANN) topologies were devised that used a number of input nodes equal to the number of parameters present in KTH rule conditions and a number of output nodes equal to the number of parameters that a KTH rule action could change.

The rules Bresin considered affect the performance of individual notes according to local context effects: "In this model the performance is regarded as a relation that computes time, and/or loudness deviations for the current note depending on some meaningful parameters possessed by the note itself. Thus we are dealing with a local model, based on a non-linear function with a short context" (1998, 242–243).

The networks trained to mimic the KTH rules use input and output nodes derived directly from the symbolic formulations. For example, the network used to compute loudness deviations has three input nodes and one output node that indicates the amount of deviation to apply (figure 6.10).

The inputs to the network are a note's duration, pitch, and "melodic charge." The melodic charge, developed in the KTH rules, measures the dissonance of a pitch relative to an underlying harmony. For example, against a C-major tonal context, the melodic charge of

Loudness Deviation

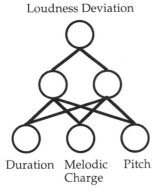

Duration   Melodic   Pitch
        Charge

Figure 6.10   Loudness Deviation Network

the pitch class C is 0 while the charge of F♯, because of its dissonance relative to C, is 6 (Sundberg et al. 1991). Bresin developed a training set from deviations output by the symbolic rules. The loudness deviation network shown in figure 6.10, for example, was trained using outputs from the symbolic rules *High loud, Durational contrast,* and *Melodic charge.* The same procedure was applied to a second network trained to make changes to the duration and off-time duration (offset-to-onset interval) of a note.

Bresin conducted a listening test in which subjects were asked to rate three performances of a Mozart fragment: (1) deadpan, with no expressive variation; (2) varied using the KTH rule set; and (3) varied using ANNs trained by the KTH rule set. The subjects clearly preferred the KTH and ANN performances to the deadpan rendering, and even showed a slight preference for the neural network performance overall.

The KTH rule set applies each rule to the score as a whole before passing to the next. "A reason for the slight preference of the ANN-versions to the rules-versions would be that the deviations in the performance depended on contributions from many rules. When only one of these contributions is responsible for the deviations, then ANNs and KTH rules give identical results. When more than one rule is activated, the additive behavior of the KTH rule system . . . and the interpolation properties of the neural networks . . . yield different results" (Bresin 1998, 251–252).

As discussed in section 6.4.1, the KTH rule system must be adapted for real-time applications because of the additive control structure used to execute them. The neural networks Bresin trained to replicate the KTH rules form just such an adaptation, as they simultaneously apply rules that in the symbolic system are executed sequentially. Interestingly, Bresin's listening experiment indicates that their simultaneous action in the neural net may produce results superior to those obtained by the sequential application regime of the original. In any case, its parallel operation and reliance on very local contexts make the Bresin ANN implementation a practical and trainable engine for real-time expressive performance.

The SaxEx system described by Arcos, Mántaras, and Serra (1998) uses a case-based reasoning system to learn expressive modifications of saxophone sounds. "Case-based Reasoning . . . (CBR) is a recent approach to problem solving and learning where a new problem is solved by finding a set of similar previously solved problems, called cases, and reusing them in the new problem situation. The CBR paradigm covers a family of methods that may be described in a common subtask decomposition: the *retrieve* task, the *reuse* task, the *revise* task, and the *retain* task" (Arcos, Mántaras, and Serra 1998, 196).

Retrieval means finding a previously solved problem, or case, by matching features of the new problem to features of the known cases. Reuse means applying a solution to the new example that was found to work with a known example, since this has been determined to be similar to the stored case. "When the solution generated by the reuse task is not correct, an opportunity for learning arises. The revision phase involves detecting the errors of the current solution and modifying the solution using repair techniques" (Arcos, Mántaras, and Serra 1998, 198). Finally, the retain process adds a newly solved problem to the collection of solved cases and the process begins again.

In SaxEx, the cases involve transforming the resynthesis of saxophone sounds such that they exhibit expressive traits similar to those produced by human performers in comparable musical situations. Notes are represented as events, and each event knows about expressive modifications of dynamics, rubato, vibrato, articulation, and types of attack. SaxEx has successfully learned strategies of expression that can be transferred from training examples to new input performances. It is unique both in its application of CBR and in its attention to the synthesis parameters of the sound of the performance. Sound examples can be found on the group's website (www.iiia.csic.es).

Gerhard Widmer has developed symbolic techniques that learn to add expressive performance variations to a "flat" score in the form of dynamic changes and tempo rubato. Early versions learned expression related to the function of notes within a context (Widmer 1993, 1995). Each note was assigned structural roles that designated its metric position, placement in a group, and the like. Widmer used MIDI recordings of performances of the analyzed work as training examples. The system learned to make particular expressive modifications to notes based on their structural characteristics. As a result, the program "discovered" some of the same expressive performance rules formulated by Sundberg and his colleagues in the KTH analysis-by-synthesis system.

More recently the focus of learning has migrated to higher-level organizations of the music: "It is by matching the observed dynamics or tempo variations against structural aspects of the piece and recognizing regularities in the way particular structures are being shaped by a performer that effective learning becomes possible" (Widmer 1996, 182). As before, learning is preceded by an analysis phase in which structural descriptors are attached to groups and the notes within them. The most important organizations are adapted from the Lerdahl and Jackendoff metric and grouping preference rules, and parts of Eugene Narmour's Implication-Realization theory. Markings indicating these structures are added to the MIDI score, some by an automated process and some by hand.

Once the structures are tagged, they are associated with prototypical shapes indicating both their dynamic and temporal evolution.

There are five shapes: even (no change), ascending, descending, ascending/descending, and descending/ascending. For example, an ascending dynamic variation is a crescendo and a descending one is a decrescendo. An ascending/descending tempo shape produces an accelerando followed by a ritardando.

Training examples for the learning phase, then, consist of musical structures paired with expressive shapes. Structures are encoded as a type (e.g., measure or phrase) together with a description of its music-theoretic features (e.g., metric placement, harmonic function, etc.). Shapes are encoded as a type (one of the five listed above) and a quantitative measure indicating the deviation of the extreme points of the shape with respect to an average loudness or tempo.

The symbolic learning component finds instances of musical structures that are associated with a particular expressive shape. It gathers together all of the feature characteristics that are found in positive examples (for example, those found to be coupled to a descending shape) and eliminates those that are also true of other shapes. Because these rules are formulated symbolically, we may examine the criteria on which its performance decisions are based. As an example, one rule produced by this process asserts that a ritardando (descending temporal shape) should be applied to triadic melodic continuations that occur early in a phrase and are also part of a "rhythmic gap fill" figure (Widmer 1996, 188).

Figure 6.11 shows a melodic fragment that fulfills the conditions required by the example. The "rhythmic gap fill" is a series of short

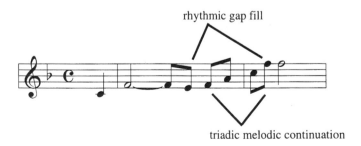

Figure 6.11 Expressive structure

durations connecting two longer ones, and the "triadic melodic continuation" outlines a triad within a larger gesture. Because all conditions of the rule are fulfilled here, a performance by Widmer's learner will play this figure with a decelerando.

The system can learn nested structures as well. That is, the phrase level figure shown in figure 6.11 might be subsumed in a larger motion that is associated with a different expressive shape. When the learner performs such hierarchically related structures it averages the effect of the two to arrive at one local variation.

Widmer tested the impact of structure-level descriptions on the efficacy of the resulting rules by comparing performances generated by three different strategies: (1) note-level simple descriptions (pitch, metric position, etc.); (2) note-level descriptions with structural backgrounds; and (3) structure-level descriptions. The training examples were taken from performances of Schumann's *Träumerei* by Claudio Arrau, Vladimir Ashkenazy, and Alfred Brendel, as collected by Bruno Repp (Repp 1992).

Rules learned by analyzing the second half of the pianists' renditions using the three strategies were subsequently applied to the first half of the composition, after which the experts' and the machine's performances were compared. A significant improvement in the agreement between the machine and expert performances emerged as more structural knowledge was incorporated. Weighted for metrical strength (a rough measure of salience), the first strategy yielded agreement of 52.19%, the second 57.1%, and the third 66.67% (Widmer 1996, 200).

Gerhard Widmer's expressive learning system relates to the goals of machine musicianship in several ways: its symbolic orientation produces rules that can be executed algorithmically as long as the relevant structural characteristics can be recognized. The application of expressive shapes to timing and dynamics can similarly be accomplished in an interactive system if a generated phrase is available for modification before it is performed.

Generally the application of expression rules requires a significant degree of planning. A program must analyze at least one full phrase before it is played to apply structural rules successfully. This corresponds to human performance, which is most expressive when musicians know where the music is heading.

As interactive systems apply such rules in real time, they may become more eloquent performers at the same time that they become more independent from their surroundings. Because they would be responding phrase-by-phrase rather than note-by-note, the correspondence between the machine musician and its human partners would rely even more critically on the program's ability to successfully predict the continuation of the performance. When the expression of hierarchical layers is added, the operation of this method becomes even further removed from real time as longer and longer spans must be analyzed to find appropriate shapes. It may be that Widmer's earlier note-level analysis, though less accurate in emulating expert performance of known scores, would yield more tractable rules for interactive systems that cannot fully predict what comes next.

7 Interactive Improvisation

Interactive improvisation poses perhaps the greatest challenge for machine musicianship. Here the machine must contribute a convincing musical voice in a completely unstructured and unpredictable environment. Accordingly, it is in improvisation that some kind of machine musicianship may be most important: because the material and the development of the material is unknown in advance, the program must be able to rely on some kind of musical common sense in order to both derive structure from what it hears, and impose structure on what it produces in response.

The difficulty of producing improvisation of any kind, but new music improvisation in particular, is evoked by Olivier Messiaen's description of his own method:

These improvisations became little by little one improvisation, always forgotten, always rediscovered, always repeated: the terrifying growls of the Beast of the Apocalypse alternated with the songs of Thrushes and Blackbirds, the sounds of water and wind in the leaves with the religious meditation and storms of joy of the Holy Spirit, Hindu rhythms combined with plainchant neumes, choruses of Larks with Tibetan trumpets, melodies of resonance and timbre with the chromaticism of duration, the most searching polymodalities, the strangest and most shimmering timbres next to the most restrained rhythmic permutations and inversions. (1997, 83 [my trans.])

In his article "Generative Principles in Music Performance," Eric Clarke postulates three principles of organization that an improviser could use during performance:

A complete performance will consist of a large number of . . . events, organized in different ways, and related to [a] first event according

*to three possible principles: (1) The first event may be part of a hierar-
chical structure, to some extent worked out in advance, and to some
extent constructed in the course of the improvisation. . . . (2) The
first event may be part of an associative chain of events, each new
event derived from the previous sequence by the forward transfer of
information. . . . (3) The first event may be selected from a number
of events contained within the performer's repertoire, the rest of the
improvisation consisting of further selections from this same repertoire, with a varying degree of relatedness between selections. (1988,
8–9)*

Clarke goes on to theorize that improvisation styles can be characterized by their combination of these three strategies. "The improvising style known as free jazz is principally characterized by
associative structure, since it eschews the constraints of a pre-
planned structure, and attempts to avoid the use of recognizable
'riffs'" (1988, 10). He similarly characterizes traditional jazz as being
more hierarchical because of the importance of the harmonic structure, and bebop as more selective "in the way in which a performer
may try to construct an improvisation so as to include as many
'quotes' from other sources as possible (ranging from other jazz
pieces to national anthems)" (1988, 10).

There is no general machine improviser yet. Though improvisation
systems do not know what will happen in performance, they generally are programmed to participate in music of a particular style. Bebop improvisers have been implemented that would sound out of
place in a performance of free jazz, and new-music-style improvisers
cannot play the blues. Ultimately the ongoing research in style
analysis/synthesis may make it possible to write a machine improviser that could recognize the stylistic characteristics of the music
being played and adapt its contribution accordingly. Style-specific
improvisers have already proven their artistic merit, however, and
still benefit from an analysis of the musical context even when that
context is essentially restricted a priori.

In this chapter I will discuss a number of case studies, systems
developed by composer/improvisers for improvising interactively

onstage. Examples in Max and C++ will be developed as a way of more fully explaining their approach. Finally, I will describe the structure of my program Cypher, though a much more complete description may be found elsewhere (Rowe 1993). In this text I will concentrate on an expansion of the original version that addresses ensemble improvisation.

7.1 Sequences in Improvisation

In chapter 5 I outlined three classes of compositional algorithms that typify interactive systems. One of these classes, sequencing, presents pre-established material in multiple guises during performance. We will discuss improvisation with sequences in connection with the work of Richard Teitelbaum, one of the first and most influential practitioners of interactive improvisation. From his beginnings as a founder of Musica Elettronica Viva through the Digital Piano (for which he won the Prix Ars Elettronica in 1986) to his current work with Max, Teitelbaum has used an improviser's sensibility to design a series of systems that produce music algorithmically in response to his live performance.

Here is a description Teitelbaum wrote of the processes operating in his *Solo for Three Pianos:* "Music played live by the pianist on one piano keyboard is sensed and instantly read into computer memory where it can be stored, overlayed, delayed, transposed, inverted, randomized, and otherwise manipulated before being passed on to the other two pianos for playback at the performer's behest. This may be done either simultaneously, or at a selectable delay time, or stored for future recall" (1982).

This study will examine some aspects of software Richard Teitelbaum developed in collaboration with Eric Singer for Teitelbaum's composition SEQ TRANSMIT PARAMMERS (1998), written for pianist Ursula Oppens and an interactive music system. Though the sequencing capabilities form only a small part of the interaction in that work, we will concentrate on it here as an example of an elaborated system developed through many years of experimentation.

Interactive systems, particularly those involving improvisation, cede a significant measure of responsibility to the performer onstage as a co-creator of the work. SEQ TRANSMIT PARAMMERS takes that collaboration a step farther by giving the player an opportunity to invent her own presets before the performance begins. During the show the patch's sensitivity to pianistic technique (velocity, articulation, etc.) ensures a direct relationship between the soloist's expression and the algorithmic response.

7.1.1 SeqSelect

Teitelbaum's improvisation systems have long included techniques for recording, transforming, and playing back musical material during the course of a performance. The Max patch developed for SEQ TRANSMIT PARAMMERS has a number of objects devoted to these operations. We will examine SeqSelect, a subpatch that provides compact management of a group of up to nine sequences. Obviously, nine is an arbitrary number and could be adjusted up or down simply by changing the number of seq objects in the patch.

SeqSelect has two inlets at the top of the patch (figure 7.1). The first accepts messages for the embedded seq objects, such as play and stop. (Seq is a Max object that records, reads, writes, and plays back MIDI files.) Note that SeqSelect uses the seq objects for playback only—all of the material to be read out has been prepared previously. The second inlet to SeqSelect gets a sequence number, selecting the corresponding internal sequence to receive subsequent seq messages through the other inlet until it is overridden by another selection.

The gate and switch objects route messages through the patch. The sequence selector arriving at the second inlet is sent to the control inlets of both gate and switch. In the case of gate, this routes all messages arriving at the right inlet to the corresponding outlet of the gate. Similarly, switch will send anything arriving at the selected input through to its outlet (switch looks and behaves rather like an upside-down gate). The switch routes the bangs that are sent when a seq object completes playback of a file.

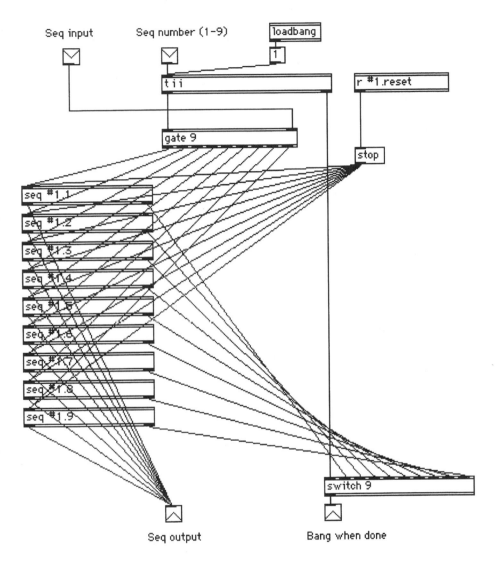

Figure 7.1 SeqSelect

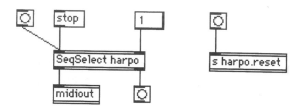

Figure 7.2 Minimal Interface

The two outlets of SeqSelect are identical to the two outlets of an ordinary seq object. The first outputs MIDI messages for transmission to midiout and the second transmits a bang when the sequence has finished playing. Finally, the #1 notation in the patch is used to set the name of a series of sequencer files and a reset message. When the SeqSelect object is instantiated, the name given as an argument will replace #1 anywhere in the patch it appears.

The minimal interface shown in figure 7.2 is the most straightforward way to address SeqSelect. The bang and stop buttons at the upper left start and stop playback of the selected sequence, respectively (note that the loadbang object in SeqSelect initially sets the sequence number to one in the absence of user input). The patch directs sequenced MIDI messages from the left outlet to midiout. The right outlet transmits a bang when the sequence has finished. Another bang is connected to a send object (abbreviated to s) that broadcasts to the receiver harpo.reset. The reset receiver built into SeqSelect sends a stop message to all nine sequencers. Note that the name argument to SeqSelect and the reset sender ("harpo") must match. The menu attached to the right inlet of SeqSelect allows the user to switch from one sequence to another.

A second interface to SeqSelect (figure 7.3) offers an automatic way to read through every file sequentially. The bang button above SeqSelect starts the first sequence playing. The bang issued at the end of the sequence increments a counter that sets the sequence number to two. The bang also travels to a switch and propagates back through to SeqSelect, starting playback of sequence two. This continues until the last sequence has been set, sequence nine. At that

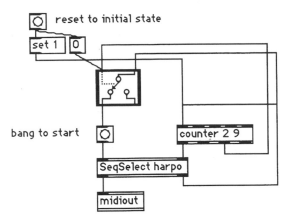

Figure 7.3 Sequential Playback

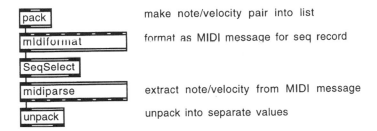

make note/velocity pair into list

format as MIDI message for seq record

extract note/velocity from MIDI message

unpack into separate values

Figure 7.4 MIDI Message Wrapping

point the overflow flag will be sent from the third outlet of the counter and change the switch to direct its input to the right outlet, leading nowhere. Now when the next bang comes from finding the end of sequence nine, it will not feed back around to SeqSelect but rather fall into empty space, ending the sequential playback. Note that at the end of this process the machine will no longer work—for one thing, the graphic switch will be set to the wrong position. The bang button at the top of the patch will reinitialize everything so that the process could be run through again.

In Teitelbaum's own use of SeqSelect, the object is wrapped with pack/unpack and midiformat/midiparse pairs as shown in figure 7.4. These surrounding pairs are used to make MIDI messages of

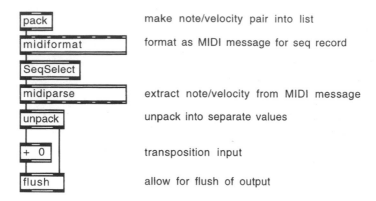

pack	make note/velocity pair into list
midiformat	format as MIDI message for seq record
SeqSelect	
midiparse	extract note/velocity from MIDI message
unpack	unpack into separate values
+ 0	transposition input
flush	allow for flush of output

Figure 7.5 Transposition

incoming pitch and velocity values, and then to unwrap the resulting MIDI messages to retrieve the original pitch and velocity. The point of the exercise is both to make available the individual components of the MIDI channel voice messages handled by the seq objects, and to allow new pitch and velocity values to be recorded inside SeqSelect.

The + object appended after unpack in figure 7.5, for example, provides for the input of a transposition value. Any new integer sent to the right inlet of the + is added to the pitch numbers of all MIDI messages coming from the sequences managed in SeqSelect. The flush object ensures that all sounding notes can be sent a corresponding note off when necessary. This is to address a common problem with transposition operators: that the transposition level may be changed between a note on and a note off, causing the transposed notes to be turned off when the time comes and the original pitches to stay stuck on.

SEQ TRANSMIT PARAMMERS takes pitch values from MIDI input to control the transposition of sequence playback as shown in figure 7.6. Under certain conditions, a MIDI pitch number will be read from the stripnote object and 60 subtracted from the value. The trigger object (here abbreviated t) then carefully times the delivery of two bangs and the calculated transposition amount. The

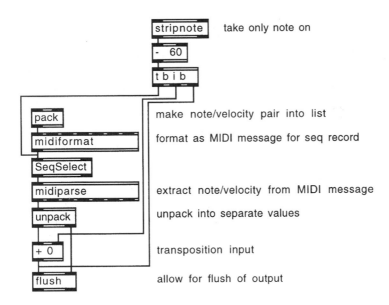

Figure 7.6 Transpose from Note Input

rightmost bang is transmitted first and flushes all sounding pitches from the output, avoiding hung notes whenever the transposition level is changed. Next the new transposition value is sent to the + object, and finally the leftmost bang will start playback of the currently selected sequence.

As each successive layer of the patch is added, we see the pattern of Teitelbaum's approach emerge: given a set of prerecorded musical materials, the improvisation software provides a range of tools for transposing, looping, and otherwise manipulating them during the performance. Figure 7.7 demonstrates how looping is added to the patch fragment developed thus far: the gate object inserted after SeqSelect feeds the bang emitted at the end of playback to the left inlet of SeqSelect. Because a bang is equivalent to a start message, playback of the same sequence will be recommenced, producing a loop of the sequence until the gate is closed.

The final extension to this fragment allows us to change the tempo of a sequence as it is being looped. Figure 7.8 shows the addition of

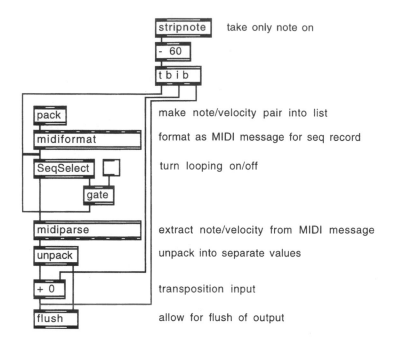

stripnote — take only note on

- 60

t b i b

pack — make note/velocity pair into list

midiformat — format as MIDI message for seq record

SeqSelect — turn looping on/off

gate

midiparse — extract note/velocity from MIDI message

unpack — unpack into separate values

+ 0 — transposition input

flush — allow for flush of output

Figure 7.7 Looping

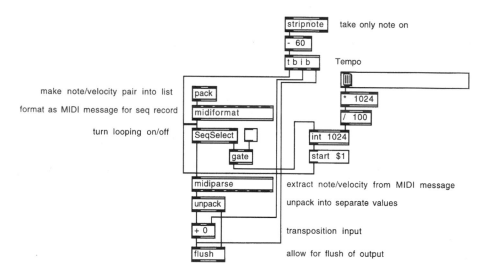

stripnote — take only note on

- 60

t b i b — Tempo

make note/velocity pair into list — pack

format as MIDI message for seq record — midiformat

* 1024

turn looping on/off — SeqSelect

/ 100

gate

int 1024

start $1

midiparse — extract note/velocity from MIDI message

unpack — unpack into separate values

+ 0 — transposition input

flush — allow for flush of output

Figure 7.8 Loop Tempo

a slider with some arithmetic attachments, an `int` object to store the output of the slider, and a start message box. Max uses integer values to set the playback tempo of a `seq` object, where a value of 1024 instructs `seq` to play back the sequence at its recorded tempo. A value of 2048 produces playback at twice the recorded tempo, a value of 512 playback at half the recorded tempo, and so on. The slider in figure 7.8 is initialized to send out values between 50 and 200. When the slider output is multiplied by 1024 and divided by 100, it will vary the playback speed of the `seq` object to between one half and twice the original tempo. At that point, the `bang` issuing from the gate (when it is open) does not proceed directly to `SeqSelect` but first passes through the `int` object (that keeps the integer value of the current tempo) and a message box that composes the message "start $1," where $1 is replaced by the value coming from the `int`. The start message is then routed to the left inlet of `SeqSelect`, causing the sequence to be looped using the most recent tempo set by the slider.

Richard Teitelbaum's interactive improvisation style makes extensive use of real-time recording and transformation of material from a human player. The Max fragment discussed in this section illustrates how programming elements are added to allow a greater variety of control over the transformation of the recorded materials. An interactive model of `SeqSelect` demonstrating several transformation techniques is included on the CD-ROM.

7.2 Influence on Improvisation Processes

When humans improvise together, players influence each other to fall in with certain kinds of textures, for example, or to adopt various melodic or rhythmic motives. The relationship is one of cooperation mixed with a degree of independence. When referring to the relationship between a human and a computer, it is more common to speak of control—that the human controls the machine. The improviser George Lewis, who has developed a highly regarded algorithmic improvisation program, often remarks that he designs the relationship between himself and the program to be one of mutual influence rather than one-way control.

Describing his Coordinated Electronic Music Studio system (1969) and Salvatore Martirano's SalMar Construction (1972), Joel Chadabe notes:

The CEMS system and the SalMar Construction were the first interactive composing instruments, which is to say that they made musical decisions, or at least seemed to make musical decisions, as they produced sound and as they responded to a performer. These instruments were interactive in the sense that performer and instrument were mutually influential. The performer was influenced by the music produced by the instrument, and the instrument was influenced by the performer's controls. These instruments introduced the concept of shared, symbiotic control of a musical process wherein the instrument's generation of ideas and the performer's musical judgment worked together to shape the overall flow of the music. (1997, 291)

Edmund Campion, in his composition/improvisation environment *Natural Selection,* similarly uses ideas of influence to organize the behavior of a large-scale algorithmic improviser written in Max. *Natural Selection* for MIDI piano and Max was composed at IRCAM in 1996, with programming by Tom Mays and Richard Dudas. Campion designed the first version of the work as an improvisation environment for himself performing on a MIDI grand piano and interacting with a Max patch called NatSel. The rules governing the operation of the patch are the same rules imparted to the performer who interacts with it. The construction and operation of NatSel express the fundamental compositional ideas of both the improvisation and the later piece: in many respects the patch is the piece. Richard Povall expresses a similar orientation to his own work: "The most difficult task at hand is to allow the *system* to *be* the composition— to allow both performer and system to interact with a degree of freedom that makes for a compelling, often surprisingly controlled outcome" (1995, 116).

NatSel's generation of material was influenced by an analysis of the harmonies and other features of the material being performed by the composer. "The patch was designed to follow the real-time composer/performer through a pre-defined, yet nonlinear landscape. The original version included a second keyboard controller as well as a Yamaha Disklavier. The second keyboard controller allowed the performer to leave the piano and take full control of every parameter of the patch, thus turning NatSel into an independent music generator. The first performance of *Natural Selection* was given in Paris on June 25, 1996 in the Espace de Projection at IRCAM" (Campion 1996).

The compositional algorithms of *Natural Selection* are predominately sequenced and generation techniques, in which stored materials are varied during performance as a function of the analysis of incoming musical gestures. There are three ways in which a human performer exerts influence over the patch: the first of these is the average onset velocity. For every incoming MIDI note event, the patch calculates the mean of the new and previous velocity values—in effect a simple low-pass filter on the performance dynamic.

The patch in figure 7.9 (avg2) keeps track of the most recent velocity, adds it to an incoming value, and returns the average of the two. Because we are using only one memory location (in the int object) to store previous velocity values, old values must be sent to the

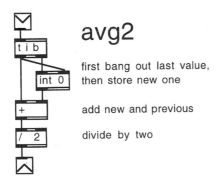

Figure 7.9 Average sub-patch

+ object before they are overwritten with the new ones. We arrange the correct order of processing with the `trigger` object. Messages are transmitted from a `trigger` in right-to-left order. The bang issuing from the rightmost outlet will first make `int` send its current value into the right inlet of +. Then the integer output of the trigger (from the left outlet) will overwrite the memory location in `int` and add itself to +. The / object divides the sum by two and sends the resulting average to the outlet of `avg2`.

Of course this patch will perform averaging on any sequence of numbers: in *Natural Selection* it is used on velocities but also to compute the average duration between successive note attacks, the second form of performer influence. Using `avg2` on these durations provides a running average of the inter-onset-intervals (IOIs) arriving from the performer. To avoid skewing the average when the performer is leaving a long rest, the program does not send IOIs beyond a certain threshold (about 1.5 seconds) to the averager.

The third and last form of influence derives from a comparison of incoming pitch combinations to a matrix. The matrix comprises 64 three-note combinations that are recognized when played either in sequence or as a chord, and 24 six-note combinations that are recognized only when played as chords. When a combination is found, the input processor issues an "influence" variable. Influence variables are used to change the presentation of sequences as well as to trigger and modify several independent note generation processes.

The performer can record sequences at will. These can be played back as recorded when triggered, or after transformation by one of the influence processes. One such process is called "3-exchange," which maps all of the notes in a recorded sequence to the pitches of the last identified tri-chord. The sub-patch `order-route` (figure 7.10) performs the mapping: MIDI note numbers enter through the inlet at the top. These are changed to pitch classes, and sent through a cascade of `select` objects. When an incoming pitch class matches one of the `select` arguments, the corresponding member of the tri-chord is passed to the outlet. C♯, F♯, G, and C are mapped to the first

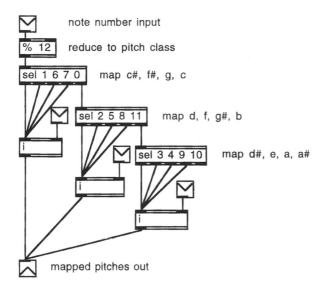

Figure 7.10 order-route

member of the tri-chord; D, F, G♯, and B to the second member; and the other pitch classes to the last.

The matrix is used not only to recognize user input, but also to organize the harmonic activity of the patch on output. The pitch collections are stored in the matrix as MIDI pitch numbers within a single octave. To realize any particular collection during performance these minimal representations are interpreted by processes that voice the member pitches of the chord. Figure 7.11 is a sub-patch that applies octave voicings to the three members of a stored tri-chord. The input to the patch is a list of three pitch values. Each member of the tri-chord is transposed by the number of octaves indicated in the voicing list. In figure 7.11 this means that every member of the incoming tri-chord will be transposed down one octave.

The transposition is calculated by the vexpr object, which repeatedly evaluates an expression on members of a vector. In this case, each member of the voicing list will be multiplied by 12, changing the value in octaves to a value in semitones. The products then are

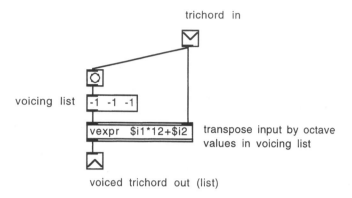

Figure 7.11 Tri-chord voicer

added to the corresponding tri-chord member. When all three tri-chord members have been transposed, the resulting list is sent to the outlet of vexpr. In figure 7.11 all members of the tri-chord are transposed by the same amount, but another voicing list (e.g., −1 2 0) might transpose the first member down one octave, the second up two, and leave the third unchanged. In *Natural Selection* the composer uses a switchable group of five voicing lists to change the transpositions of tri-chords on the fly. Moreover, tri-chords are voiced before being sent to order-route (see figure 7.10) so that the mapping of a sequence to a tri-chord will be made onto a voiced tri-chord and not the minimal representation.

When the *Natural Selection* algorithms are running in improvisation, a control structure keeps track of the compositional variables and the global quality of the input performance. For example, when the human player has stopped playing, the patch notices the lack of activity and resets certain parameters accordingly. To accomplish this, the activity patch (figure 7.12) watches for any kind of message arriving at its left inlet. As long as input keeps coming, the patch does nothing. The argument given to the patch, or any value sent to the right inlet, determines the duration of time during which activity will wait for another message to the left inlet. Once this duration has elapsed, activity will indicate the absence of incoming mes-

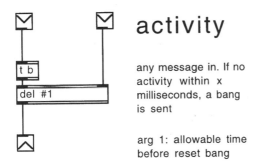

any message in. If no
activity within x
milliseconds, a bang
is sent

arg 1: allowable time
before reset bang

Figure 7.12 Activity measurement

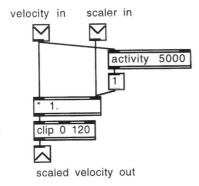

scaled velocity out

Figure 7.13 Variable reset with activity

sages by sending a bang to its outlet. The bang fires once after the last
input has been received. (Note that activity will not bang until it
has received at least one message at its left inlet).

Campion uses activity to reset certain processes to a default
state during the performance. For example, one part of the program
scales incoming velocity values using a floating point multiplier. If
no new velocities arrive within a five second window, the multiplier
is reset to the default value of one—that is, all scaling is eliminated
until more input arrives.

Figure 7.13 implements this idea in a subpatch. The left inlet
receives MIDI velocity values. The right inlet takes floating point

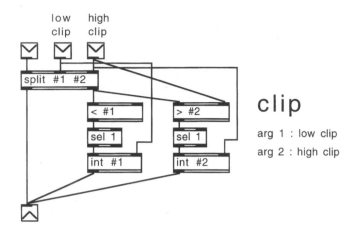

Figure 7.14 Clip object

scalers. All velocities arriving on the left side are multiplied by the scaler and clipped to a range of 0 to 120 before being sent back out. Whenever there has been an absence of velocity inputs for five seconds or more, the `activity` object will `bang` a one back into the multiplication object, effectively eliminating the amplitude scaling until a new value is received at the right inlet.

The `clip` object restricts input to a specified range (figure 7.14). Any input that falls between the upper and lower bounds of the range is passed through unchanged. If input falls above or below the bounds, it is pinned to the limit it has passed. So, if a `clip` object has bounds of 0 and 120 (as in figure 7.13), any input above 120 will be output as 120, and any input below zero will be changed to zero. `Clip` accomplishes this behavior by saving the lower and upper limits in `int` objects. A split handles the first test, passing any input between the bounds directly to the output. Inputs that do not fall within the bounds are sent to the right outlet of split, where they are tested by two conditionals. The first checks to see if the input is less than the lower bound, in which case the `int` containing the lower bound is `banged`, sending the lower bound to the outlet. The second conditional does the same operation for the upper bound, checking

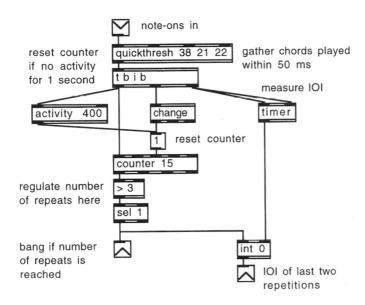

note-ons in

reset counter
if no activity
for 1 second

quickthresh 38 21 22

gather chords played
within 50 ms

t b i b

measure IOI

activity 400

change

timer

1 reset counter

counter 15

regulate number
of repeats here

> 3

sel 1

bang if number
of repeats is
reached

int 0

IOI of last two
repetitions

Figure 7.15 Repeat-notes control

to see if the input is higher than the upper bound and banging out
the upper bound if it is. Only one of these conditionals can be true
for any given input.

NatSel's independent generation processes produce material without reference to the sequences and can operate simultaneously with
sequence playback. The sub-patch repeat-notes, for example, repeats
any note played four times as long as the inter-onset interval between
any successive two of the four does not exceed 400 milliseconds.
The patch in figure 7.15 demonstrates the control structure that determines when the condition for repeat-notes has been met. Incoming note-ons are first gathered into a list by the quickthresh
object if they arrive within a 50 millisecond window. The change
object bangs a one into the counter whenever an incoming note is
different from the previous one. Therefore the counter will only advance beyond two if a pitch is repeated. The activity sub-patch
(figure 7.12) resets the counter to one if nothing happens for 400
milliseconds. When the counter advances beyond a limit set in the

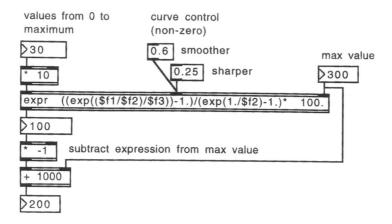

Figure 7.16 Curve control

greater-than object (>), a bang is sent to the process that produces the repeats. The inter-onset-interval between the last two of the repeated notes is used to control the speed of the generated repetitions, as shown in figure 7.16.

The repeat-notes independent process outputs a number of repetitions of the input note when the condition determined by figure 7.15 is met. The expression shown in figure 7.16 determines the timing of these repetitions as well as, indirectly, their number. (The complete repeat-notes patch can be found on the CD-ROM.) The expression calculates a quasi-exponential curve whose shape is determined by the middle inlet. In figure 7.16 two demonstration values are supplied: lower values (such as 0.25) cause the rise to be sharper at the end and higher ones (such as 0.6) make a more gradual ascent. In *Natural Selection,* this parameter is set by the velocity with which the final repetition of the input note was played, such that harder attacks produce smoother curves and vice versa.

The maximum value, determined by the third inlet, is the value that when entered in the leftmost inlet will cause the expression to output 100. Notice in figure 7.16 that the maximum has been set to 300. The value input on the left is 30, multiplied by 10 (300), which yields an output from the expression of 100. The expression outlet is then subtracted from the original maximum, producing a sum of 200. In `repeat-notes` this output is used as the duration in milliseconds between successive attacks of the echoes.

The maximum value (inlet 3) used for the echoes is the IOI between the last two repeated notes that trigger the patch. As we have seen in figure 7.15, the IOI cannot exceed 400 milliseconds because that duration causes `activity` to fire, resetting the counter to one. Therefore the upper limit on maxima sent to the rightmost inlet of the expression is 399 milliseconds. Returning to figure 7.16, as the numbers sent to the leftmost inlet are incremented, the value subtracted from the maximum will increase quasi-exponentially. The musical effect will be one of a nonlinear accelerando on the echoes of the repeated pitch. The last few echoes will be separated by only a few milliseconds. As the count of echoes increases, eventually the echo delay will become zero or less. At that point, `repeat-notes` ceases echoing the input pitch and waits again for a new series of triggers.

The NatSel patch in its entirety has been distributed with Max and is widely available. The CD-ROM includes the examples developed here as well as an audio excerpt of the composition.

7.3 Transformation in Improvisation

The preceding two sections detailed the use of sequenced and generation techniques in improvisation environments. A third algorithmic composition style concerns transformation, in which material arriving from the outside (from the performance of a human partner, or from another program) is transformed by processes that vary the material, usually based on an analysis of its properties. Amnon Wolman's composition *New York* for two player pianos was written for and premiered by pianist Ursula Oppens in 1998. The two player pianos are MIDI-equipped—one is played by the human pianist and the other by a computer program. The performance from the human is sent to a Max patch that combines pre-recorded sequences with live transformations of the pianist's material to form a counterpoint that is output on the second player piano.

Max is very well-suited to the implementation of transformations. The design of the language supports algorithms in which data arrives at the top (with `notein` or `midiin`) and is affected by some combination of objects in the middle, causing new data to be output at the bottom (through `noteout` or `midiout`). The msp extensions route audio in the same way: the program becomes a signal processor, passing input signals arriving at the top through some modifications, and then out through converters at the bottom. In *New York,* Amnon Wolman uses a number of transformation techniques based not on an analysis of the human performance, but rather on systematic random variations of the incoming material over time.

The phrase "systematically random" appears oxymoronic, but offers the most accurate description of the variation technique we will now consider. Wolman's patch applies random variations of pitch and velocity within a systematic control structure (figure 7.17).

The random part of the process is realized by the `urn` object. `Urn` outputs random numbers in some range, using them all before any one is repeated. (The name comes from the image of selecting unique items randomly from an urn until all are gone.) In figure 7.17, the argument 8 indicates that there are eight values in the `urn`, ranging from zero to seven. The right outlet emits a `bang` when the last item

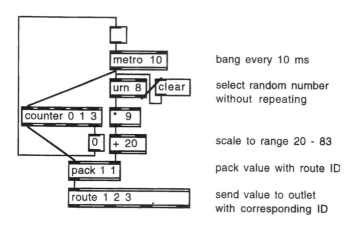

bang every 10 ms

select random number
without repeating

scale to range 20 - 83

pack value with route ID

send value to outlet
with corresponding ID

Figure 7.17 Selection from the `urn`

has been taken out. In this example we use the bang to send a clear message back to urn, refilling it with the values 0 through 7 for another round of selection.

The metro at the top of the patch sends bangs to both the urn object and a counter. The output of urn is adjusted to yield eight different values spaced evenly between 20 and 83. The counter tags these with ID numbers ranging from one to three, which control transmission of the urn values through the route object attached to pack. The counter sends a zero to the toggle controlling the metro when it has produced all three identifiers. This halts the selection of items from the urn once the three identifiers have all been associated with new values.

The values spaced evenly between 20 and 83 finally reach a set of three equality tests, as shown at the bottom of figure 7.18. These operators compare the urn outputs against the values issuing from a second counter (shown on the left-hand side of figure 7.18). The big (left-hand) counter goes from 1 to 108 over a span of 54 seconds (here I have used a metro with a pulse rate of 500 milliseconds—in the piece a tempo object gives the performer control over the speed of the big counter).

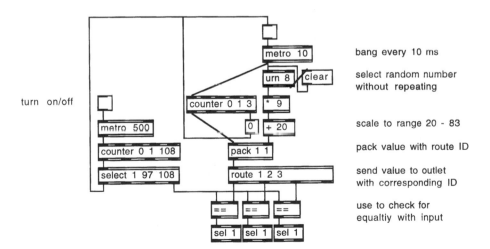

Figure 7.18 Tests for equality

Whenever the big counter strikes one, the `select` object underneath it sends a `bang` to the `metro` controlling the urn. This recommences the urn process, filling the equality operators with three new values. When the big `counter` is between 20 and 83, its output may match one of the three urn values. That span of 63 values occupies a little more than half of the full range output by the big `counter`, which will match one of them at three different points within that span. Because the values are distributed among the points { 20, 29, 38, 47, 56, 65, 74, 83 }, the hits of the `counter` will fall randomly on one of eight possible pulses spaced 4500 milliseconds apart. Figure 7.19 expands the patch to show what happens when a hit occurs.

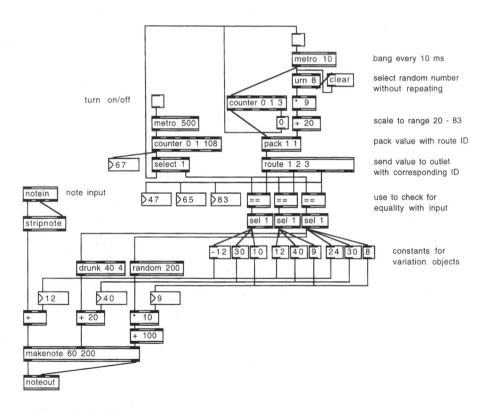

Figure 7.19 Complete example

Below each equality test is a select object. When a select finds that its corresponding equality was true (i.e., the operator output a one), it sends bangs to a group of three constants as well as to two random operations (drunk and random). The constants are scalers for the random operations and an addition value. All are used to affect the behavior of a makenote object that generates the output of the patch. Makenote has three inlets that control the pitch, velocity, and duration of a MIDI note. The first of the three constants set by the select objects is added to any incoming pitches before they are fed to makenote. The effect will be to transpose any MIDI pitches played to the patch by the constant amount. Figure 7.19 shows this amount set to 12, transposing the input up by an octave.

The second constant scales the output of a drunk object that controls the velocity inlet of makenote. The arguments to drunk ensure that it will produce velocities ranging from 0 to 39. The scaling adds a constant (equal to 40 in figure 7.19) that shifts this random variation into a higher loudness range (in this case between 40 and 79). The final constant similarly affects the range of values used to determine the duration of makenote.

Playing with the example on the CD-ROM will make the effect of this mechanism clear: three different types of variation to the input are made as the counter cycles through the value triplets. The random objects ensure that the variations are always dynamic, but the constant scalers group them into audible categories of output. There is a tangibly active zone of variation as the big counter enters the range within which the equality operators switch the parameters of makenote. Experiment with the tempo of the metro to change the range and the scaling of the little counter to change the extent of the active zone.

7.4 Player Paradigm Systems

One dimension of the typology of interactive systems I have described previously (Rowe 1993) comprised three composition techniques—sequenced, generation, and transformation. Another dimension concerned types of interaction between the human and the machine. Instrument paradigm systems are those that treat the machine contribution as an extension or augmentation of the human performance. Player paradigm systems present the machine as an interlocutor—another musical presence in the texture that has weight and independence distinguishing it from its human counterpart.

Mari Kimura is a virtuoso violinist and interactive music composer. Her compositions often combine notated music and improvisation performed with interaction from Max programs that elaborate on her material. Her 1998 composition, *Izquierda e Derecha* (Left and Right) is a player paradigm interactive system, a dialog between the human violin performance and machine reactions played on a MIDI piano. The piece gives equal prominence to the human and machine components, though at times the violin takes over and controls the piano directly. Usually the Max patch operates through a collection of compositional algorithms that the violinist can influence through her own performance, much as Campion's NatSel patch is designed around the idea of influence. The Chromatic subpatch is emblematic of the texture-producing modules Kimura combines in her piece (figure 7.20).

Chromatic generates chromatic scales running up from a constant starting pitch through a randomly generated range. There are two metro objects that determine the rate of Chromatic's operation: the leftmost metro sends bangs to a counter object that outputs pitch transpositions. The transpositions from the counter are added to the constant starting pitch, yielding the scalar motion. The second metro controls the rate of change of the upper bound of the counter. The upper bound affects the length of the scales produced, as the counter will reverse direction whenever the boundary is reached. In figure 7.20, the upper bound metro is set to fire every two seconds, banging out a new random limit between 6 and 40. These values establish that the length of the scales will vary between 6 semitones (a tritone) and 40 semitones (three octaves and a tritone). The split object that controls the range of variation also introduces some uncertainty in the regularity of limit change: if a random num-

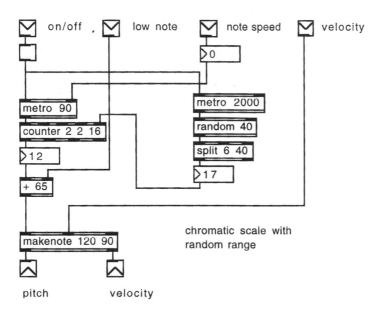

Figure 7.20 Chromatic

ber is produced that is less than 6, it will fall into empty space from
the right outlet. This means that 15% of the time, no limit change
will be made, interrupting the regular 2 second rate of variation.

Figure 7.21 demonstrates one way in which Kimura makes the
chromatic patch interactive. MIDI pitch numbers coming from the
pitch-to-MIDI converter of her Zeta violin are mapped to start numbers for the chromatic scale generator. Two conditions affect the interaction: first, the patch is only sensitive to violin pitches within
the range 54–70 as determined by the split object. This means that
notes from the bottom of the violin range through the B♭ above middle
C will affect the scales. Second, the insertion of the table object
provides a layer of indirection between her own melodic output and
the base notes of the scales. Rather than a slavish imitation of her
performance, the table gives the machine's output a relationship to
the melodic material of the violin that nonetheless remains distinct.

The patch in figure 7.22 demonstrates another of the texture generators from *Izquierda e Derecha*. This one produces variations on a

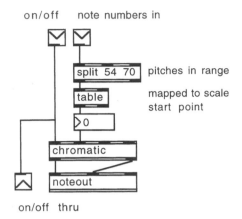

on/off thru

Figure 7.21 Chromatic interaction

number of triads based on the C-major scale that are saved in a coll file. There are five stored triads, which are accessed in random order by the urn object. The urn first outputs the five addresses for the coll file in random order, at a rate of four per second (determined by the metro object at the top of the patch). Once all of the addresses have been generated, as in Amnon Wolman's *New York* patch, the urn refills its collection and turns off the metro. While the addresses are being produced, they retrieve new triads from the coll file and set these into a note list. The notes are associated with velocities through a table and played out, along with a copy that is transposed by 0–6 semitones. The transposition is not random but linear, generated by the counter object at the left of the patch. The counter is banged only every six seconds, meaning that the transposition level changes slowly relative to the quick successions of triads.

Figure 7.22 is included on the CD-ROM under the name "C Chords" and is written to operate independently. In her composition, Kimura interacts with the C Chord generator by turning the metros on and off and changing their speeds interactively based on certain pitch triggers. Here again we see her technique of using quasi-random texture generators that are activated and influenced by her onstage improvisation.

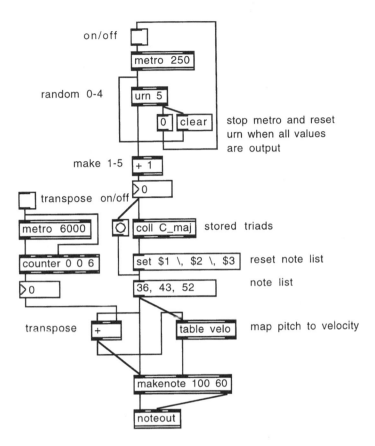

Figure 7.22 Chord textures

We have seen now a number of examples of controlled random textures used as a backdrop for interactive improvisations. The urn object is well-suited to the task as it exhaustively explores a given range of values and can refill itself or turn off an associated process once all have been used. Another Max object that works well for such textures is drunk, which performs a random walk within limits defined by the inputs. In a random walk a step of a determined size is made in a random direction from the current position, much as a human drunk will make steps of the same size but with no particular heading. "Brownian motion" is another name for this

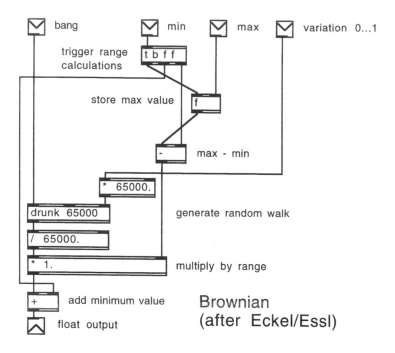

Figure 7.23 Brownian

type of random behavior, and the Brownian subpatch developed by Gerhard Eckel packages the Max drunk object in a way that presents the user with somewhat different controls (figure 7.23). In Brownian, the inlets from left to right receive a bang to generate a new value; the minimum value to return; the maximum value to return; and the degree of variation between the minimum and maximum to generate, expressed as a floating point value between zero and one.

Karlheinz Essl's *Lexicon-Sonate* is an extensive Max environment and composition that has been made available by the composer on the Internet. The library supporting the composition (RTC-lib) includes many valuable and well-documented sub-patches that fit the discussion here. The Brownian sub-patch, for example, plays a prominent role in Essl's work. One of the distinguishing characteristics of the urn object, relative to Brownian and other random pro-

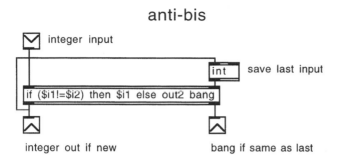

Figure 7.24 anti-bis

cesses, is that it does not repeat any value until all possible values have been output. The RTC-lib includes a small filter called anti-bis that can add this functionality to other kinds of random objects as well (figure 7.24).

The anti-bis subpatch protects against repetition of the integers presented to its inlet. When an integer arrives, it is compared against the number last input to the right inlet of the expression object. If the two numbers are different, the new input is fed through to the left outlet of anti-bis and stored in the int object above the right inlet of the expression. When the number reaches the int, it is both stored there and transmitted through to the expression. Because the expression is only evaluated when a number reaches its left inlet, the number from the int simply waits to be compared to a subsequent new input whenever it arrives. If the expression finds the two values to be the same, it outputs a bang from its right outlet. This bang can be used to elicit another value from the process sending inputs to anti-bis, thereby running it continually until it does not repeat.

Figure 7.25 demonstrates how anti-bis can be used in conjunction with Brownian to provide random walk outputs without repetitions. The metro continually bangs out values from Brownian. Whenever one of its outputs proves to be a repetition, the bang from the right outlet of anti-bis is fed back into Brownian, eliciting other values until one is generated that is not a repetition of the last.

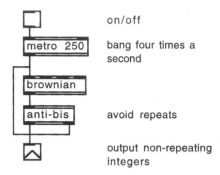

on/off

bang four times a
second

avoid repeats

output non-repeating
integers

Figure 7.25   Non-repetition of random values

The same technique can be used with any random generator that produces output on receiving a bang.

The CD-ROM includes Brownian, anti-bis, and their combination. The reader is referred to Karlheinz Essl's clear and instructive RTC-lib and the *Lexicon-Sonate* itself for more examples of their use.

7.5   Ensemble Improvisation

Every interactive system we have examined in this chapter is built around the scenario of one improviser playing with one program. This is by far the most common application of these ideas and the one most easily conceptualized. Though he is not speaking of algorithmic improvisation, Philippe Manoury points to the problems of programming for a larger ensemble when he states:

One can connect a computer with a flute, a soprano, or a piano in a way that is profound and even quite practical. One can detect very subtle elements and make use of them. But one can't do the same thing with a collective such as an orchestra. It would be unmanageable to put a sensor on every instrument. I am, at best, an experimenter in this discipline. Experimentation is more difficult when one is faced with a large collective. (Derrien 1995, 17 [my trans.])

Despite the difficulties involved, there are many environments that allow algorithmic improvisation as an ensemble. David Berhman describes some of his early work: "In the live electronic pieces I composed in the 1960s and early 1970s . . . it seemed to make sense to double, triple or quadruple the amount of hardware for use in performances. The sound textures were enriched and several performers could play together. The 'scores' consisted of general instructions, rather than of specific commands governing moment-to-moment actions. Inevitably a kind of counterpoint would result as the performers pursued their individual paths while listening to one another" (Kuivila and Berhman 1998, 15).

One of the oldest and best-known collectives is The Hub, a group of six programmer/improvisers who have developed various strategies for performing interactively with composing computers (Gresham-Lancaster 1998). The development of MIDI allowed them to formulate a fully interconnected network arrangement in which the computer of any member could communicate MIDI messages to the computer of any other. Tim Perkis devised the piece *Waxlips* (1991) for this configuration: "*Waxlips* . . . was an attempt to find the simplest Hub piece possible, to minimize the amount of musical structure planned in advance, in order to allow any emergent structure arising out of the group interaction to be revealed clearly. The rule is simple: each player sends and receives requests to play one note. Upon receiving the request, each should play the note requested, then transform the note message in some fixed way to a different message, and send it out to someone else" (Perkis 1995). The rule applied by each member remained constant during each section of the piece. One lead player could change sections by sending a message to the other players, and simultaneously kick the new section into motion by "spraying the network with a burst of requests" (Perkis 1995).

Another collective is Sensorband, three improvisers (Edwin van der Heide, Zbigniew Karkowski, and Atau Tanaka) who have specialized in the use of new controllers, some of which require the manipulations of all three. One of these is the Soundnet, a very large web of ropes in which sensors are embedded. Sensorband performs on the instrument by actually climbing on it—the resulting sound is produced from their combined movements on the net.

The rope, the metal, and the humans climbing on it require intense physicality, and focus attention on the human side of the human-machine interaction, not on mechanistic aspects such as interrupts, mouse clicks, and screen redraws. Sensorband has chosen to work with digital recordings of natural sounds. The signals from Soundnet control DSPs that process the sound through filtering, convolution, and waveshaping. Natural, organic elements are thus put in direct confrontation with technology. The physical nature of movement meeting the virtual nature of the signal processing creates a dynamic situation that directly addresses sound as the fundamental musical material. Through gesture and pure exertion, the performers sculpt raw samples to create sonorities emanating from the huge net. (Bongers 1998, 15)

The problem with ensemble improvisation, beyond the basic technical difficulties mentioned by Manoury, is one of designing an appropriate control structure. As with many of the analytical systems discussed in this text, arbitration between competing sources of information becomes harder as the number of discrete sources increases and their interaction becomes more complex. In the case of Soundnet, the integration of three "information sources" is accomplished by the interface itself. The input to the sound-producing algorithm is simply the output of the web as a whole.

7.5.1 Multiple Cypher

I have developed several control structures for ensemble improvisation that work with Cypher, a program I wrote for real-time analysis and improvisation. Because of the extensive discussion of Cypher in my book *Interactive Music Systems* (1993), I will provide only a capsule description of the architecture of the program here. Moreover, the objects for algorithmic analysis and composition described in the present text can be used to build Cypher and Cypher-like programs directly. The CD-ROM contains a full implementation of Cypher and a listing of the source code.

The program comprises two large conceptual components, the listener and the player. The listener applies a number of feature analyzers to incoming MIDI events and stores the classifications produced by each of them. The features analyzed are register, inter-onset-interval rate, vertical density, loudness, articulation, and harmony. The program responds to these classifications by channeling the input through some number of transformation processes in the player. A user of Cypher configures the player to apply certain transformations when particular combinations of feature classifications are received. For example, one rule might specify that when low, loud, chords are found at the input, the player should respond by transforming that material through deceleration and thinning processes.

A higher level of the listener segments incoming events by looking for simultaneous discontinuities across several features. Within the current group, the listener typifies the behavior of each feature individually in terms of its regularity. That is, if a feature is invariant within the current group (e.g., always loud) it is called regular, but if the feature changes frequently (e.g., alternating loud and soft) it is called irregular. These regularity/irregularity judgments can also form the conditions of rules that the user specifies. For example, the user might require that irregular articulations within a group should trigger a drone note in the player.

In one multiple player strategy, each individual player is analyzed by a separate copy of the Cypher listener. Single streams are identified by MIDI channel number, so each performer must take care to set their instrument to a unique channel. Each player can elicit a distinct set of responses from the program based on the characteristics of her individual performance. The interface offers different screens for each player to manage the correspondences between analysis and response. Figure 7.26 illustrates the strategy under discussion: each performer is analyzed by a separate listener. Listener messages are passed to several players, all contributing their individual responses to the output of the program as a whole.

The problem with this model is readily apparent: the program is responding to several individuals as if they were not all playing together. Cypher's contribution to the whole, therefore, is the sum of

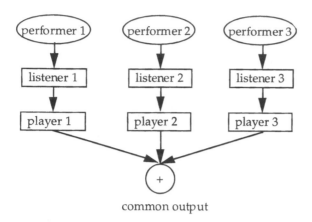

Figure 7.26 Multiple copies

its reactions to each part and is likely to be far too dense to be useful in an ensemble setting. Given the problems inherent in simply proliferating copies of the program with each additional player, the second strategy was to employ a critic. The Cypher critic is a separate copy of the listener that reviews output from the program before it is played. If the critic finds certain conditions are true of the incipient output, it can change the material before the actual performance. Instructing the critic to reduce the density of response when several players are active improves the contribution of the program noticeably. Figure 7.27 illustrates this revision to the architecture.

The computer is a better member of an ensemble when it has a sense of what the group as a whole is doing. The next strategy of Multiple Cypher, then, was to develop a meta-listener that compares the analyses of individual players within an ensemble to arrive at a global characterization of the performance.

Figure 7.28 shows how the meta-listener fits in the architecture of the program as a whole. As before, each player is tracked by a separate copy of the Cypher listener. Now, these individual listener reports are passed to the meta-listener, which compares and summarizes the individual reports before passing the information on to a single player. The user of the program determines how the player

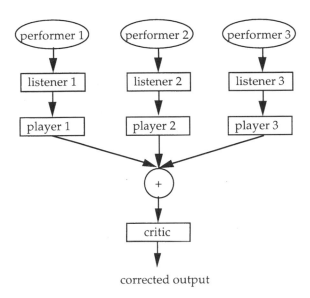

Figure 7.27 Multiple copies with critic

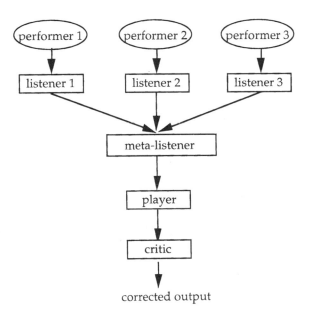

Figure 7.28 Meta-listener

will react to meta-listener messages. The range of messages transmitted, however, has grown to reflect the diversity of input. The individual listener classifications are tagged with an identifier showing which performer corresponds to which analysis. This player ID allows a user to make the program respond in different ways to different individuals. A correspondence using this type of message might look like this:

```
if (Speed(Player 2) == kSlow)
    Accelerate(Input(Player 2));
```

Along with characterizations of each player individually, the meta-listener sends a global characterization of the ensemble performance as a whole.

Let us consider how feature analyses from individual players can be combined to arrive at an ensemble classification. An obvious possibility is what I will call the mean-value strategy. To arrive at a mean loudness classification, for example, one would sum the loudness values of all members of the ensemble and divide by the number of players. While the mean loudness is certainly useful, it can also mislead the program as to the musical nature of the performance. For example, if one member of a three-player ensemble is playing an extremely loud solo, the mean-value strategy would still find that the group as a whole was playing softly (because the other two performers are not playing at all).

To compensate for this type of confusion, the meta-listener sends as part of its global report a continually updated analysis of the players' relative levels of activity. A player who is not performing is certainly considered inactive. Moreover, the program takes players who are at significantly lower levels of loudness, speed, and density to be less active as well. Now a mean loudness for all active players can be computed and sent as a message distinct from the overall mean loudness report. A rule using some of these messages might be:

```
if ((Loudness(activePlayers))==kLoud)) &&
    (Number(activePlayers)>1))
        Silence();
```

Such a rule would instruct the program to stop playing entirely if more than one partner in the ensemble is already playing loud and actively.

The proliferation of information available when an ensemble is under analysis means that the meta-listener must be available for queries. The single-player listener always makes the same report with every event. The meta-listener has a standard report format as well, as we have seen: the ID-tagged individual reports plus mean-value feature analyses and indications of relative activity. In many situations, however, the player can usefully ask the meta-listener for more specific information. For example, a rule might ask whether players 2 and 3 are playing loudly but with an average speed below that of the entire ensemble. Such a state can certainly be found by the meta-listener, but the information is not generally useful enough to be included in a standard report.

We have looked at ways in which analyses of an ongoing performance can be used to shape an algorithmic musical response that becomes part of that same performance. Now we will examine how such analyses can affect responses realized through media other than the production of more music. Changing the display of imagery, such as video or animation, is one of the most common forms of interactive multimedia. Another well-developed approach is to interpret visual or gestural input in such a way that it can be used to generate music interactively. Motion sensors tracking dancers (Siegel and Jacobsen 1998) or the movement of viewers before an installation (Ritter 1996) are common in such works. A general problem in composing for interactive multimedia is that the cross-modal interpretation of musical information can be difficult to make clear to an audience. This chapter will consider both the technology and the aesthetic questions arising from the use of music to control image, and vice versa.

Interactive multimedia environments are those in which more than one medium is used either as input to a computer system gathering information from sensors and producing a related response or as output from such a system. Examples would include sending MIDI input (musical sensors) to an interactive system controlling the movement of an animated figure (image output), or using the gestures of dancers (motion sensors) to change the onstage lighting. In this chapter we will be exclusively concerned with systems that use music as one or more of the input or output media.

Using analysis of music to control or influence the generation of additional musical material calls on compositional craft that has been developed through centuries of polyphonic writing. Musical training naturally leads to the ability to create relationship rules such as: "If the input material is in F major, generate a response in F major," or even, "If the input material is in F major, generate a response in D♭ major." We know from experience that the first relationship would entail a response that is consonant to the extent that it shares the same key, while the second would create a response more dissonant but still related because F is the third degree of D♭ major.

Operating from a predominately musical background, or even a predominately visual one, it is more difficult to imagine the effect of relationships such as: "If the input material is in F major, make the ball spin faster." One can imagine how this would look easily enough, but it is more difficult to predict whether an observer would recognize the relationship simply by watching it.

In his text *Analyzing Multimedia,* Nicholas Cook describes different ways of relating media compositionally: "Kandinsky conceived intermedia relationships as triadic; a colour corresponds to a sound inasmuch as both correspond to an underlying emotional or spiritual meaning. We can, then, distinguish this triadic variety of conformance from what might be called the unitary and dyadic varieties. Dyadic conformance means that one medium corresponds directly to another, in the way that the faster luce part of Prometheus corresponds to the sequence of 'mystic chord' roots. (The term 'dyadic' does not, of course, mean that there can be only two constituent media; it means that there is a direct, pair-wise relationship between each medium and each of the others). Unitary conformance, by contrast, means that one medium predominates, and that other media conform to this" (Cook 1998, 101).

In this chapter we will see examples of both dyadic and unitary conformance. (The extent to which Kandinsky's triadic conformance is operative depends on one's emotional or spiritual lexicon). Essentially Cook's distinction marks the level of symmetry between two media: either both contribute more or less equally to the artistic whole, or one leads the aesthetic argument and is augmented by the other. When multimedia becomes interactive, another aspect of the relationship comes to the fore: the degree to which computational relationships between media are experienced by observers.

8.1 *Intimate Immensity*

Composer Morton Subotnick's large-scale work for interactive multimedia, *Intimate Immensity*, was premiered as part of the Lincoln Center Festival in New York in the summer of 1997. The work has four performers: three humans (He, She, and the Cyber-Angel) and one projected image (the Hand). The music consists of stored sound files and live generation played on two MIDI-controlled pianos. The lighting, laser disc projection, and music are all affected by interaction with the human performers.

The work is a meditation on our love affair with technology. In our quest to be empowered, to be in control of our destinies and to be free of the constraints of nature, we are constantly creating new tools. The hand was the first tool and thus takes on a prominent role in the work. We invented magic and our gods to empower us as well. The Cyber-Angel represents magical empowerment (Subotnick 1997).

The Cyber-Angel guides the audience through a technological journey from the earliest tool (the hand) to "a world without time . . . a world without space." The role of the Cyber-Angel is played by a traditional Balinese dancer (I Nyoman Wenten), who makes his technological revelations through mysterious control of the music, video, voices, and lights. The opening of the work is a dialog between the Cyber-Angel and the Hand, whom the Cyber-Angel calls to life and gradually teaches to talk and play music (figure 8.1).

The composition's software is able to randomly access video images on five laser discs. Any frame can be called up at any point. Once a frame is loaded, it can be displayed in a frozen state (still image), or used as the starting point for video playback either forward or back at any speed. This kind of real-time control enabled interactive choreography of the images as part of the composition, for example, when the movements of the Cyber-Angel direct the animation of the Hand coming to life.

Figure 8.1 Cyber-Angel and the Hand

The program notes suggest the intricate interaction between the live performers and the computer environment: "He and She sit at their work tables. He is reading; She is writing. Both move in and out of a daydream state [Intimate Immensity] from which they eventually do not return. With arm gestures they trigger light, video and sound events. They are seen and heard as if in different locations (futuristic telephonic 'sites'), each performing a meditation on His/Her sense of Intimate Immensity, a duet of parallel performances. We hear what they sing and speak mixed with what they 'think' through amplified computer versions of their voices" (Subotnick 1997).

The interaction of *Intimate Immensity* is carefully composed and controlled, with an evident attention to the salience of the relationship between the performers' motions and the machine-generated audio and video responses. The video Hand is considered a fourth performer in an ensemble with three humans, but its range of behavior and connection to the Cyber-Angel in particular is made clear in the performance itself through the opening "teaching" segments.

8.1.1 Interactor

The entire application of *Intimate Immensity* was written in Interactor, a graphic interaction programming environment for Apple Macintosh computers. Interactor was designed by Mark Coniglio and Morton Subotnick and implemented by Coniglio. Interactor programs process several types of events, including most notably MIDI, timing, and Macintosh events. Statements in Interactor generally follow an if-then logic flow, where attributes of incoming events are evaluated to determine whether they match some conditions listed in the if part of a statement. When a condition is found to be true, additional operators (the then part) are executed. Such if-then sequences can occur several times in a single statement; whenever a conditional operator returns a false value, the current statement ends and the next one begins.

Figure 8.2 shows a scene edit window. Three statements, made up of *operators,* from the basic building blocks of Interactor. Operators evaluate conditions or execute actions. One operator in the first statement will evaluate true when the scene (collection of statements) is opened, but not again until the scene is restarted. Indicated by the small x at the side, this kind of operator is used to initialize various conditions in the scene. In this case the statement simply informs the user that the rest of the scene is now active.

In the other two statements, the first operator is a conditional looking for a MIDI note on message within a particular velocity range.

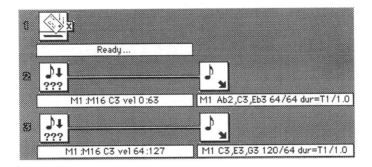

Figure 8.2 Interactor example

The box below the operator is a comment showing the values of the operator's parameters. These parameters can be modified simply by double-clicking on the operator, which brings up a dialog box wherein parameters values can be textually modified. In the figure we see that statement 2 will react to a middle C played on any MIDI channel with a velocity between 0 and 63. The first operator of statement 3 evaluates true when the same pitch is played but with a velocity between 64 and 127. In effect, statement 2 is the "soft C" handler, while statement 3 is the "loud C" handler.

In both cases, an action operator (send note) that outputs a triad engages next. Action operators are always true—that is, any additional operators after an action will be executed until a conditional operator is encountered that tests false, or the end of the statement is found. Notice that the "soft C" send note operator will trigger an A♭-major triad just below middle C played with a velocity of 64 and a duration of one beat. The "loud C" handler triggers a C-major triad with a velocity of 120.

Interactor supports eight simultaneous multi-channel sequencers. There are also eight independent timebases so that each sequencer can have its own temporal behavior. Scheduling operators use the timebases as well, e.g., the Delay Timer which postpones the execution of subsequent operators in a statement by some number of ticks. Time is expressed in measures, beats, and ticks, where 480 ticks equal one quarter note. This allows tempo to be varied while individual events maintain their relationship to an underlying metric structure. We see a timebase in operation in the send note operators of statements 2 and 3 in figure 8.2: the duration of the triads is specified relative to the first timebase (T1) and given a value of 1.0 beats. The actual duration in milliseconds of the triads, then, depends on the speed of T1 and will change as T1 changes.

Interactor shows some obvious similarities to Max, in both its graphic orientation and the kinds of interactive applications it was written to support. There are important differences as well: (1) Interactor's left-to-right statement construction enforces a particular graphic convention that is consistent and clear. What graphic regu-

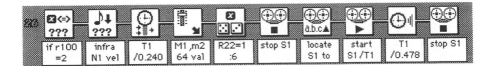

Figure 8.3 Cyber-Angel/Hand interaction

larities exist in Max arise from the execution order, namely that control flows from top to bottom and from right to left. Any consistency beyond that is left up to the user. (2) The use of registers and lists to store input information and pass data between operators is a significant departure from Max's patchcords. (3) The combination of sequencers and timebases in Interactor provides particularly powerful support for the interactive performance of sequenced material. Max's seq and mt can be used to accomplish the same things that Interactor does, but the environment itself is not organized around them to the same extent that Interactor is based on its sequencers.

Figure 8.3 shows a characteristic Interactor statement from the opening sections of *Intimate Immensity*. This is the 26th statement in a collection of 63 contained in one scene, all simultaneously comparing their start conditions with the state of the onstage performance. In figure 8.3, the first operator tests the contents of the r100 register. If r100 contains the value 2, execution advances to the following operator. This looks for any Note On event coming from the "infrared" channel, corresponding to one of the motion sensors that transmits information to the computer by way of MIDI messages. The infrared sensing is so acute that even the blinking of the Cyber-Angel's eye (figure 8.4) can be used to trigger events.

When such an event from the infrared channel is found, it is sent through a "time filter" (the third operator). The time filter performs the same function as Max's speedlim; in other words, it filters out repetitions of events that occur before a certain duration has passed.

When a note passes the time filter, operators 4 through 10 perform the following actions: (4) continuous controller 64 is changed from 127 to 0 over a duration of 4 beats; (5) a random number between 1 and 6 is stored in register 22; (6) the first sequencer (S1) is

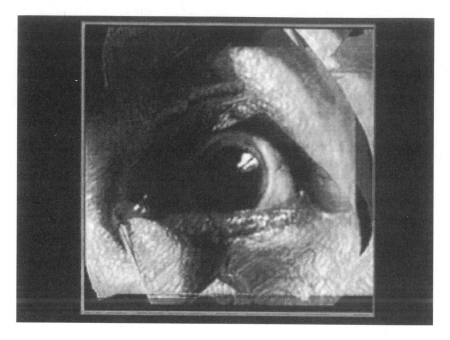

Figure 8.4 Cyber-Angel's eye

stopped; (7) S1 is reset to a new location; (8) playback from S1 is started; (9) a delay of 0.478 beats of the first timebase passes; after which (10) the playback is stopped again. This combination of effects demonstrates how Interactor can describe a complex series of actions in a compact and clear notation.

The use of the sequencers, so prominent in figure 8.3, is part of an approach to the music of the piece that combines the computer performance with that of the human players onstage: "The music plays two roles. The music of the performers, which includes the live piano music, supports the 'narrative' development on the stage. There is also music, played by the computer, which is a collage of modifications of pre-recordings of the piano (including inside piano sounds), the two vocalists and the Balinese dancer. This music acts like an interior dialogue. It is the world of the inner self, or perhaps, the Intimate Immensity. Sometimes the two musics act alone and sometimes are juxtaposed" (Subotnick 1997). The CD-ROM includes audio excerpts with some slide shows that demonstrate visual aspects of the composition.

8.2 *A Flock of Words*

A Flock of Words was a collaboration between video artist/holographer Doris Vila and myself, with programming and animation design by Eric Singer. It was premiered at New York University in the spring of 1995, and a subsequent installation version was shown in Berlin in the fall of 1996. *A Flock of Words* was based on some musical ideas and the visual imagery of bird flocks, particularly the large swarms that appear to perform swirling aerial acrobatics in northern European skies in the fall. Some video shot by Doris Vila of such flocks formed one of the initial guides to the composition. We were struck by the similarities between that image and the descriptions of large collections (of wheat, water, birds, and people) written by Elias Canetti in his masterwork *Crowds and Power* (1984). Doris Vila had the idea of making Canetti's words fly in flocks the way the birds do in the video, and the work began to assume its ultimate shape.

The media used in *A Flock of Words* incorporated real-time animation, video, lighting, large-scale holograms, and algorithmically generated computer music. These were interactive because their behavior was controlled by a machine analysis of the performance of an instrumental ensemble consisting of violin, viola, cello, MIDI keyboard and two percussionists. The elements of the technical setup of the piece were as follows: 3 Apple Macintosh computers, 3 video projectors, 3 robotic lighting elements, a MIDI-controlled light board, a laser, 2 large holograms and sound synthesis equipment. The general equipment arrangement is shown in figure 8.5. Two of the computers were used to cue up and play back video clips and to generate animations in real time. One of these (video computer 1) sent an identical signal to two video projectors, each projecting onto large scale holograms on either side of the instrumental ensemble. The second video computer projected a different set of videos and animations onto a large screen at the back of the stage.

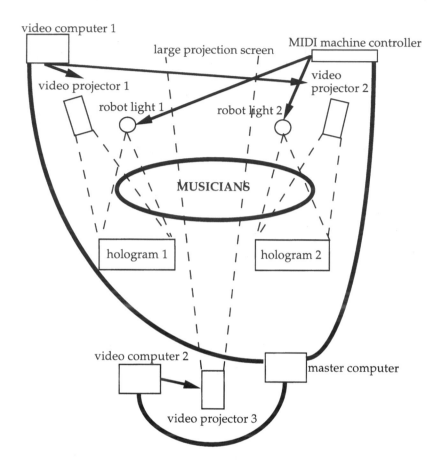

Figure 8.5 Stage setup for *A Flock of Words*

All of the software for *A Flock of Words* was written in C by Eric Singer and myself. Performance information from the ensemble was analyzed by a program running on the master computer that looked at musical attributes such as register, density and articulation. Software on the video computers was responsible for receiving control messages from the analysis machine and sending video and animation to the display projectors. The analysis and video software communicated through MIDI connections and a set of MIDI messages we redefined. The master computer also generated a stream of MIDI-encoded music that was sent to a synthesizer and effects processor to accompany the live ensemble and control lighting effects through a dedicated show controller. Video, animations and lights were projected onto the screen behind the ensemble as well as onto the holograms flanking the ensemble, changing the holograms' appearance as the piece progressed.

Displayed video consisted of prerecorded video clips and real-time animation. The video clips were stored and played back from QuickTime movie files. The animation was based on Craig Reynolds's *Boids* algorithm (1987), adapted from an implementation by Simon Fraser. Reynolds's work was an early and influential algorithm in the field of artificial life. Boids are graphic objects that travel in groups and plot their movement based on characteristic relations they wish to maintain with the other Boids around them. These relations include things like preferred distance from other members in a group, preferred speed of movement, a tendency to move toward a particular point on the screen, and so on. The motion of the group as a whole is not specified directly but emerges from the local interactions of each individual with all of the other Boids. The resulting group movement is strikingly similar to that of bird flocks, schools of fish, and other collections of natural organisms.

To create the *Flock of Words* animation, a set consisting of 10 to 30 words was selected from *Crowds and Power* and animated using the Reynolds algorithm. The center point of each word (or "Woid") was treated as the center of a Boid and animated under real-time control. Numerous parameters were used to change the flocking attributes and thereby influence the look of the flock. These included the speed and acceleration of the Woids; their tendency to stay close to the center of the flock; to avoid each other; to follow a point on the screen; and to avoid the edges of the screen.

Figure 8.6 shows four characteristic Woid flocks in mid-flight. The flock in the lower left, for example, is moving toward a point of attraction centered near the bottom of the screen. The flock above shows the Woids in a pattern of greater dispersal due to a change of direction or increase in neighbor avoidance. Because the objects are

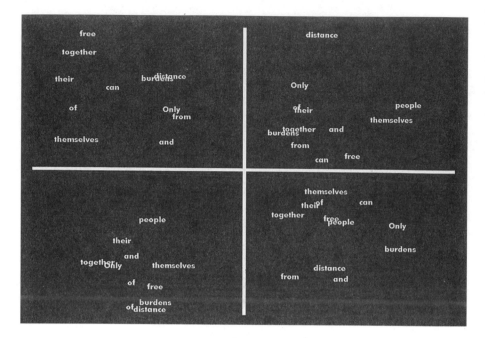

Figure 8.6 Screen displays of Woid flocks

words, they continually enter into new grammatical relationships with each other as they fly, sometimes aligning as in the original text, and at other times garbling the syntactic order entirely. This continual fluctuation between sense and nonsense was one of the motivations for this approach: the force of Canetti's original text is always preserved through the normal-order presentation in the video clips and balances with the nonlinear presentation in the animation.

The analysis software sends MIDI messages to the video programs to control their display. (MIDI communication between machines is indicated by the thick black lines in figure 8.5.) Various MIDI messages were defined to be interpreted as control messages. For example, note on messages were used to initiate playback of QuickTime video, with the note number selecting the particular video clip to be played. Continuous-controller messages were used to change the values of flocking parameters. Video control messages were sent by the analysis software based on cue points in the musical score, as well as musical gestures and playing attributes of the live performers. In this manner, the displayed video is guided by the musical performance.

Because various flocking parameters are linked to messages sent by the analysis software, which are in turn derived from musical gestures of the performers, the behavior of the flock is effectively controlled by the performers. The full set of video controls available to the analysis software includes selection of video clips, selection of word sets from the text, color of the Woids and background screen, and twelve flocking parameters. The QuickTime video clips combined footage of flocking birds, animation of flying phrases and close-ups of hands and mouths pronouncing vowels. After-effects were applied to make sparks fly out of the mouths (figure 8.7).

Doris Vila created two large rainbow holograms (22″H × 42″W) for the piece. Triple-exposure images on the hologram mix the spectral colors into bright fields filled with found objects, words and

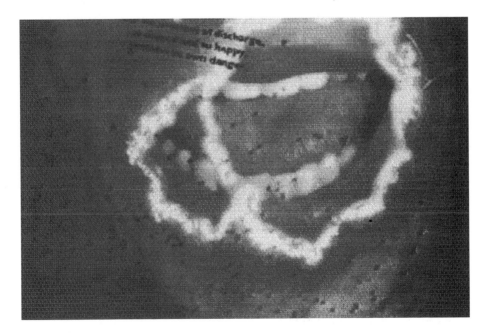

Figure 8.7 Still from *Flock of Words* video clip

diagrams. Ordinarily, holograms are displayed by shining a point-source of light on the plate at the reconstruction angle. However, in *A Flock of Words,* video projectors illuminated the hologram. The holographic surface became a diffractive screen for the Woids animation. As the color of the Woids changed, it filtered the color in the holographic reconstruction. In the piece's second movement, robotic controls drove mirrors that altered the apparent location of the reconstruction light, making the holographic imagery cross and turn in response to the music.

Another implementation of the project was developed for presentation at the Musik + Licht exhibition in Berlin in the fall of 1996. For this application, a screen was set in front of an active floor equipped with pressure sensors. The motion of the Woids across the screen corresponded to the position of viewers on the floor. Similarly, parameters of a compositional algorithm generating music through a synthesizer were tied to the presentation of the Woids and controlled by the placement of the viewers. In this case, the analysis of musical performance was replaced by position mapping of participants in front of the screen, which directed both the flight of the Woids and the production of the music.

8.2.1 Woids

The CD-ROM includes two applications with source code, one called Woids and the other Flock. Woids animates word sets from the Canetti text using parameters set in a dialog box, while Flock performs animation and launches video clips from an analysis of a performance arriving over a MIDI line. In this section I will briefly introduce some of the calculations that produce the flocking behavior demonstrated by the Woids. The code is my C++ port of Eric Singer's Woids program, itself adapted from Simon Fraser's implementation of the Boids algorithm by Craig Reynolds.

The AvoidWalls function is typical of the routines that collectively compute the direction and speed of a Woid's motion (figure 8.8). The Velocity struct records how much horizontal and how much vertical movement each Woid should make at the end of a

```
typedef struct Velocity {

     float h;      // horizontal movement

     float v;      // vertical movement

} Velocity;


Velocity Woid::AvoidWalls(void)

{

     Rect      flyRect = flock->FlyRect();

     Point     testPoint;

     Velocity tempVel = { 0, 0 };


     testPoint.h = oldPos.h + oldDir.h * speed * flock->EdgeDist();

     testPoint.v = oldPos.v + oldDir.v * speed * flock->EdgeDist();


     // change horizontal direction if outside screen

     if (testPoint.h < flyRect.left)

          tempVel.h =   fabs(oldDir.h); else

     if (testPoint.h > flyRect.right)

          tempVel.h = - fabs(oldDir.h);


     // change vertical direction if outside screen

     if (testPoint.v < flyRect.top)

          tempVel.v =   fabs(oldDir.v); else

     if (testPoint.v > flyRect.bottom)

          tempVel.v = - fabs(oldDir.v);

     return tempVel;

}
```

Figure 8.8 AvoidWalls() function

calculation cycle. A flock does have certain global parameters that are not simply the sum of the behaviors of its members. For example, the flyRect is a specification of the screen rectangle within which the Woids are allowed to move. AvoidWalls first calculates a testPoint that shows where the Woid would end up if it continued in its current direction at its current speed. If the testPoint shows the Woid flying off the screen, its current motion in that direction is reversed.

The code fragment in figure 8.9 demonstrates how the AvoidWalls() function is used within the full calculation of a Woid's movement. The velocity returned by AvoidWalls() is saved in a variable, avoidWallsVel. Each of the determining tendencies

```
avoidWallsVel = b->AvoidWalls();              // move away from walls


/* compute resultant velocity using weights and inertia */
b->newDir.h = inertiaFactor * (b->oldDir.h) +

                    (centerWeight  * goCenterVel.h        +

                    attractWeight * goAttractVel.h        +

                    matchWeight   * matchNeighborVel.h +

                    avoidWeight    * avoidNeighborVel.h +

                    wallsWeight    * avoidWallsVel.h)   / inertiaFactor;
b->newDir.v = inertiaFactor * (b->oldDir.v) +

                    (centerWeight  * goCenterVel.v        +

                    attractWeight * goAttractVel.v        +

                    matchWeight   * matchNeighborVel.v +

                    avoidWeight    * avoidNeighborVel.v +

                    wallsWeight    * avoidWallsVel.v)   / inertiaFactor;
```

Figure 8.9 Velocity calculation

(motion toward the center, attraction to other Woids, matching the motion of other Woids, avoiding other Woids, and avoiding the walls) is multiplied by its corresponding computed velocity. This sum then is used in an equation with the old direction and an inertia factor to compute the new horizontal and vertical displacement of the Woid.

The Woids application on the CD-ROM provides a dialog box with which the various tendency weights can be adjusted manually. Entering different weights by hand gives a direct impression of how these values affect the movement of the flock. The Flock application, on the other hand, changes the tendency weights (and several other parameters) through an analysis of the performance arriving in a MIDI stream. Flock is best viewed while improvising on a MIDI instrument, when the correlations between the musical texture and the behavior of the flock can be experienced most readily.

The routine MatchHeavy() is an example of the functions called by Flock when certain configurations of musical features are found in the input (figure 8.10). Both the matching weight and the centering

```
void Flock::MatchHeavy(void)

{

        matchWeight    = 100.0;        // tendency to match neighbors

        centerWeight   = 100.0;        // tendency to fly to center

        avoidWeight    =  10.0;        // tendency to avoid neighbors

        attractWeight  =  10.0;        // attraction to attract point

        accelFactor    =  50.0;        // acceleration

        inertiaFactor  =  10.0;        // inertia

        prefDist       =   2L;

        prefDistSqr    =   2L * 2L;

}
```

Figure 8.10   MatchHeavy() listing

weight are set to the maximum while avoidance and attraction to a point other than the center are minimized. This produces a distinctive behavior in the flock in which all of the Woids are shouldering each other aside, as it were, to get as close as possible to the center of the screen. Such extreme behaviors are easily recognizable and so contribute to a visible relationship between the musical performance and the graphic output.

8.3 *In Transit*

Roger Dannenberg's composition *In Transit* is an interactive multimedia work in which the performance of the composer on trumpet influences and is influenced by the simultaneous generation of computer music and real-time animation. As Dannenberg plays the trumpet, his audio signal is captured by a microphone and sent to a pitch-to-MIDI converter, producing a stream of MIDI messages corresponding to his improvisation. Software written by the composer analyzes these messages and outputs commands affecting algorithmic composition routines and the animation engine. The images are projected on a large screen behind the performer as he plays, while the compositional algorithms output MIDI messages destined for synthesis gear that produce the sounding output to accompany the trumpet.

The animations are produced using the system *Bomb,* developed by Scott Draves in collaboration with Roger Dannenberg (*Bomb* is now available as a Max external). The particular images of *In Transit* arise from "heat-diffusion models and iterated function systems to create pulsing, organic forms that both respond to and initiate musical ideas" (Dannenberg 1998, 69). We will examine two primary facets of the musical processing here: on the analysis side, a statistical style recognizer; and on the compositional side, a method for chord selection and voicing.

8.3.1 Style Recognition

In his text, *Jazz Improvisation,* David Baker suggests that there are "three basic tune types found in jazz up through the post-bebop era: (1) vertical tunes, that is, tunes which are essentially concerned with chords or vertical alignments, i.e., 'Tune Up' and 'Giant Steps,' (2) horizontal tunes, that is, compositions which have few chord changes or compositions in which the chord changes move very slowly, i.e., 'So What' and 'Maiden Voyage,' and (3) tunes which are a combination of vertical and horizontal, i.e., 'Speak Low,' 'Dear Old Stockholm,' and the blues" (1983, 19).

Baker's classification system basically entails a measurement of the average speed of harmonic change. Though we will not build it now, the germ of a "tune type classifier" can be found here: a combination of chord detection (chapter 2) and meter induction (chapter 3) produce an evaluation of rate of harmonic change. A division of the evaluations into three classes according to Baker's scheme can group slowly changing tunes into the horizontal class, intermediate speeds into the combination class, and quickly changing tunes into the vertical class.

This simple sketch suggests that there are techniques for the algorithmic analysis of style, even in real time. Though it is a relatively new development, current research is directed both to the algorithmic analysis and synthesis of style. On the synthesis side, Brad Garton and his colleagues have written several style generators. Garton's models are organized as layers of rules that ultimately control the parameters of sound synthesis algorithms. The physical layer mimics the kinematic constraints of performing on an instrument—requiring a slight delay between the attacks of successive strings in a strummed guitar sound, for example. "The [inflection] layer codes information about performance inflections appropriate to a given musical style. The manner in which pitch bends occur, the types of vibrato used, grace notes and quick rhythmic figurations are all examples of these inflection rules" (Garton and Suttor 1998, 484).

Figure 8.11 illustrates the six rule layers involved in Garton's model. Though they are laid out hierarchically in the figure, the interactions between the layers are not so strictly regulated in practice. "When assigning parameter values to a synthesis algorithm, the rules do not function in a hierarchical manner. Instead, rules are accorded precedence in a context-dependent, probabilistic manner. Finding the exact locus of 'compositional decisions' or 'performance

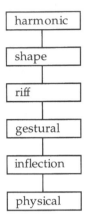

Figure 8.11 Garton Style Rule Layers

decisions' in one of our models is nearly impossible because the rules all function interdependently in making musical choices" (Garton and Suttor 1998, 484).

The Garton style synthesis work is already operative as an interactive system. The rule sets and underlying sound production algorithms are implemented in RTcmix, a real-time version of the venerable cmix software synthesis system (Garton and Topper 1997). All of the code for RTcmix and the style synthesis rules can be found on the Columbia Computer Music Center website.

The style recognition algorithm described by Dannenberg, Thom and Watson (1997) was designed to recognize any of four improvisation styles during performance within five seconds. The four initial style types were "lyrical," "frantic," "syncopated," and "pointillistic" (other styles were added later). The goal was to make the computer identify the style that corresponded to the player's intention.

Rather than hand-code recognizers, the group recorded a number of training sets and used them as input to supervised learning processes. To gather the training sets, a computer screen would prompt a trumpeter to improvise in one of the target styles. The improvisations were recorded and later rated by the improviser to identify how well they represented a particular style. Five-second segments of the improvisations together with the assigned ratings yielded 1200 training examples. An example could be rated as representative of more than one style: e.g., a segment might have a high "frantic" rating and a moderate "syncopated" score as well.

Of particular interest for the feature-based analysis systems under discussion in this text is the collection of features extracted from the training examples that were used as parameters for learning: "To build a classifier, we first identified 13 low-level features based on the MIDI data: averages and standard deviations of MIDI key number, duration, duty factor, pitch, and volume, as well as counts of notes, pitch bend messages, and volume change messages. (Pitch differs from key number in that pitch-bend information is included. Duty factor means the ratio of duration to inter-onset interval)" (Dannenberg et al. 1997, 345).

The `ListenProp` analysis style provides for some number of feature analyzers to be called with each incoming MIDI event. We can easily amend the design to provide averages over the preceding five seconds by consulting the time fields of `Events` in the buffer. In this way we could construct 13 `ListenProps` corresponding to each of the Dannenberg group's parameters, or one large `Averager` `ListenProp` that would keep track of all 13 simultaneously.

The supervised learning techniques used in the study included a naive Bayesian classifier, a linear classifier, and a neural network. We have already investigated neural networks, though the net Dannenberg's group used was of a different type from the ones implemented in chapter 3: the Cascade-Correlation network begins with only input and output nodes and then adds successive hidden layers (of one node each) as learning progresses (Bishop 1995).

The naive Bayesian classifier learns a mean feature vector for each target class. Then new vectors are classified by finding the target vector that is closest to it, using a "normalized distance." "The 'normalized distance' is the Euclidean distance after scaling each dimension by its standard deviation" (Dannenberg et al. 1997, 345).

The linear classifier computes a weighted sum of features. The learned feature weights change for each class to be identified. All three techniques resulted in classifiers with a high degree of accuracy in identifying the target styles. With four targets, the Bayesian classifier correctly identified the style 98.1% of the time. Using eight targets, the identification accuracy was 90%.

Machine learning makes it possible to recognize styles using correlations of features that may not be readily apparent. "Casually guessing at good features or combinations, plugging in 'reasonable' parameters and testing will almost always fail. In contrast, machine learning approaches that automatically take into account a large body of many-dimensional training data lead to very effective classifiers" (Dannenberg et al. 1997, 347).

The goal of the Dannenberg group's study was to train a classifier that could be used in an improvised performance. In that they manifestly succeeded, as the Bayesian classifier was actually used as part of the software for *In Transit.* High-level gestural characterizations, then, can not only be learned but also recognized onstage.

8.3.2 Chord Selection and Voicing

Roger Dannenberg uses a pre-defined collection of chords to generate the harmonies of *In Transit.* The collection is maintained in a text file (chords.dat) that is read into the program prior to performance. The chords are typed into six groups { major, minor, augmented, diminished, suspended, dominant } and are associated with a frequency of occurrence that determines their relative probability. Dannenberg derived a statistical profile of chord transitions from an analysis of jazz standards: chords in the originals were reduced to the six classes listed above. A transition is defined by the type of the first chord, the type of the second chord, and the interval between their roots. Using an intervallic representation means that only one V7-I progression is identified (for example) rather than twelve related progressions corresponding to the twelve possible root combinations.

In the *In Transit* application on the CD-ROM, the chords.dat collection is used to initialize an array of IntervalChord objects. Fields in the IntervalChord class include the chord's frequency, root,

```
class IntervalChord {

private:

        enum  ArraySizes { kIntervalMax = 8 };

        int    frequency;        // probability of selection per type

        int    root;

        int    bass;

        int    intervals[kIntervalMax];


public:

        IntervalChord(void);

        IntervalChord(const IntervalChord& rhs);


        friend class ChordGenerator;

};
```

Figure 8.12 `IntervalChord` class

bass note, and a list of intervals (figure 8.12). The root is a pitch class
and forms the lower member of all of the intervals recorded in the
intervals list. That is, if root is 5 it represents the pitch class F (5
semitones above C). An interval of 10 in the intervals list, then,
would be mapped to E♭, 10 semitones above F.

The intervals list is zero-terminated. There may be up to `kInter-
valMax-1` intervals in any `IntervalChord`, but following the final
interval in the list there must be a zero.

The frequency values in a chord collection are normalized such
that the sum of frequencies for each chord type is equal to the constant value `kCertain`. The function `Select()` uses these frequency
values to determine which chord of a given type to choose (figure
8.13). The first operation is to generate a random number between 0
and `kCertain-1`. `Select()` then scans through all of the chords of

```
void ChordGenerator::Select(int type, int inRoot, IntervalChord* chord)
{
        // choose a random number from 0 to kCertain-1, inclusive:
        int  r    = fastrand(0, kCertain-1);
        int  sum  = 0;
        long i    = chordTable[type];
        long last = chordTable[type+1];


        // scan all chords, find the one whose probability spans r
        while (i < last) {
                sum += chordData[i]->frequency;
                if (sum > r) break;           // found it
        }


        if (i == last)                        // if failed to find a chord
                i = chordTable[type];         // take first of type


        (*chord)    = (*chordData[i]);
        // add input root to root of chord
        chord->root = (inRoot + chord->root) % 12;
}
```

Figure 8.13 ChordSelect() function

the requested type, adding the frequency associated with each chord to sum. Once sum exceeds the random number, the chord currently reached in the search is chosen and returned. In this way, the frequency associated with a chord corresponds to the likelihood that it will be chosen with Select(). Finally the root of the output chord is determined by adding inRoot to the root of the chord selected from the collection.

The full selection process used for *In Transit* combines the Markov selection with a constraint that tries to harmonize predicted pitches against a chord to be played. When the program is about to complete a chord transition, learned from a series of jazz standards, it assumes that the performer will move up a half-step when the second chord of the transition is played. Therefore it tries to select a chord that contains or is consonant with the pitch one halfstep above where the performer currently is. In this way the actual chord selected will be affected by both the probabilities and the influence of the player, who can direct the harmonization to a certain zone by leading to the desired pitch.

The chord identification processes developed in chapter 2 reduce a chord to a collection of pitch classes in which the relative and absolute locations of the component notes are discarded. Certainly one of the most critical aspects of chord performance in jazz piano playing, however, is voicing. Voicing refers to the distribution of the constituent pitches of a chord across the keyboard. When we move from chord analysis to chord synthesis, therefore, we quickly encounter the necessity of describing the voicing that will be used to perform any particular abstract type.

Roger Dannenberg represents chords in two different ways in the *In Transit* software. The first is an IntervalChord, shown in figure 8.12, and is used for the calculation in Select(). The second representation is a VoicingChord (figure 8.14). A VoicingChord maintains the pitches of the chord as MIDI note numbers, not as intervals above a root. There are two arrays of note numbers, one for the "left hand" (lh) and one for the "right" (rh). Both lists are zero-terminated and each is assumed to record note numbers in ascending order. The

```
class VoicingChord {

    private:

    enum  ArraySizes { kNoteMax = 8 };

    int   lh[kNoteMax];

    int   rh[kNoteMax];


    public:

    VoicingChord(void);               // constructor

    VoicingChord(int int1, ...);  // constructor with initialization


    friend class ChordGenerator;
};
```

Figure 8.14 VoicingChord class

VoicingChord constructor takes a variable number of note names with zeroes marking the end of the left- and right-hand lists.

The allocation new VoicingChord(36, 42, 46, 0, 63, 70, 75, 0), then, will produce a VoicingChord with C2, G♭2, and B♭2 in the left hand and E♭4, B♭4, and E♭5 in the right. Once an IntervalChord has been chosen with Select(), it is changed into a VoicingChord to prepare it for performance. The function

VoicingChord* Voice(VoicingChord* last, IntervalChord* next)

takes the previous VoicingChord and a newly selected IntervalChord as arguments and returns a new VoicingChord generated with the intervals from next using appropriate voice-leading from last.

Dannenberg's technique is ideally suited to real-time improvisation because it does not depend on information about the future to work. In jazz harmony texts, however, chord voicings and substitutions are often described with reference to the immediately following context: "players may choose to precede a major, minor, dominant, or half-diminished chord in a progression by a dominant chord whose root is either a fifth or a half step above that of the structural chord or by a diminished chord whose root is a half step below it" (Berliner 1994, 86).

The technique of chord insertions that Berliner describes is algorithmic in its formulation. That is, given a chord progression we can write a program that will make the insertions Berliner suggests at the appropriate points. To realize the insertions in performance, however, the program would need to know the progression being played, just as a human musician would. Human players have access to the progression because it is written on a lead sheet on their music stand, because they are told the name of the progression before the band begins to play, or because they recognize it as it is being played.

We would like to assume as little as possible about the composition-specific information available to the program. The pattern processing techniques of chapter 4, however, may make it possible for a machine musician to recognize chord progressions as they are underway. Once a known progression is found, planning for Berliner-style substitution could be carried out based on the anticipated continuation of the series.

8.4 Multimedia Improvisation

Italian computer scientist and composer Leonello Tarabella has been working for years with a team of programmers, musicians, and visual artists on new programs and interfaces for real-time multimedia improvisation. Their project has been carried out under the auspices of the CNUCE, a branch of the Italian National Research Council, in the Computer Music Research laboratory in Pisa.

8.4.1 Controllers

The most striking aspect of performances by this group is their use of several original and highly expressive controllers. Tarabella's very definition of the term interaction suggests the degree to which their work is involved with the development of novel interfaces: "The term interaction has referred to the activity of a performer on a controller which detects gesture[s] and translates them into data that a computer uses for controlling synthesizers" (Tarabella 1993a, 180).

One of their best-known controllers is called the Twin Towers, in which a pair of infrared rectangles projected up from a base unit are played by a human performer who moves his hands through the beams (figure 8.15). The changing orientation of the performer's

Figure 8.15 The Twin Towers

hands relative to the device can be calculated from the reflection of the beams back to the base. This results in a controller with (in the simplest case) six degrees of freedom: the height, side rotation, and front rotation of each hand. When the timing of gestures is included, many more possibilities arise: for example, the speed of motion through the beams could be used as a control parameter as well.

In the composition *Flexible Links* written for the NYU New Music and Dance Ensemble, Tarabella used the Twin Towers to control the recording and processing of sounds from the ensemble. Microphones were used to make hard-disk recordings of the musicians as the piece progressed. The composer could start and stop recording at will by making predefined hand gestures over the Twin Towers. Once a large chord of material was accumulated, it was played back through effects processing whose parameters were also changed with the controller. Tarabella's hand gestures manipulated filter cutoffs, reverberation, and other effects applied to material recorded earlier in the performance.

The group has produced several other controllers that are used in dedicated performances or together with the Twin Towers in large-scale interactive multimedia shows. These include the Light Baton, PAGe, the UV Stick, and the Imaginary Piano. All of them use video tracking in some way, a technology that the group has developed to a high degree of flexibility. The Light Baton, for example, is a conducting baton with a light emitter in the tip. A video sensor tracks the motion of the baton in real time and derives a number of fundamental conducting gestures whose recognition can be used to control the speed of playback of standard MIDI files or to send parameter values to compositional algorithms.

In PAGe (Painting by Aerial Gesture), another video-detection based system, a performer moves his hands through the active video area. The software tracks the hand motions and generates color graphics on a large screen behind the performer. Algorithmic computer music is generated at the same time under the influence of the hand movements to accompany the graphics. A more recent system performs Fourier analyses of hand images to detect different postures (fist, splayed fingers, etc.) used as inputs to interactive graphics and sound synthesis algorithms (Tarabella et al. 1998).

The UV Stick employs, as the name suggests, a stick lit by an ultraviolet lamp. Video tracking calculates the three-dimensional rotations of the stick, which control real-time synthesis parameters and interactive graphics. Finally, the Imaginary Piano tracks hand motions in the video field and interprets these as piano-playing gestures. The software translates the detection into control parameters for an algorithmic composition process sounding through piano samples. The effect is of someone playing on an invisible piano.

Tarabella has designed and implemented a number of computer languages for interactive programming, the most recent of which is GALileo (Graphic ALgorithmic music language) (Tarabella and Magrini 1998). GALileo uses a graphic interface to programming objects, like Max, but can also open a text editing window to allow users to modify the underlying code. Both high-level constructs and sound synthesis, using a csound-like protocol, can be programmed and combined into patches for real-time performance.

8.4.2 Composition Techniques

As a composer, Leonello Tarabella writes a new set of composition functions for each new work. A number of techniques, however, find repeated use in his pieces. One of these is the generation of rhythmic textures based on random numbers. To produce these rhythms, a constant (short) duration is specified. Then a random number is generated with a number of bits equal to the length of the desired pattern. A bit mask moves along the random number, and if a bit is on (equal to one), a note is produced with the constant duration. If the bit in the random number at the location of the mask is off (equal to zero), a rest with the same duration is produced. The code in figure 8.16 demonstrates a version of this process that was used in Tarabella's work, *Algorithm Blues*. In this instance the rhythm generator performs patterns on cymbals as part of a blues combo.

Mark Coniglio, composer for the interactive dance company, Troika Ranch, uses a similar procedure. In Coniglio's version, ASCII

characters instead of random numbers generate the rhythmic patterns. The drum patterns he produces, then, can actually "spell out"
words composed of strings of characters played by the generator in
a kind of computer-age Morse code.

The Algorithm Blues application on the CD-ROM provides a simple interface to the Cymbals() procedure listed in figure 8.16.
Whenever the Make Pattern button is pushed, Cymbals() is called
with a pattern size of eight. The OMS output menu can be used to
select the desired recipient of the generated MIDI messages. All of the
source code is included with the application; the reader may wish
to vary the operation of the example by changing the pattern size

```
void AlgorithmBlues::Cymbals(int pattern)

{

    long dur     = 150L;   // constant duration

    int   Piatto1 = 63;     // pitch number of cymbal sound


    // generate a random number with # of bits equal to the pattern length

    int n     = rand()%((int)pow(2.0, (float)pattern));

    int mask = 1;

    for (int j=0; j<pattern; j++) {

        // if the mask finds a bit in the random number is set

        // then generate a new note

        if (n & mask)

            Nota(j*dur,Piatto1-(rand()%2),(rand()%80)+40,0,0.90,dur);

        mask <<= 1;        // shift the bit mask left

    }

}
```

Figure 8.16 Algorithmic rhythm generator

randomly every time the button is pushed, for example, or by using different output pitch numbers. Note that Algorithm Blues as it stands will only sound like a cymbal if note 63 on channel 0 is a cymbal sound.

Tarabella's Nota() sound output function is interesting because of the care with which it treats the NoteOff() call for a MIDI note. The MIDI standard requires two messages to be sent for a complete note: one when the note goes on, and another when it is to go off. A full MIDI note process makes a single conceptual unit of these with one routine that handles the scheduling of both MIDI transmissions. An advantage of this message structure is that a full note has a duration attached to it, whereas a simple MIDI note on has no concept of time and does not know when it will end. Many full MIDI note processes (including my own Event::Play() and the MakeNote object in Max) treat the note's duration as an undifferentiated span of time. The Nota() function, on the other hand, implements the idea of a duty cycle within the overall duration of the note. Rather than simply scheduling the note off message to be sent when the duration of the full note has elapsed, the note off will be sent at the end of a duty cycle within that duration.

Figure 8.17 lists the code for a version of Tarabella's Nota() function using the *Machine Musicianship* library's Event representation. The duration of the event is given in milliseconds as a long integer, and the duty cycle as a floating point value. The note on is called after onset milliseconds, and the note off scheduled to occur duty * duration milliseconds after the onset.

There are two primary uses for the duty cycle concept. First, synthesized or sampled sounds are often designed with a decay phase, a part of the sound that is to be produced after its release. The duty cycle allows the composer to think of the duration of the note in terms of its total length, while still allowing time for the decay to occur. Durations might be expressed as a series of quarter notes, conceptually, while the duty parameter could force each duration actually to be shortened by 20%, thereby leaving time for the decay

```
void AlgorithmBlues::Nota(long onset, int pitch, int velocity, int
                          channel, float duty, long duration)
{
        Event event, *e = &event;


        e->SetIOI(onset);

        e->SetChans(1, channel);

        e->SetChordSize(1);

        Note *n = e->Notes(0);

        n->SetPitch(pitch);

        n->SetVelocity(velocity);

        n->SetDuration(duration*duty);

        outPort->Play(e);
}
```

Figure 8.17 Nota() listing

phase. Certainly this requires that the synthesis method be tuned to the duty cycle, so that the sound actually has a decay to fill the requisite time.

Another application of a duty cycle is to add articulations to MIDI notes. If the release time is not being filled by a decay phase, it simply will be heard as a shortening of the note, as in staccato. A composer can determine the degree of staccato by changing the duty parameter while keeping the duration equal to the conceptual length of the note, much as a dot is placed over a quarter note in traditional notation. In fact the duty cycle can be much more precise than a notated dot, as the composer can specify exactly how much of the conceptual duration a performed note should fill. Duty cycles with a value greater than one produce legato, with the end of a note extending beyond the presumed duration.

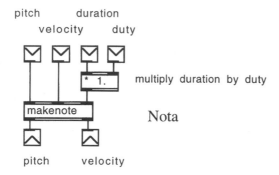

Figure 8.18 Nota Max object

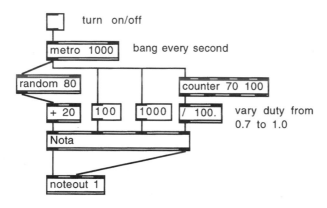

Figure 8.19 Nota Max patch

Figure 8.18 shows Nota, a Max object implementing the duty cycle parameter. It is simply makenote with a multiplication added to the duration inlet that changes the length of the note according to the duty value. The duty is initialized to 1.0, so that it will have no effect until it is changed. Nota retains the most recent duty value whenever one is sent. The outlets of Nota are normally sent to a noteout object.

Figure 8.19 shows Nota being used to vary the articulation of random notes. With every bang from the metro object, the counter will increase the duty parameter linearly from 0.7 to 1.0. (The counter uses integer values, so we divide integers ranging from 70

to 100 by 100.0 to derive floating point duty values.) Whenever the
`counter` reaches the upper bound (100), it jumps back down to 70
and begins counting up again. This results in a series of notes with
steadily increasing durations that snap back to their shortest staccato
form every thirty notes.

8.4.3 Continuous Controls

A large part of the compositional order developed in Tarabella's programs centers on continuous control of synthesis parameters. Essentially the technique involves the production of breakpoint line
segments over specified durations of time. Max/msp is particularly
well suited to such continuous controls: a combination of a `line`
object with `ctlout` accomplishes what is needed for MIDI devices.
The patch shown in figure 8.20 will change the volume of a MIDI
synthesizer to off or full over a span of five seconds whenever the
corresponding button is pushed.

The function `CtlLine()` will continually update the value of a
MIDI continuous control from some beginning value to a target value
over a specified duration (figure 8.21). The variables needed to accomplish this behavior are:

- id   The number of the MIDI continuous control
- from   The begin value
- duration   The time within which to change
- to   The target value
- channel   The MIDI channel number

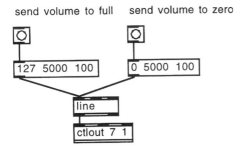

Figure 8.20   Max control change

```
void CtlLine(int id, ...)

{

  va_list args;

  int      from, to, channel;

  long     duration;


  va_start(args, id);

  from     = va_arg(args, int);

  duration = va_arg(args, long);

  to       = va_arg(args, int);

  channel  = va_arg(args, int);

  va_end(args);


  if (outport->controlTask) scheduler->AbortTask(outport->controlTask);

  outport->CtlOut(id, from, channel);

  if (duration <= kGrain) {

      outport->controlTask = scheduler->Schedule_Task(Now+duration, 0,

                        2, 0, CLiner, 0L, to, 0, 0, channel, id);

      return;

  }

  steps = duration/kGrain;

  if (steps == 0) return;              // avoid division by zero

  range = to - from;

  inc   = range/steps;

  if (inc != 0) {

      from += inc;
```

Figure 8.21 Control change routine

```
outport->controlTask = scheduler->Schedule_Task(Now+kGrain, 0, 2,

                0, CLiner, kGrain, from, inc, steps-1, channel, id);

} else {

    inc       = (range>0)?1:-1;

    steps     = abs(range);

    duration /= steps;

    outport->controlTask = scheduler->Schedule_Task(Now+duration, 0,

            2, 0, CLiner, duration, from, inc, steps-1, channel, id);

    }

}
```

Figure 8.21 Continued

CtlLine() is called initially by the application program, and thereafter by itself. Because calls to CtlLine() are usually run through the scheduler, they must follow the variable argument conventions described in <stdarg.h>. Conformance to the variable argument conventions means that any function can be scheduled for later execution—the scheduler does not enforce any particular limit of the number or types of arguments.

CtlLine() calculates the increment needed for each step of the continuous control change and schedules CLiner() for repeated execution to actually transmit the necessary MIDI messages. The OMS output port (outPort) keeps track of the scheduler record associated with the continuous control process. This makes it possible for the outPort to abort the control change at any time. In the example there is only one controlTask, which means that only one continuous control process can be active at a time. In more complex applications this can be replaced by an array of task pointers, implementing an unlimited number of simultaneous controllers.

9 Installations

Beyond stage presentations, musically aware installations provide another venue for interaction between humans and machine performers. In many cases, the humans interacting with such machines need not be trained musicians themselves—the musicianship of the system can respond to input from the users in such a way that they are able to use simple physical gestures to control or influence complex musical results. Installations often make a visual, as well as an audible response to the visitor. As such, they resemble most closely the interactive multimedia environments presented in chapter 8.

Artists creating such installations are again faced with the problem of cross-modal influence—how to make the relationship between visual, audible, and physical gestures meaningful. In some ways, these relationships are exposed more directly in installations than they are in the types of staged multimedia presentations discussed in chapter 8. When watching a performance, observers deduce relationships between the humans onstage and their machine partners. When faced with an installation, observers must explore the nature of the relationship by interacting with the environment themselves.

9.1 Multimedia Installations

The traditional form of multimedia installation is a location where machines and visitors interact. Motion, force, or video sensors that can locate the placement and movement of visitors in the space typically provide input. Video, animation, lighting, and motorized objects are possible output modalities, though we will be most concerned with such environments that also involve sound.

9.1.1 Audio and Imagery

Felt Histories (re: the fact of a doorframe) is an interactive video and sound installation designed by Thecla Schiphorst. The installation projects a video image of an old woman's body onto a screen of raw silk suspended within a doorframe. "As the visitor approaches the doorframe, the image within the frame responds very slightly to the proximity of the visitor. The image quivers and waits. As the visitor touches or caresses the image within the frame, the visitor's own hands and perhaps their face, appear momentarily reflected within the image they caress. This mirroring occurs only during the moments of contact. As the visitor caresses the surface of the image, a very small breeze (controlled by miniature fans embedded within the frame) moves very slightly over the face of the visitor, the image within the frame moves in response to the caress, and a complex sound environment is constructed in direct response to the gesture and movement of contact" (Schiphorst 1996).

By design, *Felt Histories* confronts visitors with questions about their own aging, decay, and sexuality. Because the piece responds to touch, visitors must overcome their reluctance to caress the body of another, albeit video, person. The technology of the installation uses proximity and force detection sensors to notice when a visitor has approached the doorframe or touched the silk screen. Information from the sensors is interpreted by a Max patch to control four types of response: (1) movement of the video, (2) sound, (3) mixing of the stored video with live video of the visitor, and (4) manipulation of small fans in the doorframe.

The audio is stored in sound files that are played back as an ambient background, as a function of the user's interaction. What the user does determines both which sound files are heard and the level of their playback within the overall mix: "The soundscape is constructed in such a way as to create an intimate local sound response based on movement of the hand over the surface. The movement and proximity of the participant's body literally mixes the sound. The interface invites whole body movement which 'falls into' the work. The local sounds trickle outward and affect the ambient soundscape

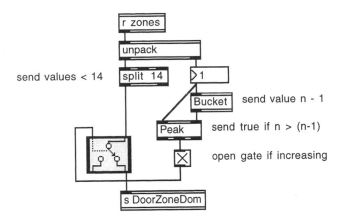

send values < 14

send value n - 1

send true if n > (n-1)

open gate if increasing

Figure 9.1 Dominant Zone

depending on the level of activity that occurs on the surface of the work" (Schiphorst 1996).

The Max patch, programmed by Ken Gregory, Grant Gregson, and Norm Jaffe, receives and parses sensor inputs and distributes their signals to the appropriate response algorithms. One of the subpatches that does this is Dominant Zone (figure 9.1). Dominant Zone uses a clever combination of objects to change the primary zone of reaction within the doorframe. The send/receive variable zones sends lists of two values to Dominant Zone, the first of which is a zone number and the second a controller.

The control passes through Bucket, a Max object that implements a bucket brigade message passing regime in which incoming messages are sent incrementally out the outlets from left to right as new messages arrive. The patch uses only one outlet of Bucket, so the output from the object will be the previous input received each time a new value arrives. This delayed value is sent to the right inlet of Peak, a Max object that detects when a new value has been received that is higher than some peak threshold. Values sent to the right inlet change the threshold variable without triggering any output.

Now the original input to Bucket is passed to the left inlet of Peak. Because we are comparing the original input with the previous one

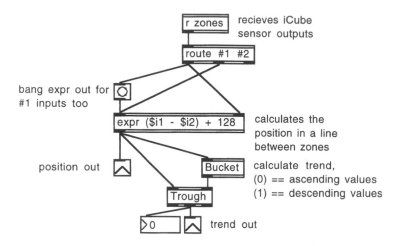

Figure 9.2 Liner

(comparing input *n* to input *n-1*), Peak will only be true when the current input is higher than the last. In that case the gate on the left-hand side of the patch is opened and the new zone value allowed to pass through to the DoorZoneDom transmitter.

The Liner patch (figure 9.2) performs an operation similar to but more general than that of Dominant Zone. The input to Liner is information from the iCube device merging all of the sensors trained on the visitors. Any sensor that changes sends its ID number and new value to the zones send/receive pair. The expression object then calculates a new position in a line between the two zones tracked by a given instance of Liner (which two IDs are tracked depends on the arguments #1 and #2 used to instantiate the object). This position is sent through the left outlet together with a trend that tracks ascending or descending motion of the expression value, similar to the ascending sensitivity of Dominant Zone. The trend is determined by Bucket, this time connected to a Trough object. Trough compares input *n* to *n-1* and outputs a zero if *n* is greater than *n-1* and a one if it is not.

Thecla Schiphorst's installation work not only encourages the visitor to explore the relationship between their actions and the technical environment but causes them to confront their habitual forms of interaction with other people, and their own bodies as well. The CD-ROM includes a sample Max patch that tracks the "trend" of mouse movements over a surface.

Don Ritter has produced a number of interactive multimedia installations, including *Fit* (1993) and *Intersection* (1993–95). *Intersection* deals with the interaction between people and machines:

Visitors to the installation encounter the sounds of speeding cars travelling across a completely dark room, typically 13 by 8 metres. The illusion of traffic is created through digital audio devices and eight audio speakers arranged to create four invisible lanes of traffic. If a visitor stands in the lane of an approaching car, this car will "screech" to a halt and remain "stopped" with its engine idling. Traffic will continue in the other lanes. When a visitor leaves a lane containing a "stopped" car, this car will quickly accelerate and continue travelling across the space. When a visitor remains in a lane with a "stopped" car, however, subsequent cars travelling down that lane will "smash" into the "stopped" car. Like an actual freeway, "safe areas" exist between each lane where a visitor may stand without affecting the flow of traffic. An unlimited number of visitors can be accommodated by the installation at one time. (Ritter 1996)

The purely audio relationship between the visitors and their darkened environment often provokes a quite visceral reaction. The threatened violence of the aural situation even makes it impossible for some to cross the space.

Fit produces another kind of physical reaction: the work consists of a video image of an aerobics instructor. "When a viewer moves in front of the image, music begins and the instructor starts exercising. When a viewer stops moving, the instructor also stops exercising and the music becomes silence. Each time a viewer begins moving his or her body, the instructor begins a new exercise with music. If a viewer moves non-stop, over time the instructor will exercise faster and change every 6 seconds to increasingly quicker routines. If a viewer exercises for 30 seconds non-stop, the instructor and music are presented at a dizzying rate" (Ritter 1996). Though the visitor controls the presentation of the instructor, many become engaged enough to follow the video image into wearying exertions. The CD-ROM includes a video clip of *Intersection* and of a human interacting with *Fit*.

9.1.2 Large-Scale Interaction

Tod Machover's *The Brain Opera* (1996) was, among other things, an attempt to combine the staged and installation types of interaction in one work: "*The Brain Opera* is an attempt to bring expression and creativity to everyone, in public or at home, by combining an exceptionally large number of interactive modes into a single, coherent experience. The project connects a series of hyperinstruments designed for the general public with a performance and a series of real-time music activities on the Internet. Audiences explore the hands-on instruments as preparation for the performance, creating personal music that makes each performance unique" (Machover 1996).

Before the performance of the staged part of the work, audience members interacted with installations that stored their material and brought it back later during the onstage performance. Websites collected further input from participants away from the concert hall and weaved this into the performed presentation as well. The design of *The Brain Opera* introduces another element into the contrast between performed and installed interaction: by collecting material from installed interaction and recalling it in performance, the audience is able to experience the genesis of the music firsthand and recognize it later as an observer. The work engages the audience's memory as well as its ability to see immediate relationships.

The Brain Opera's interactive material was collected in a large installation, named the "Mind Forest" or "Lobby." The environment comprised 29 separate interactive components powered by circa 40 networked computers. The components were conceptually part of several groups, each typified by its own interface and outputs. For example, a device called the Singing Tree used a microphone to sample the voice of a visitor. A dedicated PC analyzed 10 features of the singing voice: as these indicated an increasingly stable tone at a single pitch, a resynthesis of the visitor's voice became more "pleasing," and an animated image appeared on a monitor before them. "When the voice falters, the animation rewinds into a set of simpler images. The audio and video feedback on the singing voice has proven quite effective; the tonal and visual rewards encourage even poor amateurs to try for a reasonable tone" (Paradiso 1999, 133).

Another large component was the Rhythm Tree, a collection of 320 drumpads grouped into 10 strings of 32 pads each. Each drumpad detected when it was struck by a visitor's hand and identified the type of stroke used. (See the CD-ROM for a video clip of visitors interacting with the Rhythm Tree.) The information generated by visitors' input controlled percussion sounds and illumination of the pads struck.

Material sampled from the interactive environment was woven into the staged composition, itself performed using a group of three interactive hyperinstruments. *The Brain Opera* was a groundbreaking experience in the organization and performance of very large-scale interactive works: beyond its impressive technical prowess, the piece explored several aesthetic issues surrounding the integration of input from non-musicians and the synthesis of unrelated amateur performances.

The Brain Opera*'s musical mappings and parametric sequences ran independently on each Lobby instrument. Although this satisfied individual players (many of whom wore acoustically isolated by wearing headphones or were near appropriate speakers), the overall sound of* The Brain Opera *Lobby quickly dropped to the familiar, stochastic level of an arcade. . . . In general, future research is needed to address the balance between overall and local experiences, e.g., selecting and coordinating the audio responses over a network to enable large installations like* The Brain Opera *to sound more* *musically coherent to an outside observer while still retaining enough deterministic action-to-response musical feedback to satisfy individual participants. (Paradiso 1999, 147)*

The CD-ROM includes diagrams and video clips of the interactive part of *The Brain Opera,* and more can be found in *The Brain Opera* section of the Media Lab website (www.media.mit.edu).

9.2 Animated Improvisation

The combination of computer music and real-time animation is a natural manifestation of interactive multimedia that has been realized in several guises. In this section I will concentrate on the *Interactive Virtual Musicians* (IVM) system. New York University's Center for Advanced Technology developed IVM through collaboration between music and animation programmers. The complete environment consists of two major software subsystems: IMPROV and the IVM control software.

Developed by Ken Perlin, AThomas Goldberg, and others, the IMPROV system creates animated characters with individual personalities (Perlin 1995; Perlin and Goldberg 1996). Characters in IMPROV, known as *virtual actors,* are autonomous and directable. They are endowed with a library of animated actions, movements and gestures as well as individual personalities created by a programmer or animator using a scripting system. Characters are then able to generate their own animation sequences based on external information and influences (such as user input, musical analysis software, and the actions of other characters) and in accordance with their personality traits.

The IVM control software extends the functionality of the virtual actors to include music performance, thereby turning them into virtual musicians (Rowe and Singer 1997). IVM is responsible for receiving and interpreting the various forms of input, generating and playing the musical performance, and directing the graphical performance of IMPROV. The results of real-time musical analysis are communicated to the virtual musicians and influence their performance. Characters are controlled on several levels simultaneously. Low-level commands specify physical actions of the characters, such as movement of the virtual saxophonist's fingers. Higher-level commands communicate information about the musical performance, user input and other environment variables. This information influences the animated performance in various ways based on each character's programmed personality.

The ability to endow characters with personalities is one of the major innovations of IMPROV. A scripting system enables authors to create decision rules which use information about an actor and its environment to determine the actor's preferences for certain actions over others. The author specifies which information is relevant and how the information is weighted in making each decision. For example, an author might define a *nervousness* attribute for an actor that increases as other actors get closer. Furthermore, the author could specify that an increase in *nervousness* will cause the actor to choose fidgeting actions, such as shuffling its feet or biting its fingernails. Then, as other actors move closer, the character will appear to fidget more. IMPROV's personality scripting gives the virtual musicians a "body language," a set of actions that reflect various moods of playing, and "musical personalities" to select and control these actions. Among their many capabilities, virtual musicians can groove along to the music, tap their feet in time and raise their horns in the air during their solos.

Figure 9.3 shows an interactive virtual saxophone player named Willy (in recognition of Clilly Castiglia, author of his animation scripts). Willy is able to improvise solo lines above chords played on a MIDI keyboard, using the chord identification process described in section 2.1. Eric Singer developed the improvisation algorithm, which is based on a collection of pentatonic scales. In the flow of control during a performance, MIDI information arrives at the chord analysis module, which informs the improvisation process (called *Scales*) as to the root and type of the current input chord. Scales

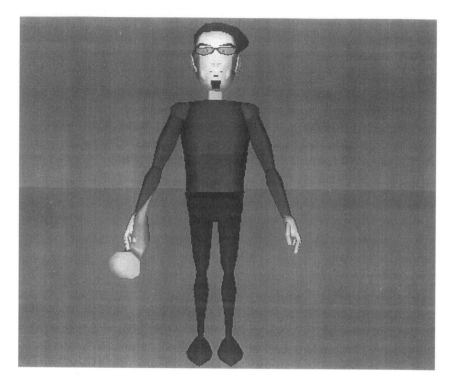

Figure 9.3 Willy, interactive virtual musician

selects intervals from one of a number of stored scales and adds these to the found chord root. Rhythmic constants specified by the user determine how many notes may be played per beat and what percentage of the possible beats will actually be articulated by performed notes.

As the musical improvisation is being generated, messages are sent to IMPROV that influence the animated behavior of Willy on the screen. Typical messages include instructions to turn right, turn left, lean back, tap foot, and so on. The system currently runs on two computers: music analysis and generation is written in C++ and performed on an Apple Macintosh, while IMPROV is implemented in Java and VRML and runs under any VRML2-compliant browser (currently, the CosmoPlayer on an SGI). Communication from the analysis machine to the animation engine is accomplished using Telnet/ TCP and UDP connections across a local-area network.

9.2.1 Improvisation with Scales

Eric Singer's improvisation algorithm generates solo saxophone lines using a number of stored scales. Particular scales are linked with chord types such that when the identification process recognizes an input chord of the corresponding type, its associated scale is activated. Figure 9.4 lists the definition of the Scales class.

The scaleList is a collection of scales used by the process in generating melodic lines. AddPattern takes a scale and stores it in scaleList at the position indicated by the chord type. Rather than restrict the length to pentatonic scales, AddPattern uses the C/C++ variable argument conventions to allow scales of any length (see section 5.1).

The following is a typical call to AddPattern():

```
AddPattern(kMaj, 5, C, D, G, A, B);// Major
```

This call associates a pentatonic scale with the chord type kMaj. Any number of pitch classes up to kScaleMax can be specified. The pitch names describing the scale are a convenience for the reader— in practice they specify a series of intervals above the first member. If this scale were to be played above a D-major chord, for example, the pitches used would be D, E, A, B, C♯ (the same sequence of intervals based on D instead of C). Beyond the scales themselves, the algorithm maintains a set of paths to read through any given scale. An example of a set of paths:

```
int path[kNumPaths][kPathLen] =
          {{1, 1, -2, 1}, {2, 1, -2, 1}, {1, 1, 1, 1}};
```

These paths are used to step through a scale. An index into the chosen path picks each step size in turn, which is added to another index pointing into the scale. Whenever the calculated index goes past the end of the scale, it is wrapped around back to the beginning. For example, if the third path in the list above is chosen (1,1,1,1),

```
class Scales {
public:
        enum ToneNames { C=0, Cs=1, Db=1, D=2, Ds=3, Eb=3, E=4, Es=5,
                         Fb=4, F=5, Fs=6, Gb=6, G=7, Gs=8, Ab=8, A=9,
                         As=10, Bb=10, B=11, Bs=12, Cb=11 };
        enum ChordType { kMaj = 0, kDom9, kDom13, kMin7, kMaj7, kDoms11,
                         kLast, kNumChords };
        enum            { kNumPaths = 3, kPathLen = 4, kScaleMax = 11 };


private:
        long        beatDuration;           // length of a beat in ms
        int         beatNumber;             // which beat in the bar
        int         beatsPerBar;            // how many beats per bar
        int         chordRoot;              // pitch class of root
        ChordType   chordType;              // type: one of ChordType
        int         lastIndex;              // last index into scale
        int         lastNote;               // last pitch output
        int         notesPerBang;           // subdivisions per beat
        int         pathIndex;              // index into path
        int         pathNum;                // which path
        int         path[kNumPaths][kPathLen]; // paths
        int         rangeHi;                // high note of output range
        int         rangeLo;                // low note of output range
        int         scaleList[kNumChords][kScaleMax];
        int         scaleSize[kNumChords];  // size of scale per type
        float       swingness;              // swing regulator
        float       timeAdj;                // timing deviation variables
```

Figure 9.4 Scales class

```
        float           timeDev;

        float           velBase;                // velocity deviation vars

        float           velDev;

        float           velPush;


        class EventBlock* events;               // output events

public:

        Scales(void);

        ~Scales(void);

        int             Bang(long bangTime, long beatDuration);


private:

        void            AddPattern(int chordIndex, ...);

        void            SetNotesPerBang(int notesPerBang);

};
```

Figure 9.4 Continued

each note from the scale will be taken in order. No matter which member of the path is selected, the scale index will always be incremented by one. If, instead, the first path were chosen (1,1,−2,1), the scale would be read in order except once every four notes, when the scale reader would jump back two places instead of ahead one. Taken with the scale C, D, G, A, B, the first path would produce C, D, E, C, D, E, F, D, E, F, G, E, etc.

The FindIndex() routine is the first step in finding the address of the scale member to be used at any given moment (figure 9.5). It begins by calculating the distance between the last scale degree produced and the first degrees past the end or before the beginning of the scale. This is to cover the case in which a scale should be

```
/*

 * FindIndex: find the closest member of the scale, wrapping around

 * beginning or end of the scale

 */

int Scales::FindIndex(int* scale, int lastDegree, int length)

{

  int toneDiff;    // find closest tone, accounting for wraparound

  int toneIndex;

  int extendUp   = abs(scale[0] + 12 - lastDegree);

  int extendDown = abs(lastDegree + 12 - scale[length-1]);

  if (extendUp < extendDown) {

      toneDiff  = extendUp;

      toneIndex = length;      // set the index past the end of the list

  } else {

      toneDiff  = extendDown;

      toneIndex = -1;    // set the index before the start of the list

  }

  for (int i=0; i<length; i++) {

      int newDiff = abs(lastDegree - scale[i]);

      if (newDiff < toneDiff) {

            toneDiff  = newDiff;

            toneIndex = i;

      }

  }

  return toneIndex;

}
```

Figure 9.5 FindIndex() method

continued in another octave. Consider a C-major scale that is to be played in order: when the B at the top of the scale is played, the scale index will loop back around to zero in order to point at the C that initiates the scale. The C that should be played, however, is the one found one half-step above the B, not the C a major seventh lower. FindIndex() will notice that the half-step C is closer to B and return an octave-switching index accordingly.

The combination of FindIndex() with a collection of scales will produce endlessly meandering melodies that fit with particular chord types and roots. To give them more of a shape and direction in time, however, they must first be joined with a rhythmic presentation. One of the functions with which this is done in Scales is GenRest(), which generates a rest in the output according to a fixed set of probabilities (figure 9.6).

```
bool Scales::GenRest(int subdivision)

{

    switch (subdivision) {

        case 0:     return RndPosFloat() < 0.55;

        case 1:     return RndPosFloat() < 0.55;

        case 2:     return RndPosFloat() < 0.43;

        case 3:     return RndPosFloat() < 0.16;

        case 4:     return RndPosFloat() < 0.29;

        case 5:     return RndPosFloat() < 0.35;

        case 6:     return RndPosFloat() < 0.51;

        case 7:     return RndPosFloat() < 0.30;

        default:    return RndPosFloat() < 0.05;

    }

}
```

Figure 9.6 GenRest() method

The subdivision argument refers to the position of the output note within a measure. The values 0–7 represent eighth note positions such that zero is the initial eighth note of the measure, one is the second half of the first beat, two is the first eighth note of the second beat, and so on. `RndPosFloat()` is a macro that returns a floating point random number between 0.0 and 1.0. The fixed probabilities of the `GenRest()` method make it most likely that a note will be played on the first, second, or seventh eighth note of a 4/4 bar. In other words, both halves of the first beat and the first eighth of the last beat are the most probable subdivisions to be articulated. The least likely position is the second eighth of the second beat.

The `Scales` application on the CD-ROM implements the melodic improviser outlined here. A control panel allows the user to change parameters such as notes per beat, percentage of rests, etc. `Scales` will improvise against chords played either on a MIDI keyboard or entered in the control panel.

9.2.2 Improvising Melodic Lines

David Baker's *Jazz Improvisation* (1983) teaches beginning improvisers some basic techniques of melodic and rhythmic elaboration in the jazz idiom. In it he discusses three approaches to improvising melodic lines above chord changes: "We may approach any composition in a number of ways, three of which follow: (1) The first approach is a scalar approach where we reduce each chord or series of chords to basic scale colors. . . . In this approach we are less concerned with outlining the particular chords than with presenting a scale or mode that would sound the key area implied by the chords. (2) In the second approach the player articulates each chord. He might simply use arpeggios and seventh chords in a rhythm of his own choosing or he might use what I have labeled root-oriented patterns such as 1-2-1-2, 1-2-1-2; or 1-2-3-1, 1-2-3-1; or 1-2-3-5, 1-2-3-5, etc. . . . (3) The third approach involves the use of patterns either predetermined or spontaneously conceived" (Baker 1983, 19).

The `Scales` algorithm can directly model Baker's first approach. The stored scales "sound the key area implied by the chords" and

Figure 9.7 Scales against Tune I

will be transposed correctly by the root delivered from the analysis. The second approach is readily implemented as well. Using the pentatonic scale C, D, G, A, B, we can define simple paths to realize Baker's root-oriented patterns. The path (1,−1) will output 1-2-1-2, the path (1,1,−2) will output 1-2-3-1, 1-2-3-1, and so on.

Jazz Improvisation goes on to show several examples of using approaches (1) and (2) against a simple tune (Tune I). Let us use the Scales algorithm to reproduce these examples. Tune I is a four-bar chord progression: two bars of C-major 7th, followed by one bar each of F minor 7th and B♭-minor 7th. Baker's first example recommends playing a major scale against the major seventh chord, followed by a 1-2-1-2 root-oriented pattern over both minor seventh chords (figure 9.7).

To realize this example, we can use a major scale for all the recommended patterns. In this case, we need to associate a path number, and not the scale itself, to the type of the chord being played. A function similar to AddPattern can be used to initialize the paths array and place the desired path in the location corresponding to a given chord index. These two calls will produce the behavior required by Baker's example 1:

```
AddPath(kMaj7, 1, 1);        // Major Seventh
AddPath(kMin7, 2, 1, -1);    // Minor Seventh
```

Baker's third melodic improvisation approach—"the use of patterns either predetermined or spontaneously conceived"—calls to mind the pattern processing techniques of chapter 4 and in fact represents one of the strongest motivations for pursuing such techniques in the first place. In his description of an algorithmic improvisation program, Philip Johnson-Laird calls into question the pattern-based mode: "A common misconception about improvisation is that it depends on acquiring a repertoire of motifs—'licks' as they used to be called by musicians—which are then strung together one after the other to form an improvisation, suitably modified to meet the exigencies of the harmonic sequence. There are even books containing sets of 'licks' to be committed to memory to aid the process" (Johnson-Laird 1991, 292).

Johnson-Laird is right to question the pattern-chaining model as an explanation of all that occurs during improvisation. That there is an important element of pattern repetition and variation, however, is echoed in a wide range of scholarly writing on the subject: "Charlie Parker, like all improvisers, built his solos from a personal collection of melodic building blocks of various lengths. In his best work, he employed these melodic units creatively as connective components and as raw material for creation. In his more routine work (especially in the 1950s), he used them more mechanically, in lieu of real discovery" (Woideck 1996, 57). Here Woideck even uses the degree of literal repetition as a gauge of the creativity involved in a solo.

Lewis Porter's analysis of the solos of the young John Coltrane reveal clear instances of this strategy in the playing of the budding genius: in two recordings made on July 13, 1946, when Coltrane was 19 years old, the saxophonist repeatedly employs a motive that Porter labels "lick c." "Coltrane uses certain figures or 'licks,' as musicians call them, repeatedly on this session. For example, his short chorus on 'Sweet Miss' . . . employs a little phrase-ending figure (marked a on the example) four times, and figure c is used to begin three phrases. In fact c and a are teamed up two of those times" (Porter 1998, 45). Though Johnson-Laird's point is well taken, the truth lies somewhere in the middle—improvisers do use a repertoire of learned licks, but the good ones modify these in unpredictable ways through the course of a performance.

9.3 Multimodal Environments

Antonio Camurri and his colleagues have spent several years researching and building interactive multimodal environments (MEs) "conceived of as an audio-visual environment which can be used to

communicate with other humans and machines, other actors partici-
pating in the same event (including autonomous robots) or external
spectators of the action" (Camurri and Leman 1997, 496).

Multimodal environments can adapt their behavior to interaction
with a human partner or other machine agents. The system extracts
information about the actions of other agents in the environment (human or machine) by reading a collection of motion sensors. In one
application, a software agent tracked the motion of a human dancer
and generated computer music in response. "We can imagine that
the agent is trying to identify features of the 'style of movement' of
the dancer. If the latter starts moving with a given nervous and rhythmic gestures in roughly fixed positions in the space, therefore evok-
ing the gestures of a percussionist, the agent, after a few seconds,
initiates a continuous transformation toward a sort of 'dynamic
hyper-instrument': a set of virtual drums located in points of the
space where the dancer insists with his/her movement" (Camurri
and Ferrentino 1999, 33–34).

There are two important points to notice about this example: first,
that the agent is able to recognize a particular style of gesture; and
second that it can calculate an appropriate response to that movement and adapt it to the placement in space initiated by the dancer.
The environment continually adapts to the motion of the human
agent: if a particular drum is not played for some time, it begins to
"fade away," changing its sound or intensity. Alternatively, the
dancer may animate virtual agents onstage and, once they are constructed and playing, move on to create others while the previous
ones continue with the actions they were given.

The role of the designer (or composer) in such a complex system
is one of describing modes of interaction and degrees of freedom
within and between multiple agents. "The designer of the performance introduces into the system the sound and music knowledge,
the compositional goals, the aspects of integration between music
and gesture (including a model of interpretation of gestures), and
decides the amount of (possible) degrees of freedom left to the agent
as concerns the generative and compositional choices" (Camurri,
Ricchetti, and Trocca 1999).

The complexity of the environments in which MEs are situated is handled by a hybrid approach, combining symbolic and sub-symbolic components as required by different aspects of the problem. The symbolic and sub-symbolic parts are coordinated in a knowledge base, organized as shown in figure 9.8. In the notation of the figure, concepts are represented by ellipses, double arrows designate IS-A links, and boxes indicate roles. An IS-A link represents a hierarchical relation between objects or concepts: a robin IS-A bird, for example, and in Camurri's ontology, navigation IS-A type of action.

The two large symbolic categories of the knowledge base are *actions* and *situations*. These two subsume all other categories that are characterized by a duration and/or point in time. Situations represent relatively static states of the environment. An action always has an initial situation, from which is it begun, and a final situation that it produces. There may be identifiable intermediate situations between these as well. That all of these relations are true of navigation is concisely represented by figure 9.8 (taken from Camurri et al. [1995]).

An action on the symbolic level is executed sub-symbolically by an agent. An agent is a class that is expert in some domain and able to perform actions within it. In the dance interpretation application outlined above, the system architecture trains a number of observer

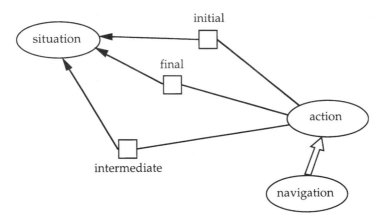

Figure 9.8 Knowledge base fragment

agents (OAs) on the output of a double video camera sensing device. The task of the OAs is to recognize and interpret the gestural and emotional content of the dancer's movements onstage. OAs are implemented using a variety of techniques, depending on their specialization. The posture analysis agent, for example, is a neural network, trained by users of the system to recognize certain postures of human figures. The input to the network is the low-level visual information from the video cameras, generating an output classification of the posture type.

Camurri deals with the coordination of multiple agents thus: "OAs can read concurrently the data produced by the preprocessing module. OAs can communicate [with] each other to cooperate or compete to analyse and understand high-level movement and gesture parameters. For example, a posture analysis OA can provide a gesture analysis OA with the recognized posture time marks on the input stream: then, the gesture OA can use them as candidate segmentation points to start gesture recognition processes" (Camurri, Ricchetti, and

Figure 9.9 Multimodal environment children's robot

Trocca 1999). Camurri's group has used multimodal environments in live performance, video production, and museum installations. They are designed for implementation on several parallel computers, which means that they can execute real-time sound synthesis, animation, and robotic control simultaneously using a network of dedicated machines.

Figure 9.9 shows a multimodal robot that is permanently installed in a children's science museum in Genoa, Italy (Città dei Bambini).

10 Directions

This volume has demonstrated ways to implement some of the fundamental concepts of musicianship in software and shown how this knowledge level can be used to support real-time performances, improvisations, and interactive installations. In conclusion I would like to review some of the main themes of the text and suggest both immediate and longer-term ways in which these could be projected into future research.

10.1 Research Synergy

Practitioners recognize that there is a significant pooling of interest in the fields of computer music composition, algorithmic analysis, and music cognition. It is normal to see researchers specialized in one field presenting work at a conference nominally devoted to a different area. There is an awareness of cross-disciplinary research in centers ranging from psychology laboratories to music production facilities. Within individual lines of work, however, the reigning strategy remains one of "divide and conquer." For example, algorithms for pitch rarely consult rhythmic aspects of the material and vice versa. Symbolic processes rarely are written to interact with sub-symbolic ones and vice versa. Even within one division, further simplifications may lead to powerful but limited results: key induction programs, for example, are often written to address only monophonic or only chordal input. Beat trackers may assume only slowly changing tempi or previously quantized inputs.

The "divide and conquer" approach has led to notable successes and accounts for much of the progress in these fields to date. It is an old and honored scientific tradition and certainly represents one of our most productive methodologies. I hope to have established, however, that so much strong work has now been accomplished from a reductionist standpoint that the field has become ripe for more synthetic research. We all know—and reductionist researchers are the first to point out—that humans experience music as a whole, not as the simple concatenation of independent and mute processes.

The reductionist impulse is strong because scaling systems to address a more complete musical context is difficult. Without such breadth, however, even some restricted problem areas may remain intractable. At the end of an article describing several attempts to separate the voices of a polyphonic composition using production system techniques in Prolog, Alan Marsden writes: "It seems clear, though, that deterministic production-system-like models are too rigid for modelling the complex interactions which underlie listening to, or even analysing, music. . . . But even if we use a more flexible framework, whether a constraint system, network or hybrid system . . . a full and faithful model of any one domain is unlikely to arise without also being a model of the full musical domain (and possibly beyond) because the interactions between domains appear to multifarious—the modeller must be humble in his or her objectives" (Marsden 1992, 262).

Marsden points out a phenomenon well known from artificial intelligence research, that after an initial period of great success, restricted problem domains have a tendency to run up against obstacles that cannot be easily overcome without consulting a wider context.

10.2 Research Directions

The best way to address a larger context in music modeling, in my view, is to coordinate the operation of multiple processes. Synthesis of existing research can be realized by implementing published algorithms within a common framework. Groups of such processes must then be coordinated to make their individual outputs contribute to the emergence of higher-level structures.

This line of research evokes the agenda of multi-agent systems, and a number of agent architectures have already proven the viability of these techniques for interactive music systems. The NetNeg program, Camurri's EyesWeb project, the Beat Tracking System and others have established a promising foundation for multi-agent systems in music and multimedia performance.

Isolating components of the system into relatively autonomous agents will help smooth the transition from MIDI or performance-based sensing to auditory inputs. As reviewed in chapter 4, adding an auditory component to interactive systems brings them much closer to the human experience of music. One of the primary impediments to auditory systems has been the relative expense of the input hardware. Now that digital signal processing has migrated to the CPU of even laptop computers, that boundary has fallen away. Though the additional information of an audio stream should greatly enhance the responsiveness of machine musicians, we should not lose the functionality already achieved by analyzing performance data. Combining dedicated components as necessary can aid the design of analysis and composition systems that approximate as closely as possible the desired behavior.

Finally, I believe there is important work to be done in realizing the potential of these systems by pursuing a much wider range of interaction with human musicians. They can and have assumed a critical role in music education, as well as in analysis, performance, and composition. Commercially, the term "interactive music" describes systems that make music without any musical input from the user at all, providing audio that changes in synchrony with game-playing—a byproduct of joystick movement, for example. If machine musicians are to encourage human musicmaking, a motivation explored at some length in chapter 1, we need to find better ways to employ them as assistants and teachers rather than simplistic prostheses.

In this text I concentrated on the modeling of the classical repertoire, particularly when testing analysis systems. I think there is much to be gained by demonstrating the power of these systems in situations where their performance can be readily gauged by a wide population, particularly when that population may have little prior experience with them. An equally important compositional standpoint holds that computers should be used to construct previously unknown musical worlds: "Perhaps a musical relativity admitting multiple points of view, frames of reference and operating models is what we require. We must educate the populace to understand that music making can involve creating entire musical universes, each built on its own unique assumptions and provided for inquiring souls to explore" (Rosenboom 1997, 39).

In these pages I have demonstrated a variety of tools, and some strategies for combining them. There are relatively few ready-to-run solutions here, but many templates for development. Ultimately, tools are only useful for building something else; the attraction of computational tools is that they can be used equally for emulating known worlds or devising completely new ones. I hope that I have provided readers with something more valuable than a collection of useful applications: ideas to catalyze new creation.

References

Allen, P., and R. Dannenberg. 1990. Tracking musical beats in real time. In *Proceedings of the 1990 International Computer Music Conference*. San Francisco: International Computer Music Association, 140–43.

Arcos, J., L. Mántaras, and X. Serra. 1998. Saxex: A case-based reasoning system for generating expressive musical performances. *Journal of New Music Research* 27(3):194–210.

Ashley, R. 1989. Modeling music listening: General considerations. *Contemporary Music Review* 4:295–310.

Baisnée, P., J.-B. Barrière, O. Koechlin, and R. Rowe. 1986. Real time interactions between musicians and computer: Live performance utilisations of the 4X musical workstation. In *Proceedings of the 1986 International Computer Music Conference*. San Francisco: International Computer Music Association.

Baker, D. 1983. *Jazz improvisation: A comprehensive method for all musicians*. Van Nuys, CA: Alfred Publishing Company.

Bent, I. 1980. *Analysis*. New York: W.W. Norton & Company.

Berg, P. 1998. *Using the AC Toolbox*. Distributed by the author at http://www.koncon.nl/ACToolbox/

Berliner, P. 1994. *Thinking in jazz: The infinite art of improvisation*. Chicago: The University of Chicago Press.

Berry, W. 1987. *Structural functions in music*. New York: Dover Publications.

Bharucha, J. 1987. Music cognition and perceptual facilitation: A connectionist framework. *Music Perception* 5:1–30.

Bharucha, J. 1999. Neural nets, temporal composites, and tonality. In *The psychology of music. 2nd Ed.* Ed. D. Deutsch. London: Academic Press.

Bharucha, J., and P. Todd. 1989. Modeling the perception of tonal structure with neural nets. *Computer Music Journal* 13(4):44–53.

Bigand, E. 1993. The influence of implicit harmony, rhythm, and musical training on the abstraction of "tension-relaxation schemas" in tonal musical phrases. *Contemporary Music Review* 9(1,2):123–137.

Biles, J. 1994. GenJam: a genetic algorithm for generating jazz solos. In *Proceedings of the 1994 International Computer Music Conference*. San Francisco: International Computer Music Association.

Biles, J. 1998. Interactive GenJam: Integrating real-time performance with a genetic algorithm. In *Proceedings of the 1998 International Computer Music Conference*. San Francisco: International Computer Music Association.

Bilmes, J. 1993. *Timing is of the essence: Perceptual and computational techniques for representing, learning, and reproducing expressive timing in percussive rhythm*. Master's thesis, Massachusetts Institute of Technology.

Bishop, C. 1995. *Neural networks for pattern recognition*. Cambridge, England: Clarendon Press.

Bloch, J., and R. Dannenberg. 1985. Real-time computer accompaniment of keyboard performances. In *Proceedings of the 1985 International Computer Music Conference*. San Francisco: International Computer Music Association.

Bobrow, D., and T. Winograd. 1977. An overview of KRL, a knowledge representation language. *Cognitive Science* 1(1):3–46.

Boden, M. 1994. What is creativity? In *Dimensions of creativity*. Ed. Margaret A. Boden. Cambridge, MA: The MIT Press.

Bongers, B. 1998. An interview with Sensorband. *Computer Music Journal* 22(1):13–24.

Bregman, A. 1990. *Auditory scene analysis*. Cambridge, MA: The MIT Press.

Bresin, R. 1998. Artificial neural networks based models for automatic performance of musical scores. *Journal of New Music Research* 27(3):239–270.

Brown, H., D. Butler, and M. Riess Jones. 1994. Musical and temporal influences on key discovery. *Music Perception* 11:371–407.

Butler, D. 1989. Describing the perception of tonality in music: A critique of the tonal hierarchy theory and a proposal for a theory of intervallic rivalry. *Music Perception* 6:219–242.

Butler, D. and W. Ward. 1988. Effacing the memory of musical pitch. *Music Perception* 5:251–260.

Cambouropoulos, E. 1997. Musical rhythm: A formal model for determining local boundaries, accents and metre in a melodic surface. In *Music, gestalt, and computing: Studies in cognitive and systematic musicology*. Ed. M. Leman. Berlin: Springer.

Camurri, A., A. Catorcini, C. Innocenti, and A. Massari. 1995. Music and multimedia knowledge representation and reasoning: The HARP system. *Computer Music Journal* 19(2):34–58.

Camurri, A., and M. Leman. 1997. Gestalt-based composition and performance in multimodal environments. In *Music, gestalt, and computing: Studies in cognitive and systematic musicology*. Ed. M. Leman. Berlin: Springer.

Camurri, A., and P. Ferrentino. 1999. Interactive environments for music and multimedia. *Multimedia Systems* 7:32–47.

Camurri, A., M. Ricchetti, and R. Trocca. 1999. EyesWeb: Toward gesture and affect recognition in dance/music interactive systems. In *Proceedings of IEEE multimedia systems 1999, Florence*.

Canazza, S., G. De Poli, G. Di Sanzo, and A. Vidolin. 1998. A model to add expressiveness to automatic musical performance. In *Proceedings of the 1998 International Computer Music Conference*. San Francisco: International Computer Music Association.

Canazza, S., G. De Poli, A. Rodà, and A. Vidolin. 1997. Analysis by synthesis of the expressive intentions in musical performance. In *Proceedings of the 1997 International Computer Music Conference*. San Francisco: International Computer Music Association.

Canetti, E. 1984. *Crowds and power*. trans. Carol Stewart. New York: Farrar Straus Giroux.

Carreras, F., M. Leman, and M. Lesaffre. 1999. Automatic description of musical signals using schema-based chord decomposition. *Journal of New Music Research*.

Chadabe, J. 1989. Interactive composing: An overview. In *The music machine*. Ed. C. Roads. Cambridge, MA: The MIT Press.

Chadabe, J. 1997. *Electric sound: The past and promise of electronic music*. Upper Saddle River, NJ: Prentice-Hall.

Chafe, C., B. Mont-Reynaud, and L. Rush. 1989. Toward an intelligent editor of digital audio: Recognition of musical constructs. In *The music machine*. Ed. C. Roads. Cambridge, MA: The MIT Press.

Clarke, E. 1985. Structure and expression in rhythmic performance. In *Musical structure and cognition*. Ed. P. Howell, I. Cross, and R. West. London: Academic Press.

Clarke, E. 1987. Levels of structure in the organization of musical time. *Contemporary Music Review* 2:211–238.

Clarke, E. 1988. Generative principles in music performance. In *Generative processes in music*. Ed. J. Sloboda. Oxford: Clarendon Press.

Clarke, E. 1999. Rhythm and timing in music. In *The psychology of music*. 2nd ed. Ed. D. Deutsch. London: Academic Press.

Cook, N. 1987. *A guide to musical analysis*. Oxford: Oxford University Press.

Cook, N. 1998. *Analysing musical multimedia*. Oxford: Clarendon Press.

Cope, D. 1990. Pattern matching as an engine for the computer simulation of musical style. In *Proceedings of the 1990 International Computer Music Conference*. San Francisco: International Computer Music Association.

Cope, D. 1991. *Computers and musical style*. Madison, WI: A-R Editions, Inc.

Cope, D. 1993. A computer model of music composition. In *Machine models of music*. Ed. S. Schwanauer and D. Levitt. Cambridge, MA: The MIT Press.

Craik, F., and R. Lockhart. 1972. Levels of processing: A framework for memory research. *Journal of Verbal Learning and Verbal Behavior* 11:671–684.

Cuddy, L. 1993. Melody comprehension and tonal structure. In *Psychology and music: The understanding of melody and rhythm*. Ed. T. J. Tighe and W. J. Dowling. Hillsdale, NJ: Lawrence Erlbaum Associates.

Dannenberg, R. 1984. An on-line algorithm for real-time accompaniment. In *Proceedings of the 1984 International Computer Music Conference*. San Francisco: International Computer Music Association.

Dannenberg, R. 1989. Real-time scheduling and computer accompaniment. In *Current directions in computer music research*. Ed. M. Mathews and J. Pierce. Cambridge, MA: The MIT Press.

Dannenberg, R. 1993. Music representation issues, techniques, and systems. *Computer Music Journal* 17(3):20–30.

Dannenberg, R. 1998. *In Transit* program note. Program of the 1998 International Computer Music Conference.

Dannenberg, R. 1999. Personal communication.

Dannenberg, R., and B. Mont-Reynaud. 1987. Following an improvisation in real time. In *Proceedings of the 1987 International Computer Music Conference*. San Francisco: International Computer Music Association.

Dannenberg, R., B. Thom, and D. Watson. 1997. A machine learning approach to musical style recognition. In *Proceedings of the 1997 International Computer Music Conference*. San Francisco: International Computer Music Association.

Deliège, I., M. Mélen, D. Stammers, and I. Cross. 1996. Musical schemata in real-time listening. *Music Perception* 14(2):117–160.

De Poli, G., A. Piccialli, and C. Roads, eds. *Representations of musical signals*. Cambridge, MA: The MIT Press.

Derrien, J. 1995. Entretien avec Philippe Manoury. In *Philippe Manoury: Les cahiers de l'Ircam*. Paris: Editions Ircam—Centre Georges-Pompidou.

Desain, P. 1992. A (de)composable theory of rhythm perception. *Music Perception* 9(4): 439–454.

Desain, P. 1993. A connectionist and a traditional AI quantizer: Symbolic versus subsymbolic models of rhythm perception. *Contemporary Music Review* 9(1,2):239–254.

Desain, P., and H. Honing. 1989. The quantization of musical time: A connectionist approach. *Computer Music Journal* 13(3).

Desain, P., and H. Honing. 1994a. Foot-tapping: A brief introduction to beat induction. In *Proceedings of the 1994 International Computer Music Conference*. San Francisco: International Computer Music Association, 78–79.

Desain, P., and H. Honing. 1994b. Rule-based models of initial-beat induction and an analysis of their behavior. In *Proceedings of the 1994 International Computer Music Conference*. San Francisco: International Computer Music Association.

Desain, P., and H. Honing. 1994c. Advanced issues in beat induction modeling: Syncopation, tempo and timing. In *Proceedings of the 1984 International Computer Music Conference*. San Francisco: International Computer Music Association.

Desain, P., and H. Honing. 1999. Computational models of beat induction: The rule-based approach. *Journal of New Music Research* 28(1):29–42.

Deutsch, D. 1999a. Grouping mechanisms in music. In *The psychology of music. 2nd Ed.* Ed. D. Deutsch. London: Academic Press.

Deutsch, D. 1999b. The processing of pitch combinations. In *The psychology of music. 2nd Ed.* Ed. D. Deutsch. London: Academic Press.

Deutsch, D., and J. Feroe. 1981. The internal representation of pitch sequences in tonal music. *Psychological Review* 88:503–522.

Dobbins, B. 1994. *A creative approach to jazz piano harmony*. Advance Music.

Dolson, M. 1991. Machine tongues XII: Neural networks. In *Music and connectionism*. Ed. P. Todd and G. Loy. Cambridge, MA: The MIT Press.

Dowling, W. and D. Harwood. 1986. *Music cognition*. New York: Academic Press.

Duckworth, W. 1998. *A creative approach to music fundamentals. 6th Ed.* Belmont, CA: Wadsworth Publishing Company.

Ebcioglu, K. 1992. An expert system for harmonizing chorales in the style of J.S. Bach. In *Understanding music with AI: Perspectives on music cognition*. Ed. O. Laske and M. Balaban. Cambridge, MA: The AAAI Press/The MIT Press.

Forte, A. 1973. *The structure of atonal music*. New Haven, CT: Yale University Press.

Friberg, A. 1991. Generative rules for music performance: A formal description of a rule system. *Computer Music Journal* 15(2):56–71.

Gabrielsson, A. 1988. Timing in music performance and its relations to music experience. In *Generative processes in music: The psychology of performance, improvisation, and composition*. Ed. J. Sloboda. Oxford: Clarendon Press.

Gabrielsson, A. 1995. Expressive intention and performance. In *Music and the mind machine*. Ed. R. Steinberg. Berlin: Springer-Verlag.

Garton, B., and M. Suttor. 1998. A sense of style. In *Proceedings of the 1998 International Computer Music Conference*. San Francisco: International Computer Music Association.

Garton, B., and D. Topper. 1997. RTcmix: Using CMIX in real time. In *Proceedings of the 1997 International Computer Music Conference*. San Francisco: International Computer Music Association.

Gjerdingen, R. 1988. *A classic turn of phrase: Music and the psychology of convention*. Philadelphia: University of Pennsylvania Press.

Gjerdingen, R. 1990. Categorization of musical patterns by self-organizing neuronlike networks. *Music Perception* 8:339–370.

Gjerdingen, R. 1999. Apparent motion in music? In *Musical networks: Parallel distributed perception and performance*. Ed. N. Griffith and P. Todd. Cambridge, MA: The MIT Press.

Goldman, C., D. Gang, J. Rosenschein, and D. Lehmann. 1999. NetNeg: A connectionist-agent integrated system for representing musical knowledge. *Annals of Mathematics and Artificial Intelligence* 25:69–90.

Goto, M., and Y. Muraoka. 1994. A beat-tracking system for acoustic signals of music. In *ACM multimedia 1994 proceedings*. San Francisco: Association of Computing Machinery.

Goto, M., and Y. Muraoka. 1997a. Real-time rhythm tracking for drumless audio signals: Chord change detection for musical decisions. *Working notes of the IJCAI-97 workshop on computational auditory scene analysis*, 135–144.

Goto, M., and Y. Muraoka. 1997b. Issues in evaluating beat tracking systems. *Working notes of the IJCAI-97 workshop on issues in AI and music*, 9–16.

Gresham-Lancaster, S. 1998. The aesthetics and history of The Hub: The effects of changing technology on network computer music. *Leonardo Music Journal* 8:39–44.

Griffith, N., and P. Todd, eds. 1999. *Musical networks: Parallel distributed perception and performance*. Cambridge, MA: The MIT Press.

Handel, S. 1989. *Listening: An introduction to the perception of auditory events*. Cambridge, MA: The MIT Press.

Hewlett, W., E. Selfridge-Field, D. Cooper, B. Field, K. Ng, and P. Sitter. MIDI. In *Beyond MIDI: The handbook of musical codes*. Ed. E. Selfridge-Field. Cambridge, MA: The MIT Press, 41–72.

Hillis, W. 1992. Co-evolving parasites improve simulated evolution as an optimization procedure. In *Artificial life II*. Ed. C. Langton, C. Taylor, J. Farmer, and S. Rasmussen. Reading, MA: Addison-Wesley.

Holloway, R. 1989. Word—Image—Concept—Sound. *Contemporary Music Review* 5:257–265.

Honing, H. 1993. Issues on the representation of time and structure in music. *Contemporary Music Review* 9(1,2):221–238.

Howell, P., R. West, and I. Cross. 1991. *Representing musical structure*. San Diego: Academic Press.

Huron, D. 1992. Design principles in computer-based music representation. In *Computer representations and models in music*. Ed. A. Marsden and A. Pople. London: Academic Press.

Huron, D. 1994. *The Humdrum Toolkit reference manual*. Menlo Park, CA: Center for Computer Assisted Research in the Humanities.

Huron, D. 1997. Humdrum and Kern: selective feature encoding. In *Beyond MIDI: The handbook of musical codes*. Ed. E. Selfridge-Field. Cambridge, MA: The MIT Press, 375–401.

Jackendoff, R. 1992. Musical processing and musical affect. In *Cognitive bases of musical communication*. Ed. M.R. Jones and S. Holleran. Washington, DC: American Psychological Association.

Järvinen. 1985. Tonal hierarchies in jazz improvisation. *Music Perception* 12:415–437.

Johnson-Laird, P. 1991. Jazz improvisation: A theory at the computational level. In *Representing musical structure*. Ed. P. Howell, R. West, and I. Cross. London: Academic Press.

Jordan, M. 1986. Attractor dynamics and parallelism in a connectionist sequential machine. *Proceedings of the 8th Annual Conference of the Cognitive Science Society*. Hillsdale, NJ: Cognitive Science Society.

Kendall, R., and E. Carterette. 1990. The communication of musical expression. *Music Perception* 8(2):129–164.

Kohonen, T. 1984. *Self-organization and associative memory*. Berlin: Springer.

Kosslyn, S., and J. Pomerantz. 1977. Imagery, propositions, and the form of internal representations. *Cognitive Psychology* 9:52–76.

Knuth, D. 1973. *The art of computer programming. Vol. 3, Searching and sorting*. Reading, MA: Addison-Wesley.

Krumhansl, C. 1990. *Cognitive foundations of musical pitch*. Oxford: Oxford University Press.

Krumhansl, C. 1992. Internal representations for music perception and performance. In *Cognitive bases of musical communication*. Ed. M.R. Jones and S. Holleran. Washington, DC: American Psychological Association.

Krumhansl, C., and E. Kessler. 1982. Tracing the dynamic changes in perceived tonal organization in a spatial representation of musical keys. *Psychological Review* 89:334–368.

Kuivila, R., and D. Behrman. 1998. Composing with shifting sand: A conversation between Ron Kuivila and David Behrman on electronic music and the ephemerality of technology. *Leonardo Music Journal* 8:13–16.

Large, E. and J. Kolen. 1994. Resonance and the perception of musical meter. *Connection Science* 6:177–208.

Lee, C. 1985. The rhythmic interpretation of simple musical structures. In *Musical structure and cognition*. Ed. P. Howell, I. Cross, and R. West. London: Academic Press.

Lee, M., and D. Wessel. 1992. Connectionist models for real-time control of synthesis and compositional algorithms. In *Proceedings of the 1992 International Computer Music Conference*. San Francisco: International Computer Music Association.

Leman, M. 1992. Artificial neural networks in music research. In *Computer representations and models in music*. Ed. A. Marsden and A. Pople. London: Academic Press.

Leman, M. 1995. *Music and schema theory: Cognitive foundations of systematic musicology*. Heidelberg: Springer-Verlag.

Leman, M., and F. Carreras. 1997. Schema and gestalt: Testing the hypothesis of psychoneural isomorphism by computer simulation. In *Music, gestalt, and computing: Studies in cognitive and systematic musicology*. Ed. Marc Leman. Berlin: Springer.

Lenat, D., and E. Feigenbaum. 1992. On the thresholds of knowledge. In *Foundations of artificial intelligence*. Ed. D. Kirsh. Cambridge, MA: The MIT Press.

Lerdahl, F., and R. Jackendoff. 1983. *A generative theory of tonal music*. Cambridge, MA: The MIT Press.

Lindemann, E., F. Dechelle, B. Smith, and M. Starkier. 1991. The architecture of the IRCAM musical workstation. *Computer Music Journal* 15(3):41–49.

Lippe, C. 1997. Music for piano and computer: A description. In *Proceedings of the U.S.A/Japan computer music conference 1997*. Tokyo: Kunitachi Conservatory.

Longuet-Higgins, H., and C. Lee. 1982. The perception of musical rhythm. *Perception* 11:115–128.

Longuet-Higgins, H., and C. Lee. 1984. The rhythmic interpretation of monophonic music. *Music Perception* 1(4):424–441.

Loy, D. 1985. Musicians make a standard: The MIDI phenomenon. *Computer Music Journal* 9(4). Reprinted in *The music machine*. Ed. C. Roads. Cambridge, MA: The MIT Press.

Loy, D. 1989. Composing with computers: A survey of some compositional formalisms and music programming languages. In *Current directions in computer music research*. Ed. M. Mathews and J. Pierce. Cambridge, MA: The MIT Press.

Maes, P. 1995. Modeling adaptive autonomous agents. In *Artificial life: An overview*. Ed. C. Langton. Cambridge, MA: The MIT Press.

Machover, T. 1999. Technology and the future of music. Interview by F. Oteri, August 18, 1999. *NewMusicBox* 6. http://www.newmusicbox.org.

Manoury, P. 1984. The role of the conscious. *Contemporary Music Review* 1:147–156.

Manoury, P. 1991. *Jupiter*. Paris: Éditions Musicales Amphion.

Marsden, A. 1992. Modelling the perception of musical voices. In *Computer representations and models in music*. Ed. A. Marsden and A. Pople. London: Academic Press.

Marsden, A., and A. Pople, eds. 1992. *Computer representations and models in music*. London: Academic Press.

Marslen-Wilson, W., and L. Tyler. 1984. The temporal structure of spoken language understanding. *Cognition* 8:1–71.

Martin, K., E. Scheirer, and B. Vercoe. 1998. Music content analysis through models of audition. *ACM multimedia 1998 workshop on content processing of music for multimedia applications*. San Francisco: Association of Computing Machinery.

Maxwell, H. 1992. An expert system for harmonic analysis of tonal music. In *Understanding music with AI*. Ed. M. Balaban, K. Ebcioglu, and O. Laske. Cambridge, MA: The MIT Press.

McAdams, S. 1987. Music: A science of the mind? In *Contemporary Music Review* 2(1):1–62.

McClelland, J., and D. Rumelhart. 1988. *Explorations in parallel distributed processing*. Cambridge, MA: The MIT Press.

McEwan, I. 1998. *Amsterdam*. London: Jonathan Cape.

Meehan, J. 1980. An artificial intelligence approach to tonal music theory. *Computer Music Journal* 4(2):64.

Messiaen, O. 1997. *Traité de Rythme, de Couleur, et d'Ornithologie* (Tome IV). Paris: Alphonse Leduc.

Minsky, M. 1985. A framework for representing knowledge. In *Readings in knowledge representation*. Ed. R. Brachman and H. Levesque. Los Altos, CA: Morgan Kaufmann Publishers.

Miranda, E., ed. 1999. *Readings in music and artificial intelligence*. The Netherlands: Harwood Academic Publishers.

Mitchell, M. 1996. *An introduction to genetic algorithms*. Cambridge, MA: The MIT Press.

Mozer, M. 1991. Connectionist music composition based on melodic, stylistic, and psychophysical constraints. In *Music and connectionism*. Ed. P. Todd and D.G. Loy. Cambridge, MA: The MIT Press.

Mozer, M. 1993. Neural net architectures for temporal sequence processing. In *Predicting the future and understanding the past*. Ed. A. Weigend and N. Gershenfeld. Reading, MA: Addison-Wesley.

Myers, C., and L. Rabiner. 1981. A level building dynamic time warping algorithm for connected word recognition. *IEEE Transactions on Acoustics, Speech, and Signal Processing* ASSP-29(2):284–297.

Narmour, E. 1977. *Beyond Schenkerism: The need for alternatives in music analysis*. Chicago: University of Chicago Press.

Narmour, E. 1990. *The analysis and cognition of basic melodic structures: The implication-realization model*. Chicago: University of Chicago Press.

Narmour, E. 1999. Hierarchical expectation and musical style. In *The psychology of music*. 2nd ed. Ed. D. Deutsch. London: Academic Press.

Nigrin, A. 1993. *Neural networks for pattern recognition*. Cambridge, MA: The MIT Press.

Nordli, K. 1997. MIDI extensions for musical notation (1): NoTAMIDI meta-events. In *Beyond MIDI: The handbook of musical codes*. Ed. E. Selfridge-Field. Cambridge, MA: The MIT Press, 73–79.

Odiard, P. 1995. De la confrontation à la conjonction: a propos de *Sonus ex machina*. In *Philippe Manoury: Collection «compositeurs d'aujourd'hui»*. Paris: Editions IRCAM—Centre Georges-Pompidou.

O Maidin, D. 1992. Representation of music scores for analysis. In *Computer representations and models in music*. Ed. A. Marsden and A. Pople. London: Academic Press.

Ossowski, S. 1999. *Co-ordination in artificial agent societies: Social structure and its implications for autonomous problem-solving agents*. Berlin: Springer.

Owens, T. 1974. *Charlie Parker: Techniques of improvisation*. Ph.D. diss., University of California, Los Angeles.

Palisca, C. 1996. *Norton Anthology of Western Music*. 3rd ed. Vol. 2. Ed. C. Palisca. New York: W.W. Norton & Company.

Palmer, C. 1989. Mapping musical thought to music performance. *Journal of Experimental Psychology* 15:331–346.

Paradiso, J. 1999. The Brain Opera technology: New instruments and gestural sensors for musical interaction and performance. *Journal of New Music Research* 28(2):130–149.

Parncutt, R. 1988. Revision of Terhardt's psychoacoustical model of the roots of a musical chord. *Music Perception* 6:65–94.

Parncutt, R. 1989. *Harmony: A psychoacoustical approach*. Berlin: Springer.

Parncutt, R. 1994. A perceptual model of pulse salience and metrical accent in musical rhythms. *Music Perception* 11:409–464.

Parncutt, R. 1997. A model of the perceptual root(s) of a chord accounting for voicing and prevailing tonality. In *Music, gestalt, and computing: Studies in cognitive and systematic musicology*. Ed. Marc Leman. Berlin: Springer.

Pennycook, B., D. Stammen, and D. Reynolds. 1993. Toward a computer model of a jazz improviser. In *Proceedings of the 1993 International Computer Music Conference*. San Francisco: International Computer Music Association.

Perkis, T. 1995. Liner notes to the audio CD, *Wreckin' Ball*. Artifact Recordings ART 1008.

Perlin, K. 1995. Real-time responsive animation with personality. *IEEE transactions on visualization and computer graphics*. New York: IEEE.

Perlin, K., and A. Goldberg. 1996. IMPROV: A system for scripting interactive actors in virtual worlds. In *Proceedings of SIGGRAPH 96, Annual Conference Series*. New York: ACM SIGGRAPH.

Pope, S., ed. 1991. *The well-tempered object: Musical applications of object-oriented software technology*. Cambridge, MA: The MIT Press.

Popper, K. 1992. *The logic of scientific discovery*. London: Routledge.

Porter, L. 1998. *John Coltrane: His life and music*. Ann Arbor, MI: The University of Michigan Press.

Povall, R. 1995. Compositional methods in interactive performance environments. *Journal of New Music Research* 24(2):109–120.

Pressing, J. 1988. Improvisation: Methods and models. In *Generative processes in music: The psychology of performance, improvisation, and composition*. Ed. J. Sloboda. Oxford: Clarendon Press.

Puckette, M. 1993. Contributions to "Putting Max in perspective." Ed. R. Rowe and B. Garton. *Computer Music Journal* 17(2):3–11.

Rai, T. 1998. Program note to *Kinetic Figuration: Five works with computers*. Audio CD, Toshiba-EMI DAC-1210.

Reis, B. 1999. Simulated music learning: On-line, perceptually guided pattern induction of context models for multiple-horizon prediction of melodies. In *Proceedings of the 1999 workshop on pattern processing in music*.

Repp, B. 1992. Diversity and commonality in music performance: An analysis of timing microstructure in Schumann's "Träumerei." *Journal of the Acoustical Society of America* 92(5):2546–2568.

Reynolds, C. 1987. Flocks, herds, and schools: A distributed behavioral model. In *Computer Graphics, SIGGRAPH 87 Conference Proceedings*. New York: ACM SIGGRAPH.

Richter, M., C. Smith, R. Wiehagen, and T. Zeugmann. 1998. Editor's Introduction. In *Algorithmic learning theory.* Ed. M. Richter, C. Smith, R. Wiehagen, and T. Zeugmann. Berlin: Springer.

Ritter, D. 1996. The intersection of art and interactivity. In *Ars Electronica Festival 96: Mimesis.* Vienna: Springer.

Rogers, J. 1997. *Object-oriented neural networks in C++.* New York: Academic Press.

Rolland, P., and J. Ganascia. 1996. Automated motive-oriented analysis of musical corpuses: A jazz case study. In *Proceedings of the 1996 International Computer Music Conference.* San Francisco: International Computer Music Association.

Rosenboom, D. 1992. Parsing real-time musical inputs and spontaneously generating musical forms: Hierarchical form generator (HFG). In *Proceedings of the 1992 International Computer Music Conference.* San Francisco: International Computer Music Association.

Rosenboom, D. 1997. Propositional music: On emergent properties in morphogenesis and the evolution of music. Part II: Imponderable forms and compositional methods. *Leonardo Music Journal* 7:35–39.

Rosenthal, D. 1989. A model of the process of listening to simple rhythms. *Music Perception* 6(3):315–328.

Rowe, R. 1993. *Interactive music systems: Machine listening and composing.* Cambridge, MA: The MIT Press.

Rowe, R., and T. Li. 1995. Pattern processing in music. In *Proceedings of the fifth biennial symposium for arts and technology.* New London, CT: Connecticut College.

Rowe, R., and E. Singer. 1997. Two highly integrated real-time music and graphics performance systems. In *Proceedings of the 1997 International Computer Music Conference.* San Francisco: International Computer Music Association.

Rowe, R., E. Singer, and D. Vila. 1996. *A Flock of Words:* Real-time animation and video controlled by algorithmic music analysis. In *Visual Proceedings, SIGGRAPH 96.* New York: ACM SIGGRAPH.

Sankoff, D., and J. Kruskal, eds. 1983. *Time warps, string edits, and macromolecules: The theory and practice of sequence comparison.* Reading, MA: Addison-Wesley.

Sawada, H., N. Onoe, and S. Hashimoto. 1997. Sounds in hands: A sound modifier using datagloves and twiddle interface. In *Proceedings of the 1997 International Computer Music Conference.* San Francisco: International Computer Music Association.

Scarborough, D., B. Miller, and J. Jones. 1991. Connectionist models for tonal analysis. In *Music and connectionism.* Ed. P. Todd and G. Loy. Cambridge, MA: The MIT Press.

Schank, R., and R. Abelson. 1977. *Scripts, plans, goals and understanding: An inquiry into human knowledge structures.* Hillsdale, NJ: Lawrence Erlbaum Associates.

Scheirer, E. 1996. Bregman's chimerae: Music perception as auditory scene analysis. *Proceedings of the Fourth International Conference on Music Perception and Cognition.* Montreal: McGill University.

Schiphorst, T. 1996. Felt histories (re: The fact of a doorframe). Artist's description.

Schwanauer, S. 1988. Learning machines and tonal composition. In *Proceedings of the first workshop on artificial intelligence and music.* Minneapolis/St. Paul, MN: AAAI–88.

Selfridge-Field, E., ed. 1997a. *Beyond MIDI: The handbook of musical codes*. Cambridge, MA: The MIT Press.

Selfridge-Field, E. 1997b. Describing musical information. In *Beyond MIDI: The handbook of musical codes*. Ed. E. Selfridge-Field. Cambridge, MA: The MIT Press, 3–38.

Selfridge-Field, E. 1998. Conceptual and representational issues in melodic comparison. *Computing in musicology* 11:3–64.

Settel, Z. 1993. *Hok Pwah*. Program Note.

Shannon, C., and W. Weaver. 1949. *The mathematical theory of communication*. Urbana: The University of Illinois Press.

Shepard, R. 1964. Circularity in judgments of relative pitch. *Journal of the Acoustical Society of America* 36:2346–2353.

Shepard, R. 1999. Cognitive psychology and music. In *Music, cognition, and computerized sound: An introduction to psychoacoustics*. Ed. P. Cook. Cambridge, MA: The MIT Press.

Siegel, W., and J. Jacobsen. 1998. The challenges of interactive dance: An overview and case study. *Computer Music Journal* 22(4):29–43.

Simon, H., and K. Kotovsky. 1963. Human acquisition of concepts for sequential patterns. *Psychological Review* (70):534–546.

Simon, H., and R. Sumner. 1993. Pattern in music. In *Machine models of music*. Ed. S. Schwanauer and D. Levitt. Cambridge, MA: The MIT Press.

Sims, K. 1991. Artificial evolution for computer graphics. *Computer Graphics* 25(4):319–328.

Singer, E., K. Perlin, and C. Castiglia. 1996. Real-time responsive synthetic dancers and musicians. In *Visual proceedings, SIGGRAPH 96*. New York: ACM SIGGRAPH.

Singer, E., A. Goldberg, K. Perlin, C. Castiglia, and S. Liao. 1997. Improv: Interactive improvisational animation and music. *ISEA 96 proceedings: Seventh international symposium on electronic art*. Rotterdam, Netherlands: ISEA96 Foundation.

Sloboda, J. 1985. *The musical mind: The cognitive psychology of music*. Oxford: Clarendon Press.

Smoliar, S. 1992. Representing listening behavior: Problems and prospects. In *Understanding music with AI*. Ed. M. Balaban, K. Ebcioglu, and O. Laske. Cambridge, MA: The MIT Press.

Stammen, D. 1999. *Timewarp: A computer model of real-time segmentation and recognition of melodic fragments*. Ph.D. diss., McGill University.

Stammen, D., and B. Pennycook. 1993. Real-time recognition of melodic fragments using the dynamic timewarp algorithm. In *Proceedings of the 1993 International Computer Music Conference*. San Francisco: International Computer Music Association, 232–235.

Subotnick, M. 1997. *Intimate Immensity*. Program note.

Sundberg, J. 1988. Computer synthesis of music performance. In *Generative processes in music: The psychology of performance, improvisation, and composition*. Ed. J. Sloboda. Oxford: Clarendon Press.

Sundberg, J., A. Askenfelt, and L. Frydén. 1983. Music performance: A synthesis-by-rule approach. *Computer Music Journal* 7:37–43.

Sundberg, J., A. Friberg, and L. Frydén. 1991. Common secrets of musicians and listeners—an analysis-by-synthesis study of musical performance. In *Representing musical structure*. Ed. P. Howell, R. West, and I. Cross. London: Academic Press.

Tanimoto, S. 1990. *The elements of artificial intelligence: Using Common LISP*. New York: W.H. Freeman and Company.

Tarabella, L. 1993a. Introduction. *Interface* 22:179–182.

Tarabella, L. 1993b. Real-time concurrent PascalMusic. *Interface* 22:229–242.

Tarabella, L., and M. Magrini. 1998. GALileo, a Graphic ALgorithmic music language. In *Proceedings of the XII colloquium of musical informatics*.

Tarabella, L., M. Magrini, and G. Scapellato. 1998. A system for recognizing shape, position, and rotation of the hands. In *Proceedings of the 1998 International Computer Music Conference*. San Francisco: International Computer Music Association.

Teitelbaum, R. 1982. Digital piano music. Unpublished manuscript, quoted in Chadabe, J. 1997. *Electric sound: The past and promise of electronic music*. Upper Saddle River, NJ: Prentice-Hall.

Tenney, J., and L. Polansky. 1980. Temporal gestalt perception in music. *Journal of Music Theory* 24:205–241.

Temperley, D. 1997. An algorithm for harmonic analysis. *Music Perception* 15(1):31–68.

Temperley, D., and D. Sleator. 1999. Modeling meter and harmony: a preference-rule approach. *Computer Music Journal* 23(1):10–27.

Terhardt, E., G. Stoll, and M. Seewann. 1982. Algorithm for extraction of pitch and pitch salience from complex tonal signals. *Journal of the Acoustical Society of America* 71: 679–688.

Thomasson, J. 1982. Melodic accent: experiments and a tentative model. *Journal of the Acoustical Society of America* 71.

Thompson, W. 1993. The harmonic root: A fragile marriage of concept and percept. *Music Perception* 10:385–416.

Thompson, W., and M. Stainton. 1996. Using Humdrum to analyze melodic structure: An assessment of Narmour's implication-realization model. *Computing in Musicology* 10: 24–33.

Todd, N. 1985. A model of expressive timing in tonal music. *Music Perception* 3(1):33–58.

Todd, N. 1992. The dynamics of dynamics: A model of musical expression. *Journal of the Acoustical Society of America* 91(6):3540–3550.

Todd, N. 1994. The auditory "primal sketch": A multi-scale model of rhythmic grouping. *Journal of New Music Research* 23(1):25–70.

Todd, P. 1991. A connectionist approach to algorithmic composition. In *Music and connectionism*. Ed. P. Todd and D. Loy. Cambridge, MA: The MIT Press.

Todd, P. and D. Loy. 1991. *Music and connectionism*. Cambridge, MA: The MIT Press.

Toiviainen, P. 1998. An interactive MIDI accompanist. *Computer Music Journal* 22(4):63–75.

Van Immerseel, L., and J. Martens. 1992. Pitch and voiced/unvoiced determination with an auditory model. *Journal of the Acoustical Society of America* 91:3511–3526.

Vercoe, B. 1984. The synthetic performer in the context of live performance. In *Proceedings of the 1984 International Computer Music Conference*. San Francisco: International Computer Music Association.

Vercoe, B. 1997. Computational auditory pathways to music understanding. In *Perception and cognition of music*. Ed. I. Deliège and J. Sloboda. East Sussex, GB: Psychology Press.

Vos, P. 1999. Key implications of ascending fourth and descending fifth openings. *Psychology of Music* 27:4–17.

Vos, P., and E. Van Geenen. 1996. A parallel-processing key-finding model. *Music Perception* 14(2):185–224.

Watkinson, J. 1994. *The art of digital audio*. 2d ed. Oxford: Focal Press.

West, R., P. Howell, and I. Cross. 1985. Modelling perceived musical structure. In *Musical structure and cognition.* Ed. P. Howell, I. Cross, and R. West. London: Academic Press.

West, R., P. Howell, and I. Cross. 1991. Musical structure and knowledge representation. In *Representing musical structure.* Ed. P. Howell, R. West, and I. Cross. London: Academic Press.

Widmer, G. 1992. Qualitative perception modeling and intelligent musical learning. *Computer Music Journal* 16(2):51–68.

Widmer, G. 1995. Modeling the rational basis of musical expression. *Computer Music Journal* 19(2):76–96.

Widmer, G. 1996. Learning expressive performance: The structure-level approach. *Journal of New Music Research* 25:179–205.

Widrow, B. 1963. ADALINE and MADALINE. *IEEE–ICNN* 1(I):143–158.

Wiggins, G., E. Miranda, A. Smaill, and M. Harris. 1993. A framework for the evaluation of music representation systems. *Computer Music Journal* 17(3):31–42.

Winkler, T. 1998. *Composing interactive music: Techniques and ideas using Max.* Cambridge, MA: The MIT Press.

Winograd, T. 1968. Linguistics and the computer analysis of tonal harmony. *Journal of Music Theory* 12(1):2–49.

Winsor, P. 1989. *Automated music composition.* Denton: University of North Texas Press.

Winston, P. 1984. *Artificial Intelligence. 2d ed.* Reading, MA: Addison-Wesley Publishing Company.

Witten, I., L. Manzara, and D. Conklin. 1994. Comparing human and computational models of music prediction. *Computer Music Journal* 18(1):70–80.

Woideck, C. 1996. *Charlie Parker: His music and life.* Ann Arbor: The University of Michigan Press.

Wright, M., and A. Freed. 1997. Open Sound Control: A new protocol for communicating with sound synthesizers. In *Proceedings of the 1997 International Computer Music Conference.* San Francisco: International Computer Music Association.

Wright, M., A. Chaudhary, A. Freed, D. Wessel, X. Rodet, D. Virolle, R. Woehrmann, and X. Serra. 1998. New applications of the Sound Description Interchange Format. In *Proceedings of the 1998 International Computer Music Conference.* San Francisco: International Computer Music Association.

Wright, M., and D. Wessel. 1998. An improvisation environment for generating rhythmic structures based on North Indian "Tal" patterns. In *Proceedings of the 1998 International Computer Music Conference.* San Francisco: International Computer Music Association.

Zicarelli, D. 1996. *Writing external objects for Max.* Palo Alto: Opcode Systems.

Index